A Mexican Elite Family, 1820-1980

A Mexican Elite Family,

1820-1980: Kinship, Class, and Culture

LARISSA ADLER LOMNITZ

AND MARISOL PEREZ-LIZAUR

TRANSLATED BY CINNA LOMNITZ

Princeton University Press

Princeton, New Jersey

Library of Congress Cataloging in Publication Data will be found
on the last printed page of this book

ISBNO-691-07737-1   ISBNO-691-02284-4 (pbk.)

Publication of this book has been aided by a grant from the
Paul Mellon Fund of Princeton University Press

This book has been composed in Linotron Sabon type

Clothbound editions of Princeton University Press books are printed
on acid-free paper, and binding materials are chosen for strength
and durability. Paperbacks, although satisfactory for personal
collections, are not usually suitable for library rebinding

Printed in the United States of America by Princeton University
Press, Princeton, New Jersey

To the memory of my mother,
Noemi Lisa Milstein de Adler (1910-1976),
who gave me the strength to face life
with optimism
                    Larissa Adler Lomnitz

To the memory of Angel Palerm,
teacher and friend
                    Marisol Pérez-Lizaur

CONTENTS

FIGURES AND TABLES

PREFACE

WE BEGAN to gather the data for this book in 1971, without a specific project in mind, when we were both students working on different dissertations. Eventually an opportunity for a detailed study of the Gómez family presented itself, and large amounts of data were collected. Our initial contact, a young woman in her twenties, became our key informant. Although she protested that her knowledge of the family was inadequate, she produced a family genealogy of about three hundred names at one sitting. To her surprise, she was aware of the biographical details (names, parents, education, residence, business activities, personal description) of at least two hundred relatives. Gaps in the kinship information of our informant were not randomly distributed: rather, whole branches of the family seemed to have disappeared from her cognitive map. These missing branches either did not reside in Mexico City or belonged to "poor" or "black sheep" segments of the family.

Several years went by. We accumulated an amazingly extensive body of data: recorded interviews, gossip, parish records, archival material, newspaper clippings, and assorted references in the sociological or economic literature. Our most productive interviews were those with "centralizing women," self-appointed keepers of the oral traditions of the family network. Younger entrepreneurs were helpful as well, and participant observation also became a most useful method of research as access to family events was gained.

Most of our informants belonged to the wealthier branches of the Gómez family. As a result, our information on these branches is more abundant. Moreover, the ideology of this dominant group may be reflected to some extent in the ethnographic data. All data, particularly on the history of the family, have been subjected to independent checks as far as possible, but it should be remembered that the family myths still impinge on the selection of relevant actors or events and that the ideological bias of the informants cannot always be completely excluded.

In the process of our research we evolved in our way of thinking. We had started out with an economic perspective; but as we gained new insights into the family subculture we shifted our ground of discussion from process to structure and from micro- to macroanalysis. A painful, slow method, to be sure—but one that enabled us to grow closer to our subject and to evolve jointly with our material.

In the chapters that follow, family members are identified as (R,ii), where R is a Roman numeral from I to V identifying the generation and *ii* is an Arabic number. Affines are designated by e′ (first spouse) or e″ (second spouse), followed by the identification number of the family member. A list of family members will be found in the appendix. All names of persons and firms are fictitious. Because of promises of anonymity that have been made, more specific information about family enterprises could not be given.

THE PRESENTATION of our research in book form was made possible by a Guggenheim Fellowship awarded to one of us (Larissa Lomnitz). Thanks are due to Professor Cinna Lomnitz for translating the Spanish original into English and for offering helpful editorial suggestions; to Professors Guillermo de la Peña, Nelson Graburn, Robert Kemper, Claudio Lomnitz, Hugo Nutini, Raymond Smith, Eric Wolf, and Peter Worsley for critically reading all or part of the manuscript; to Alicia Castillo for her patient and efficient assistance in producing many successive typed versions; to María Elena Ducci and Agustín Piña for assistance with the figures; and to countless colleagues for their comments and encouragement at meetings where part of this research was presented. We also want to thank Cinna Lomnitz and Manuel Burgos for their support.

Last but not least, we wish to thank the Gómez for their generous help, and for being themselves: a vital presence on the complex Mexican scene.

CHRONOLOGY

Date	Mexico	The Gómez Family
1867-1872	Liberal party wins power; Benito Juárez becomes president; reform legislation put into effect.	Don Carlos Gómez (I,3), farmer and village trader, living in Puebla
1872	Beginning of the age of Porfirio Díaz and political stability	
1875		Don Carlos dies
1880		His son Leopoldo (II,16) moves to Mexico City as his cousin's employee
1910	Mexican Revolution breaks out	Leopoldo now a major entrepreneur; his brothers have all married
1917	New Mexican constitution proclaimed	
1921	Armed conflict subsides in Mexico	Leopoldo reemerges as medium-sized entrepreneur
1925		Deaths of Leopoldo and Mamá Inés (I,e″3)
1926	The Cristero uprising; religious persecution in Mexico	Pablo (III,51) and Leopoldo Jr. (III,50) take over family leadership
1928	Founding of the PNR; social peace, nationalism, and development	Cecilia (II,21) dies; third generation in control
1934-1940	Cárdenas administration; nationalism with socialistic overtones	Economic and social rise of Pablo

1940-1946	Government support of private business; "import substitution" policy	Pablo now a major entrepreneur; diversification and proliferation of investments by Pablo, Leopoldo Jr., and their cousin Pedro (III,72)
1946-1952	Alliance between business and the state; the "Mexican miracle"	
1952-1958	Beginning of a "new deal" for the working class; state also resumes negotiations with the industrialists	Death of Pablo; Pedro assumes family leadership; Leopoldo Jr. creates an industrial consortium
1958-1964	State is central planner and economic arbiter; development of new corporations; invasion of foreign capital	Fourth generation in control; marriage alliances with major capital; involvement with real estate and housing development
1964-1970	Peak of state-business alliance; foreign corporations are invited in; rise of finance corporations	Consolidation of younger family leaders; Leopoldo Jr. now family patriarch; modernization of family enterprise
1970-1976	Economic crisis; business in opposition to government; state attempts to correct socioeconomic imbalances	Some loss of confidence in the economy; flight of capital; family leaders are economically secure but now comparatively less prominent in the Mexican business world

ABBREVIATIONS

CANACINTRA Cámara Nacional de la Industria de la
Transformación (National Chamber of Industry and
Transformation)

CONAPO Consejo Nacional de Población (National
Demographic Council)

CCE Consejo Coordinador Empresarial (Entrepreneurial
Coordinating Council)

CONCAMIN Confederación Nacional de Cámaras Industriales
(National Confederation of Industrialists)

CONCANACO Confederación Nacional de Cámaras de Comercio
(National Confederation of Chambers of Commerce)

CROM Confederación Regional de Obreros Mexicanos
(Regional Confederation of Mexican Workers)

CTM Confederación de Trabajadores de México (Mexican
Workers' Confederation)

NAFINSA Nacional Financiera S.A. (National Financial Banks
S.A.)

PNR Partido Nacional Revolucionario (National
Revolutionary Party)

PRI Partido Revolucinario Institucional (Institutional
Revolutionary Party)

A Mexican Elite Family, 1820-1980

INTRODUCTION

THIS IS a study of the Gómez, an elite family of Mexico City. In the sense that the development of a kinship group is traced over a period of 160 years (1820-1980), this is a family history. Because this family is also a significant entrepreneurial group, one that has contributed to the development of modern Mexico through its involvement in the process of industrialization, this work must also take account of economic, political, and cultural history.

A basic question among social scientists concerns the relationship between the macrosocial level of analysis and the lives of real people. Two approaches are possible. On the one hand, one can ask how the lives of specific individuals have been affected by the history, economy, and culture of their society. On the other hand, one can investigate the influence of individuals or small groups on history and on society in general. We hold to the middle ground between the individualistic view that history is the outcome of the thoughts and actions of individuals and the deterministic concept of historical forces as prime movers. People live within a given historical, social, and cultural context. Decisions are made within this context, and individuals adopt different life styles and act in different ways.

Every group is distinctive in its cultural flavor, its mythology, its rituals and customs, and its position within the social structure. Distinctiveness means that members of a family or social group share an ideology and a corpus of traditions that set them apart from others. From this they derive a sense of belonging that implies the exclusion of outsiders with whom they may otherwise share a broad cultural system of nation, class, or locality. If everything were predetermined by social structure and by macrohistory, no significant variations among groups would occur within a social stratum. On the other hand, the sociocultural context is obviously essential to the understanding of individual actions and the evolution of social groups.

3

The constant interplay between these levels of analysis is a central preoccupation here. We have tried to take the facts of a specific family history and develop a sociologically valid text by placing this material—events, characters, traits, and opinions that might be trivial by themselves—into the context of place, period, social structure, culture, class, and national history.

The family history of the Gómez between 1820 and 1980 will be compared with Mexican history in three distinct periods: up to 1910, with special emphasis on the Porfiriato, a period that includes the appearance of the first family entrepreneur as well as the expansion of industrialization; from 1910 through 1950, particularly the postrevolutionary period of national reconstruction that established and consolidated the prevailing social structure and led up to the years of the "Mexican Miracle"; and the postwar years, which have seen the emergence of multinational corporations, high-technology industrial development, and the increasing role of the state in the economy.

This broader context provides a setting for the events in the Gómez family history: its rural origins and migration to Mexico City; the rise of the first family entrepreneur; the interlude of revolution; the divergent styles of the two sons, heirs to the enterprise; the rise to power and the numerical growth of the family; the stratification into family branches; and the response of the fourth generation of entrepreneurs to the challenge of the business corporations of the 1970s.

The Gómez belong to a little-studied stratum of Mexican society, the national bourgeoisie. This is not the bourgeoisie of *criollo* origin, descended from Spanish colonial landowners or mineowners. Rather, the Gómez were small merchants who later became industrialists and finally, not for profit but for prestige, landowners and ranchers. This evolution seems reminiscent of the rise of the classical industrial bourgeoisie in Europe, except that the pattern is far from uniform. Some individuals in the family seized historical opportunities; others merely followed in their footsteps. We shall describe the fortunes of nine siblings who founded distinctly different family branches and whose heirs include major industrialists, liberal professionals, and small businessmen—each group occupying a different social position in Mexico today.

Despite economic differences arising from stratification, all members of the Gómez family identify with the private sector of the Mexican political system. This sector is officially defined as comprising the owners of the means of production (e.g., industrialists, bankers), private businessmen, merchants, liberal professionals in private practice, and the white-collar employees of private business. Like the rest of Mexican society, the private sector is organized along hierarchical lines, with the major industrial and financial "groups" at the top. Among the Gómez, we find entrepreneurs who act as patrons of other members of the family; the result is a complex web of interdependent enterprises. The analysis of these levels of interaction will enable a better understanding of the relation between individuals and class politics. Above all, we must account for the salient fact that despite economic differentiation, the cohesion and solidarity of the family has been maintained.

In a different sense, this book is also a "cultural account." Kinship, rituals, and ideology are central to the cultural system of any social group. Generations of the Gómez attest to the vital role of a specific kinship pattern: the three-generation "grandfamily." This kinship pattern is not only the prescribed unit of solidarity among the Gómez but represents the predominant feature of the kinship system in Mexico and perhaps in all of Latin America. Of course it is important and useful to distinguish between a broad cultural pattern (or "grammar") of kinship and its specific realizations (or "speech"), such as the formation of households or outward expressions of solidarity. These depend on class, economy, demography, and local conditions—for example, the availability of housing. Cultural variants are produced by selection from the macrocultural pool. The Gómez emerge as a distinctive social group with specific cultural traits, which eventually revert to the national culture as an original contribution to what it means to be "Mexican." The three-generation grandfamily pattern that the Gómez have in common with the rest of Mexican society

5

largely accounts for the cultural distinctiveness of their family life as compared with that of Anglo-Saxon societies like Britain and the United States.

If we examine the ideology and the rituals of the Gómez, we see that their distinctive cultural aspects have evolved from a pool of traits shared with the rest of Mexican society. The principal Gómez rituals (weddings, funerals, christenings, and so forth) are observed by all Mexicans in broadly similar ways; yet this particular kinship group has developed nuances, variations, styles of observance, and public postures that identify its members as specifically *Gómez*. Most of the rituals are derived from the traditions of Mexican Catholicism; the variations include secular rituals or "customs" that sometimes are class-bound and sometimes seem to be entirely original to the Gómez.

The family ideology is a hodgepodge of original and borrowed elements. Some pertain to Mexican history as interpreted from a specific class position; others derive from the values of the landed gentry that was once the dominant class in Mexico. These values both clash and merge with the "Protestant ethic" of the new bourgeoisie: thrift versus conspicuous consumption, hard work versus gentlemanly leisure, and so on. Another area of ideological tension concerns ethnicity: the superiority attributed to white skin, blue eyes, and blond hair is confronted by the fact that the most revered female ancestor of the family was an Indian.

If Catholicism is recognized as the mainspring of family ideology in matters of family roles, sex roles, and the relation between individual and society, it must be added that the Catholic doctrine is also interpreted and modified from the perspective of the dominant class. The same can be said for Mexican nationalism. There are slight but nevertheless significant variations in Catholicism and nationalism from one branch of the family to another, and even from one grandfamily to another. The Gómez ideology contains enough contradictory features to allow the expression of individual and subgroup variations without danger to family solidarity.

The value system of the Gómez may be loosely described as

"Mediterranean corporativism." It affirms the priority of family over individual, group interest over personal freedom, and solidarity over development of self. Relations within the home or the business are patterned after Catholic models, and patron-client relations permeate both family and enterprise, which in fact are frequently merged into one.

The history of the Gómez kinship group may also be analyzed in terms of its evolution in urban space. The beginning of recognized family history is a rural-urban migration episode, and since 1880 the group has developed exclusively in Mexico City. Successive moves within the expanding urban limits define the type of household and the patterns of kin interaction that may be observed today. Neighborhoods rise and decline within decades, and the fortunes of each Gómez branch follow the trends of real estate values and the whims of fashion. Those who can afford it live in three-generational residential clusters, which are expressions of the powerful ideal kinship pattern that lies at the heart of the Gómez ideology.

Structure and Process

The material presented here is of a historical nature. We describe a process in time—the development of a kinship group over five generations. But at the same time we attempt to define a segment of social reality: what is constant and what is subject to change, what is essential and what is particular or circumstantial. In each chapter an effort is made to discuss change and continuity; yet each theme has its own particular dynamic of change.

Rituals represent a relatively stable aspect of group culture, but even rituals change gradually in time. Economy and ideology evolve more apace, depending on external factors, but a careful scrutiny of these aspects of social life uncovers a basic pattern that endures. The kinship pattern remains stable, but this stability only emerges if one observes the full three-generation cycle as it develops over 150 years of family history.

Our central thesis is the preeminence of the grandfamily (i.e., the three-generation extended family) as the basic meaningful unit of solidarity in Mexico. This structure is actively

7

maintained through time. Yet some of its expressions are subject to change: the household is constituted differently according to economic imperatives, for example, and the concrete expressions of kin solidarity depend on social and economic status (or on changing perceptions of what is seen as a meaningful demonstration of solidarity). Thus shantytown dwellers in Mexico City will express kin solidarity by the constant exchange of material goods and personal services; this requires close residential proximity, usually in extended family households where exchange can be maximized (Lomnitz 1977, 100-116). Among the middle- to upper-class Gómez, on the other hand, solidarity is expressed by participation in family rituals, business deals, jobs, and contracts. Nuclear families occupy separate households and daily exchange of food and personal services is not required, even though the basic unit of solidarity remains the three-generation unit of grandparents, children and their respective spouses, and grandchildren. Consanguinity is emphasized over affinity. Only after the elderly couple has died (and by that time the grandfamily may already include four generations) does segmentation take place. Even segmentation does not always imply a decrease in solidarity, because if siblings of the deceased grandparents are still alive, they are members of the now-truncated grandfamily of the previous generation.

It takes some effort to rid oneself of ingrained misconceptions. The nuclear family does not somehow represent a more "basic" unit of solidarity than the grandfamily. It makes sense to introduce a distinction between the family as a conceptual unit of meaning in the symbolic system and as the basis of the physical arrangements of the household. The latter may be more visible on the surface; the grandfamily takes forty to fifty years to unfold and complete a cycle of generational segmentation. It is a process *and* a structure at the same time.

Historical events, class differentiation, ecological constraints, and even cultural and ideological influences lumped together under the broad description of "modernization" produce changes in the outward expressions of kinship arrangements (households) or in the expressions of kin solidarity (ex-

8

change). The definitions of meaningful interaction may be modified by technological change, such as the use of the telephone as a handy means of communication in the urban setting. But continuity is maintained in the basic structure of the kinship system: the people included, the definitions of rights and obligations, and the meaning of kinship roles remain valid for all members of the group.

We have found that kinship occupies the focal point of confluence between continuity and change. Kinship unfolds and expresses itself under myriad aspects, but it maintains its identical structure through time. It completes a statement and starts over again; it is cyclical.

The continuity of kinship structure is upheld by ritual. In their essence and almost by definition, rituals should be stable. Their repetition is designed to sustain symbols through the ages. The relation between ritual and kinship is evident from the fact that the grandfamily must participate jointly in all rituals. Furthermore, interactions among different grandfamilies and among groups or strata within the larger kinship network are also expressed by rituals. Variations result in "styles" particular to each group. Rituals are arenas not only of solidarity but also of conflict. They open a window to change within continuity; thus they can ensure the permanence of kinship bonds beyond the life spans of individual kin.

Ideology is one's set of ideas, beliefs, and values about the world. The view held by the Gómez of themselves and their place in society is also an outcome of the interaction between continuity and change. The family creates history, and in so doing it makes up a historical account that is selectively contrived from the real events that occurred or did not occur in time. This "history" is transmitted orally in the family circle; it becomes the revealed truth about the family ancestry, its relevant heroes and villains, its self-image. It is a mythology.

A myth is not necessarily false. Rather, its truth or falsity is irrelevant. The gallery of family portraits becomes an idealized sequence of exemplary symbols, such as the archetypal founder, the essential grandmother, the perennial entrepreneur, the eternally devoted wife, or the black sheep par excellence. The selection of personages and events is not random but ideological, in the sense that facts are subordinated to the transmission of values: pride of kin, loyalty, hard work, status, positive and negative moral judgments, and the values attached to physical attributes. Negative examples are used to underscore the undesirable features that must be avoided if one wishes to remain a member of the family. Thus oral history is not merely a storehouse of information about the family background; the sharing and acceptance of family history are what set family members apart from nonmembers. Bloodlines do not suffice to confer membership in the kinship group; it is necessary to supplement biological descent with a common history, a mythology, and shared pseudomemories that regulate daily conduct.

Continuity and change are manifest in myth, because myth evolves from actual group experience. It is not crystallized once and for all; rather, new events and new interpretations of old events are added all the time. One might say that the theme of a family's history represents ideological continuity and that the modifications introduced by the ups and downs of its fortunes constitute ideological change. A similar analysis may be made of other aspects of the ideological system. Certain behavior patterns have become associated with class-bound values. Patriarchal authority is justified on the basis of ancestry and calls for periodic displays of generosity and conspicuous consumption. Eventually, these values conflict and then merge with bourgeois values, for example, in the self-made man who rises in the world by sheer effort and thrift. Ethnic prejudices of the old landed gentry are tempered by the acceptance of "good" Indians who are clean, hard-working, and right-thinking like the family ancestor, Mamá Inés. The Gómez version of Mexican nationalism, a major component of the family ideology, may thus be viewed as resulting from ancestral pride, emphasizing the Spanish heritage of the family, plus acceptance of its Indian component, provided that this is properly domesticated and sanctified by religion, as in the myth of the Virgin of Guadalupe.

Other instances of continuity and change may be found in the Gómez views of modernization and religion. Changing tenets of the Catholic church entail new attitudes, particularly among the younger generations, concerning education, women, birth control, and the roles of employers, workers, and the government. Such ideological changes are a source of stress among the generations; but eventually the new ideas are incorporated into the family ideology. They may not completely displace the older formations; rather, layers upon layers of ideological strata can coexist in an ideological complex. Contradictory elements within the family ideology may even be perceived as a strength rather than a weakness: tension between generations, branches, or individuals does not threaten family solidarity. In time the Gómez ideology takes on the appearance of a coherent body of beliefs and values, capable of dealing with every circumstance of an individual's life and with any historical situation the group may confront. Hence the strong feeling of identity that is shared by members of the Gómez kinship group.

The economy is the area of social life where changes are perhaps most readily detected. Each branch of the family is descended from an ancestor who differentiated himself or herself from the other siblings, thus determining the eventual class position of his or her branch. At present the social position of family members ranges over the classes or strata of urban Mexico that identify to a greater or lesser degree with the dominant sector. Gómez dominance has persisted in the face of family segmentation and class differentiation.

We shall describe how the Gómez enterprises evolved and how the Gómez entrepreneurs kept modifying their business strategies in order to stay afloat as members of the industrial elite. Yet there is also continuity in the structure of their businesses, which remain essentially family enterprises; in the importance of social networks in the economy; in the pattern of patron-client relationships; and in the general attitude of the entrepreneurs toward business as a means and a vehicle of family status rather than as an end in itself.

Economy and Meaning

A relatively recent tradition of anthropological thought is concerned with understanding the relationship between culture as a system of meanings on the one hand and the logic of economic rationality on the other. Sahlins (1976b) has attempted a critique of the idea that human cultures can be described or interpreted exclusively in terms of utilitarian or rational pursuits, that is, as adaptive formations aimed at survival. This controversy is relevant here because the Gómez kinship group is a distinct economic interest group with a particular subculture in Mexican urban society.

Sahlins argues that utilitarianism, including the Marxist view of social life as based on economics, is a peculiarly western, bourgeois viewpoint. By artificially segregating the economy from the rest of social life and endowing it with a kind of autonomy, "culture is organized in the final analysis by the material nature of things and cannot . . . transcend the reality structure manifested in production" (1976b, 207). This leads to the erroneous conclusion that material factors determine culture in a manner that is independent of human will and therefore more "real" than the symbolic system, which is supposed to adapt and yield to these material factors.

However, the practical effect of a material factor is not inherently given: rather, "the practical interest of men in production is symbolically constituted" (Sahlins 1976b, 207); it is a *cultural* datum. The problem of nature *versus* culture must not be seen as one determining the other; "rather the reverse: the action of nature unfolds in the terms of culture" (ibid., 209).

This study began as an analysis of the economy of a group, with the expectation of explaining the kinship system on the basis of the economy. Implicitly this approach was based on the western bourgeois, "practical" logic criticized by Sahlins. In other words, the phenomenon of family cohesion was to be "explained" by reference to the nature of the family enterprise, which requires close cooperation among trusted personnel such as can be found within the family circle. The economic importance of exchange of information among kin was to be stressed, the economic utility of belonging to a powerful kinship group was to be pointed out, and so on.

Yet the more we penetrated the social reality of the family, the more we realized that this economic logic, though essentially correct, was neither unique nor decisive. There were instances in the economic arena, for example, in which key decisions ran directly counter to the principle of maximization of utility. Such decisions could not simply be dismissed as irrational: they obeyed a different logic, one that informants were able to supply.

We concluded that the Gómez entrepreneurs supported a large number of relatives, spent money on rituals, and kept idle personnel on their payrolls for reasons not based on economic gain. There had to be something else: a cultural imperative, a precept of noblesse oblige, a need to be a member of a group and to earn prestige within that group. We discovered that people wasted valuable resources and made decisions against economic sense in order to gain ascendancy or to satisfy cravings for family sentiment and a feeling of belonging. In some cases the enterprise was seriously jeopardized by these decisions: in the 1960s Gómez entrepreneurs refused to incorporate because of pride and similar cultural reasons, a collective decision that cost the family its rank and financial preeminence among the upper bourgeoisie of Mexico.

We gradually came to the realization that economic logic can be subordinated to a powerful logic of a different order. People want to make money, not because money is the key resource of the economic system but to prove their personal worth. The wealthy nurture relationships with poor relatives because of a positive connotation of generosity within the ideological context of the family and because it is also a way of expressing both their social origins and their subsequent progress. The meaningful element in business for these industrialists is status and personal power; capital is not valued in itself, but rather as a means of gaining status.

Gómez entrepreneurs resist forming conglomerates or "going public" because these decisions imply forfeiting individual power over their businesses. A corporate executive can no longer provide jobs for his nephews and nieces; he cannot withdraw capital for real estate deals or for a daughter's wedding. None of this makes business sense in a world that is being

13

overrun by multinational corporations. As a result of acting according to this cultural logic, some old-style Mexican industrialists go under and are bought out by the multinational corporations they had wanted to remain separate from. Yet the case of the Gómez family shows that there is no general rule whereby "cultural reasons" can be shown to predominate over "practical reasons" or vice versa. If business is seriously threatened by the persistence of a given cultural pattern, the young entrepreneurs find new ideologies that allow them to meet the challenge. Rules of solidarity are redefined continuously in order to preserve the basic kinship structure in the face of new and unexpected material conditions.

If humans are "bi-dimensional" creatures (Cohen 1974), power relations like those found in economy or in politics represent one dimension and symbolic actions (as in kinship, ritual, and ideology) represent another. Culture is the result of the interaction between economic forces and symbolic forces. Economic survival represents one important aspect of human life; identity, beliefs, and loyalties, another. Kinship bridges the gulf between macro- and microstructure. It occupies the focal point between continuity and change and it is the arena or battleground between economic forces and abstract values in human societies. The Gómez are not merely a group of industrial capitalists and their clients, members of the bourgeoisie in a dependent capitalist country: they are also a Mexican family.

CHAPTER I

The Gómez and the Social Formation of Mexico

AFTER THE War of Independence (1810-1821), during the first half of the nineteenth century, Mexico was the scene of continuous war, economic stagnation, and regional fragmentation. Mining—the principal economic activity during the colonial period—dropped to less than half the level it had attained in the eighteenth century. Agriculture declined and landowners, bankrupt, were deeply indebted to the Church. Industry was extremely backward. The only source of capital accumulation was commerce, in particular the import trade, which was mostly in the hands of foreigners. The Church remained the country's most powerful economic and political institution.

The early period of the Mexican Republic may be described as a contest between the Liberals, who favored modernization along the lines of a secular state, and the Conservatives, who wished to maintain the status quo. The Liberals gained power in 1857; their leader, President Benito Juárez, instituted the Reform Laws, under which Church properties were expropriated and sold on the free market. The Church was also barred from economic and political activities. The Reform Laws, however, were not enforced until 1867, after the interlude of the French-Conservative reaction that put Maximilian on the imperial throne of Mexico. In his second term of office (1867-1872), President Juárez promoted basic modernization programs, including education and the reorganization and centralization of the state apparatus, to unify the nation. He also started building the México-Veracruz railroad, which was finished in 1873 (Calderon 1965). His support grew to include a new group of industrialists and bankers as well as liberal professionals. Yet the Church still retained considerable power several decades later, though its financial operations were often carried out under borrowed names (Bailey 1974; Bazant 1971; Brading 1975; Cosío Villegas 1965; Cumberland 1968; Knowlton 1976; Otero 1967; Oyarzábal 1979; Palerm 1980; Quirk 1973; Roeder 1973, 71).

The state of Puebla, ancestral home of the Gómez family, had always been dominated by the colonial capital of Puebla, which was known as an industrial city from the nineteenth century on. The city of Puebla was then a major trading center because of its strategic location on the road from Mexico City to Veracruz, the principal Mexican port. This was the normal route of entrance for foreign imports, mostly of European origin. Many members of the Puebla merchant community were foreigners who also owned the local industries. Farming and ranching were closely connected with industry and with urban life in general. The dominant power in Puebla during the nineteenth century was the Church: it owned half the real estate of the city, including its numerous and large convents, which were among the wealthiest in Mexico. But the relative prosperity that prevailed in the city did not extend to the countryside; in particular, eastern Puebla was a depressed area with a decaying agriculture (Bazant 1971, 44-45; Calderón de la Barca 1970, 34).

The Porfiriato (1876-1911)

General Porfirio Díaz became president in 1876, at a time when the country was again bankrupt and as dismembered as ever. The "Porfiriato" stressed communications, development, and the political unity of the country. The railroad project continued, involving foreign investment, and eventually foreign capital generated movement toward industrialization and modernization in the late nineteenth century. Capitalization and political integration and control allowed the consolidation of a modern central state. This development, however, was purchased at the price of economic and political dependence on the Great Powers, particularly the United States and Great Britain (Cordero 1977; Cosío Villegas 1973; Cumberland 1968; Hansen 1974, 22; Roeder 1973, 55-69).

Commercial agriculture began to produce for national as well as foreign markets. Textile and shoe factories began to displace the artisanal production in these important industries. Exports became more diversified, and imports increased year by year. The rate of growth of the national product was on the order of 2.7 percent per year against a population increase of 1.4 percent. Growth and relative prosperity were the result of political stability, foreign investments, and improvements in internal communications (Hansen 1974, 22).

The thirty-five years of the "Paz Porfiriana" gave birth to a class of professional bureaucrats known as "científicos" (literally, scientists) and to a new class, the industrialists. The per capita consumption of industrial textile goods increased by 25 percent in a ten-year period. During the same period the per capita consumption of sugar increased by 50 percent and the demand for cement, steel, glass, tobacco, and processed foods increased by comparable amounts. A process of import substitution began in the cotton goods industry (Hansen 1974, 19-22).

The earliest entrepreneurs in Mexico City were manufacturers of textiles and other consumer goods, today considered among the more traditional and less dynamic fields of Mexico's industrial economy. From the beginning, there was a differentiation between the consumer industries of central Mexico, which required a considerable marketing infrastructure with relatively low investments and low technology, and the heavy industry around Monterrey, in the north.

What was the source of capital for the industrial development of Mexico? Some early entrepreneurs were originally hacienda owners who became merchants and then industrialists. Others were merchants who became manufacturers. Many industries were begun by European immigrants and foreign investors (Derossi 1972a; Glade and Anderson 1963, 15; Hansen 1974; J. Meyer 1980, 5-9; Molina Enríquez 1979, 299; Salazar 1971). Another source of capital accumulation was the import-export business: import of consumer goods and capital goods, and export of agricultural produce and raw materials (Glade and Anderson 1968; Hansen 1974; Molina Enríquez 1979; NAFINSA 1971).

In terms of generation of capital, farming and ranching in Mexico had long been divided into two separate areas, export and internal consumption. The sisal plantations in the south provide a ready example of an export crop that was once a major source of capital. On the other hand, farming for the internal market was already stagnant in the nineteenth century and may even have been declining. Only export crops and what is commonly known as agrobusiness were potential sources of capitalization in Mexico.

The merchants were the capitalists, moneylenders, and bankers of the nineteenth century. Better communications and the inflow of capital investment fueled the development of commerce and provided the necessary income for traders to invest in industry. Not all members of this emergent class were foreigners; many were Mexicans. Yet industrial development was severely limited by the lack of a modern infrastructure and particularly by the small size and the weakness of the internal market. Most of the population was poor and was not geared to industrial consumption, which forced industrialists to look for foreign outlets. Thus industry could hardly have played a major role as a source of capitalization in the period (Molina Enríquez 1979, 311; Otero 1967; Oyarzábal 1979).

According to Walker (1979, 15-18), Mexican entrepreneurs were financed by foreign capital and by the state. The regime of Porfirio Díaz favored industrialization and provided considerable facilities for foreign capital to associate with local industrialists and merchants. Between 1896 and 1910, Mexican entrepreneurs invested 87 million pesos in new manufacturing enterprises. This is a substantial amount when compared to the total foreign investment (131 million pesos in 1911). The fact that so many new Mexican entrepreneurs emerged is surprising if one remembers that agriculture was depressed and that mining decayed throughout the nineteenth century. It seems unlikely that the capital surplus required for industrialization could have been generated internally.

There is another source of capital, however, that has often

been overlooked. Knowlton (1976, 237) estimates that between 1,000 and 1,250 million gold pesos in Church properties were nationalized during the administration of Benito
Juárez (1867-1872). Most of these lands were sold by the state
to private citizens, and the resale was a source of considerable
profit. On the other hand, it seems certain that only part of the
wealth of the Church was actually confiscated. Knowlton
(1976, 36-37), Quirk (1973, 17), and Cumberland (1968,
240) mention that fictitious "sales" of Church property to individuals considered trustworthy were commonplace. We as-
sume that such individuals became Church trustees, administrators of Church funds, and partners with the Church in a
large number of enterprises. The Church drew a regular income from such enterprises and the trustees became wealthy
entrepreneurs. Under the liberal government of Porfirio Díaz,
small entrepreneurs and traders could rise to prominence with
the help of Church loans; the government provided all kinds of
legal support and facilities (Walker 1979, 15-18) and the
Church provided the capital if conditions of confidentiality
and trust were met. The main sources of capitalization and industrial investment during the Porfirian period, then, were the
import-export trade, real estate, agrobusiness (export crops),
government subsidies, and covert operations financed by the
Church.

Racial distinctions played a part in economic differentiation
under the Porfiriato. Foreigners were at the top of the social
ladder; they included French, Americans, and British as well as
Spaniards. Next came the *criollos*, Mexican-born whites of
European extraction. This class included a few mestizos, persons of mixed Indian and Spanish origins, who were industrialists, entrepreneurs, and top-level politicians. Molina Enríquez calls them "directors." Finally there were the broad mass
of mestizos and the indigenous population. The sources of capital were fully controlled by the ruling class. Social prestige
was still largely based on the ownership of land. Thus toward
the end of the nineteenth century, the ruling class was identified as the class of landowners, and even the industrialists and

19

merchants owned estates for status reasons (Molina Enríquez 1979, 299-300).

The process of economic growth during the Porfiriato was self-limiting. The development of communications, for example, brought enormous benefits to formerly remote and disconnected regions of the country, but it also favored the growth of the metropolis at the expense of the provinces. Puebla, once a hub of commercial activities, became a provincial backwater when the new México-Veracruz railroad bypassed it. Most of the imports were now shipped directly to the capital.

Foreign investments favored capitalization, but they also produced a distorted economy geared to the export-import trade, to the detriment of the domestic market (Calderón 1965; Hansen 1974). The stick-and-carrot policy of the Porfiriato allowed unchecked development of social and economic inequalities. Social pressures rose among the peasantry and the middle class (Cosío Villegas 1973; Cumberland 1979; Hansen 1974; Molina Enríquez 1979).

Economic growth under Porfirio Díaz began to level off around the turn of the century. This was due to decreasing world demand for Mexican silver and other exports, a low capacity of growth of the internal market, saturation of the job market, and increasing socioeconomic unrest. Members of the rising middle class, reacting against the cultural and economic penetration of foreign capital, provided the leadership for revolution (Cosío Villegas 1973, 3398-3406; Cumberland 1968; Hansen 1974; Roeder 1973).

Origins of the Gómez Family (1800-1910)

During the late eighteenth century there lived, in what is now the state of Puebla, a *hacendado* (landowner) named Pedro Gómez. The family was of criollo stock; descendants claim that Pedro Gómez could trace his lineage, on his mother's side, to Spanish settlers of the sixteenth century. San Felipe de Jesús, the only Mexican saint, was reputed to have been a member of the family. The association, whether verified or not, is a way of identifying with the old Catholic and criollo gentry of New Spain.

Don Pedro had three sons and five daughters (1,1-8),[1] born at the beginning of the nineteenth century. The eldest son, a merchant, was apparently the principal heir. He had two sons and one daughter, María Guadalupe (II,11). This account of the family, however, is primarily concerned with the descendants of Carlos (1,3), the third son of don Pedro. His marriage to the daughter of a Spanish landowner in 1852 produced three sons, born between 1853 and 1858. His wife died in childbirth and Carlos remarried soon after; his second wife, Inés Aburto (1,e″3), was a poor Indian girl from a nearby village. They had seven children: two boys and five girls, born between 1862 and 1874.

By 1869 the village of Tepetlán[2] had grown into a small town, with a population over 30,000, and had become an agricultural and trading center. According to the town archives, the Gómez brothers were merchants and prominent town citizens; they seemed to have enjoyed better than average status and education. By 1871-1872 Carlos was registered as a tradesman, in partnership with his brother Antonio (1,2). As for the sisters of don Carlos, little information has been found. One (1,8) married a rich man in the city of Puebla, and her descendants were lost to the family. The other four sisters became nuns; they remained in contact with their brothers and nephews until they died. (See fig. 1, p. 52, and appendix.)

In 1876 don Carlos died, leaving little to his widow except the burden of raising nine children between the ages of one and twenty-three. The eldest son, Carlos (II,13), had already taken up residence in Puebla. Roberto (II,14), a law student at the University of Puebla, interrupted his studies upon his father's death in order to support his stepmother and his younger siblings. The last son of don Carlos's first marriage, Saúl (II,15), was therefore able to complete his studies; he became a lawyer, thanks to his brother's economic support. Both Saúl and Roberto are remembered as masculine, elegant, and very handsome: tall, blond, white-skinned, and blue-eyed.

[1] See preface and appendix for explanation of identification system.
[2] Fictitious name.

Aware of the difficult economic situation, their cousin María Guadalupe (ii,11), married to a wealthy Spanish merchant named Juan Miranda (ii,e'11), offered to take Leopoldo (ii,16), then fourteen years old, to live with them in Puebla City and work for her husband. Doña Inés and her five smaller children remained in Tepetlán and were supported by the older sons and relatives. Unlike the three older sons of don Carlos, who all eventually achieved a university education, their mestizo half brothers only completed primary school.

Young Leopoldo was now working in his cousin's store in Puebla. Don Juan Miranda was a well-known merchant dealing in imported ribbons, lace, and fabrics. His business had declined after the México-Veracruz railroad had begun operating in 1873. Eventually, he decided to relocate in the capital, a move that occurred shortly after Leopoldo joined him.

The Mexico City store was set up in partnership with a group of Catalonian businessmen; it became one of the city's better-known establishments. Leopoldo rose to be manager, and by 1886 the archives show that he became a partner of the firm, with a share of 20,000 pesos. Around the same time he went into his first textile venture, in partnership with Spanish capital, setting up the textile factory "La Paisana." In 1889 he built another textile factory, with three partners and capital of 6 million pesos. It was largely through Juan Miranda that Leopoldo was able to connect himself with the Spanish business community. After the death of don Juan in 1887, Leopoldo's half brother Saúl, by then an established lawyer, was appointed tutor to don Juan's young children (iii,27-34). Leopoldo lived downtown, in the home of his business partner, not far from the store. During the 1890s he arranged for his mother and remaining younger brothers and sisters to join him in Mexico City. His eldest brother Carlos remained in Puebla and became lost to the family. Brother Roberto moved to Mexico City at about the same time.

Thus around 1890 the core of the Gómez family was settled in Mexico City, which then had nearly half a million inhabitants. Relations with family members who had stayed behind in Puebla waned. Leopoldo bought a house in the Tacuba quarter for himself, his mother, and his younger brothers and sisters; in 1893 he married Juana Casés (11,e'16), a girl of Italian background and of modest social origins.

Tacuba in 1879 was "a poor village with a big church in the old style, flanked by a ruined convent . . . whose tall walls and tall slender tower overlooked a group of little white-topped houses in disarray among brownish adobe huts with shingle roofs, hiding a sad and miserable population" (Cosío Villegas 1974b, 99). The extended family lived together in the same home. Eventually, before the end of the century, they moved into a larger and better home on Puente de Alvarado Street in the Guerrero quarter, a better neighborhood and closer to downtown. Leopoldo, his wife, and their three young children lived upstairs; Mamá Inés and the unmarried sisters lived on the ground floor. It was a closely knit household: Leopoldo's sisters, in particular, were extremely close to each other.

In 1895 Leopoldo's brother Modesto (11,17) married a middle-class woman. They set up a clothing store in a town in the state of Michoacán. Sister Rosalía (11,20) wed a Spaniard, a friend of Leopoldo's who was employed by one of Leopoldo's most important business associates. They joined Modesto and became business partners in Michoacán.

By 1909 Leopoldo owned textile factories, lumber mills, banks, insurance companies, urban and rural real estate, tobacco mills, and shares in a wide variety of mining, industrial, and commercial ventures. Foreign and domestic corporations sought him out as a partner. One of these partners, according to some informants, was the Catholic church. No hard evidence of such an association has been found, but there were close personal friendships between family members and Church dignitaries from the earliest days to the present. The Gómez family has always been devoutly Catholic and actively interested in furthering the cause of the Church.

Saúl, the lawyer, having spent ten years as a political official in the state of Mexico, moved to Mexico City in 1907 and also settled in the Guerrero quarter, a few blocks away from Leopoldo. He was entrusted with the legal affairs of the family and remained their lawyer until his death in the 1930s.

Brothers, half brothers, and their families huddled close to the house of Mamá Inés; they were all extremely attached to her and visited her daily. Her home, where all celebrations were held, was the focus of family life. There was considerable exchange of favors and assistance among members of the family. By 1910, when the Mexican Revolution put an end to the Porfiriato, the family of Leopoldo Gómez had acquired social and economic connections with the new group of criollos and mestizos who were on the rise during the early years of the new century.

The development of the Gómez family parallels the history of Mexico prior to 1910. For a mestizo like Leopoldo Gómez, access to capitalization was to be found in commerce and under the protection of the Church. He was able to overcome his initial handicaps as an impecunious provincial mestizo lad in a criollo-dominated society thanks to family connections and, later, to social and business friendships.

The family history provides some insight into the advantages of large kin networks for social mobility. The transition from the village to the salons of urban bourgeois high society was accomplished within a few years, through the combined assistance of brothers, cousins, sons, and other relatives. The new Mexican entrepreneur was not a driving individualist (as he might have been in the United States), but the leader of a large extended family, a kinship group that he brought with him up the social and economic ladder.

Revolution and Reconstruction: 1910-1940

The 1910 revolution provided opportunities for mestizos in virtually all sectors of Mexican society. The mestizos quickly learned the game of politics: they jettisoned their alliances with the prerevolutionary dominant classes and looked for new allegiances. The economic basis for a new mestizo society was agrarian reform, based on the distribution of confiscated land; the ideological basis was the quest for the Indian past (Wolf 1967, 217-18).

Between the outbreak of the Revolution and the pacification and reunification of Mexico in 1921, the entire country underwent tremendous destruction. The population decreased from 15.2 million in 1910 to 14.5 million in 1921. The peasantry was forced to leave its homes. Many died; others eventually settled in the large cities. Industrial production was nearly paralyzed and many industries were destroyed. Manufacturing decreased by 9 percent (Hansen 1974, 43; Silva Herzog 1970; Womack 1968).

The 1917 constitution of postrevolutionary Mexico was basically nationalistic. It had four principal objectives: (1) building a sociopolitical economic structure that vested decisive control over resources in national institutions (national autonomy or independence in economic as well as in political affairs); (2) restructuring the economic system to "internalize its dynamics," that is, regrouping the dominant factors and forces of the economy and making them responsive primarily to internal rather than external conditions; (3) gradual elaboration of a more democratic structure of opportunities with a broader participation in the decision-making processes; and (4) an economic organization in which the benefits of growth would accrue primarily to Mexicans and translate into rising standards of living for the population at large (Glade and Anderson 1963, 28-29). The eventual result was the emergence of a Mexican nationality and a national consciousness. Rapid growth began immediately after pacification. The population of Mexico City doubled between 1920 and 1930, and the urban area tripled during the same period (J. Meyer 1977, 279).

The nationalistic urban middle class that rose to power in these years was largely composed of intellectuals, native businessmen, and professionals. In 1917-1918 the state invited Mexican business to create the National Confederation of Chambers of Commerce (CONCANACO) and the National Confederation of Industrialists (CONCAMIN), in a spirit of "nationalism, patriotism, business responsibility and social consciousness" (Alcaraz 1977, 34; Brandenburg 1962, 5; Shafer 1973).

Under the nationalistic administrations of the revolutionary generals Alvaro Obregón (1921-1924) and Plutarco Elías Calles (1924-1928), both leaders of the new elite and both of northern origin, the nation was unified and a powerful central state apparatus was created along the lines of the 1917 constitution. The economic foundations were laid for a capitalistic system stressing modernization, development, and industrialization. Gold and silver mining remained an important source of income, and oil appeared as a major export. Investments from the United States were again welcomed (Aguilar Camín 1977; Krauze 1977).

During the 1920s major state agencies were created to supplement and assist the economic activity of private industry and to attract foreign capital. Electric power, transport, and irrigation were major concerns. More important, the state consolidated the national banking system, which undertook to finance development with the assistance of foreign capital (Hamilton 1982).

In 1925 President Calles created the Banco de México, Mexico's federal reserve bank. He also provided support for Mexican private banks and promoted the creation of the National Association of Bankers. The Calles administration may be seen as a period of vigorous political and economic reconstruction: "economic development of the country became a priority, and politics was placed at the service of development." Because of a new emphasis on national unity, the revolutionary language of class struggle was toned down and euphemisms such as "the labor element" or "the capital factor" began to be used (Anderson 1968, 116; Hamilton 1982; Krauze 1977, 18-26; L. Meyer 1978a, 50).

A strong labor movement also began to assert its power, through the creation of the Regional Confederation of Mexican Workers (CROM). Labor–management meetings were organized to promote industrial development; one such convention took place in 1927 in the textile industry, with the participation of 119 entrepreneurs and 116 labor representatives (Krauze 1977, 189-190; J. Meyer 1977, 89-93).

A new crisis hit Mexico in 1926. Falling international prices of gold and silver produced a nationwide recession. At the same time, the revolutionary regime was seriously challenged by the Cristero Rebellion. Provincial armies under the banner of "Christ is King" rose against the authority of the central state. In this situation, the state remained victorious. It was now in a position to organize its policies of modernization, and the first step was the creation of a political apparatus that secured the concentration and survival of central power. The Church lost all its remaining formal political and economic influence but still retained its position of moral leadership. The confidential role of lay trustees in the administration of Church funds became more crucial than ever (J. Meyer 1977, 237-82).

General Obregón, the strong man of the regime and the heir apparent of President Calles, was assassinated in 1928. Alarmed at the imminent power vacuum, Calles decided to create a political party capable of reconciling and unifying the factions within the revolutionary movement. There was no other way to prevent a new round of armed uprisings. Henceforth the factional leaders would peacefully resolve their differences within the Partido Nacional Revolucionario (PNR). The president would be selected through political negotiation rather than through armed conflict. The party's constitutive assembly acknowledged that Mexico was entering a new stage of development and required a nationalistic approach to political problems. In providing an organized body in which rival claims to power could be processed in a relatively orderly way, the party consolidated, regulated, and legitimated the government created by the constituents. The party platform was self-contradictory: it was for labor and for capital, for the traditional peasantry and for modernization. It was open to anyone who agreed to respect and enforce party discipline. The PNR (later changed to Partido Revolucinario Institucional, or PRI) explicitly recognized and legitimized the existence of other interest groups and power centers outside the party, including the business community, the industrialists, the military, and the Church: no attempt was made to assimilate such groups into the party structure. The party became in effect an alliance of political leaders: a machine for the control of bosses and factions. A new value system began to be adopted by the economic, political, and intellectual elites of the country. Nationalism and support of the central government became synonymous with economic progress and the avoidance of direct

27

confrontations under the benevolent and paternalistic leadership of the state. The new values encouraged the development of political methods based on negotiation and cooptation as alternatives to armed repression. A new educational system was created in order to propagate the ideology of national unity and economic development (Glade and Anderson 1963, 27, 43; ibid. 1979; L. Meyer 1978a, 87-90; Purcell and Purcell 1977, 191-227; Stevens 1977, 230-50).

Dissident regional leaders and bosses were given the means to become entrepreneurs. This has become a pattern in recent economic history, in the sense that public officials were allowed to dip into the state coffers and to retire as businessmen when the next administration began. Eventually three kinds of capitalists emerged in Mexico: retired politicians, old entrepreneurs and bankers who had survived the Revolution, and the new entrepreneurs who were dependent on state financing or on the support of the major Mexican financial corporations (Hamilton 1982).

By 1932 the gross national product of Mexico was still below the level it had reached in 1910; yet the impact of the world depression was less severely felt in Mexico than in other Latin American countries. There was no net recession: the economy had nowhere to go but up. Basically the country was agrarian and no internal market or national industry to speak of existed (L. Meyer 1978a, 3).

The administration of Lázaro Cárdenas (1934-1940) was nationalistic with strong socialist overtones. There was an emphasis on land reform, incorporating a major sector of the peasantry into the market economy. The creation of peasant organizations and the strengthening of the labor movement increased tensions between the government and the bourgeoisie. The government sought massive popular support; the explicit socialistic trends, particularly in education, scared members of the upper middle class. In 1938, the nationalization of the petroleum industry drastically curtailed foreign as well as national investments (Cordero 1977, 6-7; Glade and Anderson 1979, 63-68; Guadarrama 1977, 62; Medina 1974, 14; NAFINSA 1971, 212-13).

The scheme of state intervention favored by Cárdenas seemed amply justified by the disastrous socioeconomic situation of the country. In 1934 Mexico could be described as "a handful of wealthy people, 15% middle class and a huge impoverished and destitute mass amounting to 84% of the population" (González 1979, 13-14). The basic industries—oil, mining, and the railroads—were in the hands of foreign capital. In spite of the Revolution, large haciendas were still common. But the textile industry was owned by Mexican entrepreneurs who initially supported the Cárdenas regime. Mexico City generated one-third of the industrial production of the country and contained most of its wealth and culture (ibid., 133).

Nacional Financiera (NAFINSA), the national credit and finance corporation, was created in 1934; it has since financed countless public and private industrial projects. The creation in 1936 of the Mexican Workers' Confederation (CTM) favored the establishment of orderly procedures of collective bargaining, a key element in industrialization. A new law of chambers of commerce and industry regulated and facilitated communication between entrepreneurs, labor, and the state. Finally, nationalization of oil and railroads eventually proved a boon to development: it enabled the transportation and power requirements of local industry to be subsidized by the state. Many economic policies initiated under Cárdenas still continue today, but they produced considerable unrest and opposition among the industrial and business communities at the time. The last months of the Cárdenas administration signaled an apparent reversal of his radical trends and a new emphasis on reconciliation with capital. His successor, Avila Camacho, continued the policy of national conciliation and implemented concrete measures to encourage industrialization (Derossi 1972b, 18; Hansen 1974, 49-50; NAFINSA 1971, 213-14).

Politically, the central state apparatus was built on the strength of a party that initially represented a coalition of regional leaders. The unifying principle was nationalism; it was sustained by an educational system aimed at involving the masses in political and economic development. A vast infrastructure of electric power and transportation was first developed and then nationalized in accordance with the prevailing state ideology. Major irrigation schemes were also developed in support of agriculture. The state continued to use local and foreign sources of capital to create the necessary financial structure for industrialization and development. The Church indirectly retained a role as a banking institution. The major social aim of the succeeding administrations during this period was to rally all social sectors and groups around these objectives of nationalism and development. Government and industry formed an alliance to lead the country toward modernization (Vázquez de Knauth 1975).

Gradually, the centralized economy broke the back of the old provincial leadership and promoted the ascendancy of strong entrepreneurial groups closely allied with the state and with foreign capital. Small entrepreneurs had to do business with the new power groups in order to survive. The agricultural countryside remained backward despite revolution, land reform, state finance agencies, and irrigation projects, an imbalance that generated an influx of population into Mexico City. It began to grow very rapidly, and real estate ventures there became another important alternate means of capitalization. At the outbreak of the Second World War, Mexico was economically ripe for accelerated development, yet serious flaws and contradictions persisted in the political, economic, and social structure.

The Gómez Family (1910-1925)

When the Revolution broke out in 1910, the process of migration and adaptation of the Gómez family to city life was complete. They had followed a standard pattern: the first migrant, a young unmarried son, joins relatives in the city. Once settled, he brings his nuclear family to the city and they live together in an extended family arrangement. Eventually they marry into urban families and sever their ties with the rural branches of the family. During the years of adaptation to the urban environment, they move repeatedly from one quarter of the city to another. Then a process of segmentation and stratification begins. Most of the descendants of Carlos Gómez clustered physically and economically around Leopoldo and Mamá Inés in Mexico City.

According to oral tradition, the Gómez family life in general and Leopoldo's interests in particular were undisturbed by the revolutionary period. The facts are otherwise: Leopoldo had been a partner of landowners and industrial leaders of the Porfirian regime. In 1913 he left the country and lived in Spain for two years; according to informants this move was simply due to business reasons. Mamá Inés remained in Mexico with two unmarried daughters plus Cecilia (II,21) and her husband. This new son-in-law, Blas Jiménez (II,e'21), had arrived in Mexico from Spain around 1880. He started out as a hacienda overseer and eventually became the administrator of a large hacienda. He was a thrifty man; around 1908 he invested his savings in public bathhouses in downtown Mexico City. These were common at the time and were among the favorite investments of the resident Spanish community. He also bought a large dairy ranch outside the city. When the Revolution broke out don Blas was a prosperous businessman, already married to Cecilia. According to family tradition, the Revolution also affected him not at all: on the contrary, he was able to increase his personal fortune to a considerable extent. Cecilia was reputed to be homely ("dark-skinned") but blue-eyed; she was also said to have been talented and courted by men. A devout woman, she remained close to her mother and sisters throughout her life.

Mamá Inés's son Modesto and daughter Rosalía returned from Michoacán to Mexico City and bought a small downtown hotel that then provided their main source of income. Their half brothers Saúl and Roberto were also in town, as was their brother Leopoldo, now trustee of the estate of his cousin and benefactor, Juan Miranda. By 1910 five of the nine children of Juan Miranda had died or had emigrated to the United States. Saúl had continued to tutor the surviving daughters. Eventually nothing remained of Juan Miranda's fortune.

As was customary for girls at the time, the education of these daughters had been rudimentary. Alone and without support, they became entirely dependent on Leopoldo. They attempted to find ways to make a living, but this was not easy. Two of them made dresses for friends and relatives, though unfortunately they were totally inexperienced in this craft. Going to a fashion school was out of the question due to their position in society. To teach themselves they borrowed dresses from relatives and friends, took them apart, copied the patterns, and then sewed the originals together again, hoping no one would notice. The other sister taught the elements of Catholic religion to all the family's small children until about 1960. The Mirandas were protected by Leopoldo and Saúl, and later by Leopoldo Jr. (III,50). Family members agreed that they had a responsibility toward the Miranda sisters and used their services as dressmakers as much as possible. In 1913, during the civil war, an epidemic broke out in Mexico City, causing the death of the mother of the Miranda girls, María Guadalupe. As single women, the daughters did not dare go out by themselves. Leopoldo, in Spain at the time, sent them black fabric to make the dresses they needed to wear in mourning; Saúl arranged for the burial. This story was told in 1976 by Juanita (III,34), the last surviving Miranda daughter.

The Mirandas were closely integrated in the Gómez network. Their presence was a prominent feature of all social occasions and their ideological influence on the religious socialization of the Gómez children was considerable. Juanita died at the age of 90 in 1977, and her funeral was a major family event, with all acknowledged kin from every branch participating.

Into the 1920s, the family lived in one particular part of town: Mamá Inés and her unmarried daughters lived with Leopoldo on Puente de Alvarado Street, Cecilia and her husband lived in the same quarter, and both Saúl and Roberto lived a few blocks away, in Santa María de la Rivera. Rosalía, Modesto, and the Miranda women lived downtown, within walking distance of the main family core. Everyone lived no more than 15 minutes from everyone else. This favored an intense family life and promoted mutual support and assistance among the relatives.

While Leopoldo was abroad, it seems that Roberto and Saúl remained in charge of his business affairs in Mexico. In this they were assisted by their cousin Bernabé (III,23), a textile engineer who had married one of Modesto's daughters (III,55). As a result of the prevailing social and political instability, Saúl's two sons (III,43 and III,46) had to work in the family business instead of getting a professional education.

Leopoldo returned to Mexico in 1915 and found he had lost a part of his enterprises but had not been singled out for persecution, at least not directly like some of his former associates who had been large landowners. On the other hand, economic activity had come to a near standstill. Even so, he apparently had little difficulty in consolidating and building up his economic interests once again. By 1920 he owned just one enterprise, the textile factory "El Buen Gusto." Much of his income during the 1920s may have originated from real estate operations in Mexico city; however, he also purchased several smaller textile firms and became a partner in a garment factory in South America. His two sons, three nephews, and one son-in-law were in charge of his various interests and industrial firms. In the latter stage of his life, he preferred to work only with relatives and close friends. It seems that the Gómez distrust of business partners who are not part of the family dates from this period. Before 1915 Leopoldo did have partners, but after his return from Spain he insisted where possible on full personal control.

He could not have managed this financial comeback without the assistance of former associates in industry and banking. He may also have had support from the Catholic church. One of Saúl's daughters and one of Roberto's took their vows at this time. According to some informants, Leopoldo agreed to manage convent funds in his own name, in order to extend protection to nuns belonging to the family. This may also have increased his financial power as well as his business reputation.

He moved to Santa María de la Rivera, a quarter where he owned real estate and an upper-middle-class neighborhood at the time. His children all went to the French school. An informant of French origin who knew the family in this period described them as "middle class" and of lower social status than her own. Mamá Inés and the unmarried daughters moved into a separate home in the San Rafael quarter, a middle-class neighborhood a few blocks away from Leopoldo. Around 1920, the family slowly began to branch out from this downtown core: Saúl and Roberto purchased some real estate and built homes in Popotla, not very far from Santa María de la Rivera and still close to Mamá Inés and the family core.

Ritually and emotionally Mamá Inés continued to be the center of family life. Her daughters and sons visited her every day with their children. Her two stepsons came less often, but they too were devoted to their stepmother. The primary social events of the family still took place at her home; with the help of her daughters she organized all kinds of parties and family reunions. Her saint's day was a major affair, with active participation expected of every member of the family (even small children took part by displaying their musical skills or by presenting a theatrical skit). During the 1920s attendance at this festivity included all consanguineous relatives, their spouses, and eventually their children's fiancés. Each family member's close personal acquaintance with the kinship network began at the home of Mamá Inés. Of course there were other social opportunities, including birthdays, saint's days, welcoming parties, and other celebrations in honor of various members of the family. When Mamá Inés, because of her age, found herself unable to attend personally to details of all social events, her daughters and granddaughters took over.

Mamá Inés and some of her descendants were what we call "centralizing women." These are women who devote their lives to creating and transmitting the family ideology and to establishing information networks within the kinship group. They represent an important cohesive force.

The interaction among relatives was not limited to reunions at the home of Mamá Inés. There was also an active exchange of social amenities between the families and between individual family members. For example, the four daughters of Mamá Inés continued attending daily mass together, even after marriage. Their children were raised together; they jointly attended the catechism classes of the Miranda sisters; and so on. Similar close attachments were formed among the men. Modesto (II,17) and his brother-in-law Ramiro Bañuelos (II,e'20) were partners. Ramiro and don Blas Jiménez (II,e'21, Cecilia's husband) had been friends before becoming related through marriage; they regularly met once a week for a card game. Saúl and Roberto lived close to each other and helped each other constantly. Eventually, as we shall see, they became in-laws through the marriage of two of their children. Leopoldo, socially aloof because of his economic position, was solicitous and protective toward all members of the family and particularly the old ladies: his mother, his unmarried sisters, and the Miranda daughters. He had a special relationship with Saúl as his trusted legal advisor. Bernabé Gómez Salinas (III, 23), who worked under Leopoldo as a technician, eventually was married to all three daughters of Modesto, one after another. Many other examples of business relations, kinship relations, and marriage relations can be found. As a result, the 1920s saw the emergence of a closely knit kinship network centered about the patriarchal figure of the aging Leopoldo Gómez.

The Process of Segmentation

The urban area of Mexico City tripled between 1920 and 1930. In 1918 horse-drawn carriages were more common than automobiles; in 1928 the use of carriages was outlawed. The city was modernizing, paving streets, building parks, markets, and public buildings, and adding residential areas. One such area was Lomas de Chapultepec, where some of the Gómez later moved (Krauze 1977, 273-86).

Leopoldo had acquired a Spanish life style during his earlier residence there. According to informants, the family changed a great deal after his return from Spain: for example, they began to prefer Spanish food to Mexican, which until then had been the only kind of food they ate.

In 1924 Leopoldo became ill and returned to Spain for treatment; he didn't trust the local doctors in Mexico City. He died in 1925, the owner of four small textile factories and some urban real estate. His eldest son, Leopoldo Jr. (III,50), inherited the main textile factory, "El Buen Gusto," and his second son, Pablo (III,51), became the owner of a smaller textile factory called "La Nacional." Two daughters inherited small textile factories, to be managed by their husbands, and the remaining three daughters received houses and other real estate in Mexico City. Leopoldo's death was followed by the deaths of Mamá Inés in 1927 and Cecilia in 1928. Cecilia was survived by a daughter, Ana María (III,69), a twelve-year-old son, Pedro (III,72), and her husband don Blas, who abruptly withdrew with Pedro to his country estate. Ana María was taken in by Aunt Anita (II,22) but almost immediately married her first cousin, Ramiro Bañuelos Gomez (III,66), a son of Rosalía (II,20).

In 1931, when his son was seventeen, don Blas retired to Spain, leaving Pedro in charge of all his business interests in Mexico. However, Blas, a conservative, retained ultimate control from Spain, permitting no new investments or ventures. He died in 1945.

Anita (II,22), the youngest unmarried daughter of Mamá Inés, finally married in 1930. Her husband, David Camarena, was a middle-class Mexican from Puebla who worked for the recently founded Banco de México. Anita made her home in the quarter of Santa María de la Rivera and provided a small apartment for her unmarried sister Magdalena (II,18), who thus continued to live very near to Anita despite her marriage. Anita is described as very beautiful: blonde, very white, and blue-eyed. She was an excellent housewife and cook; some of her recipes, such as Holy Mother cake (a kind of marzipan cookie made of pumpkin seeds), almond cheese, *buñuelos*, and other desserts, have become family traditions. She never gave recipes to the wives of her nephews: only to Gómez women, the daughters of her sisters. As a result, the art of preparing old-style Mexican food is now exclusively found among the Bañuelos branch and Cecilia's granddaughters.

Even before the death of Mamá Inés and until her own death at the age of 92 in 1966, Anita became the organizer of the emotional and social life of the family. Strong-willed and assertive, she continually stored and exchanged information about events that were of relevance to the far-flung family network. Several of her nephews, nieces, grandnephews, and grandnieces saw her every day, year after year. Not having children of her own, she adopted Carmelita (III,40), the illegitimate daughter of her half brother Roberto (II,14).

The last five years of the 1920s are strongly imprinted on the collective memory of the Gómez family. Those were the years of the Cristero Rebellion (1926-1928) and of the official persecution of the Catholic faith. Priests and nuns went underground; some found shelter with the family. Masses and other rituals were held secretly at home. Women were afraid to leave the house. The Gómez built a secret church that was never discovered by the police. Those who were young at the time recall their childhood as filled with fear and secrecy.

In the notarial archives are the documents of several property purchases by Roberto and Saúl in those years; the deeds were made out in the names of their sons. According to family informants, Saúl and Roberto were well-to-do but hardly rich at the time; Saúl had found a "treasure" in his house that enabled him to improve his financial position substantially. Since Saúl, Roberto, and their descendants never enjoyed a wealth approaching that of Leopoldo, it seems likely that some of these real estate operations may actually have concealed Church properties.

Pablo Gómez (III,51), second son of Leopoldo, was acquainted with most of his father's friends in industry, commerce, and the Church. Pablo married a middle-class mestizo girl who was related to one of the rising bankers of the time, a man connected to the Banco Nacional group. Informants who knew Pablo in this period recall that he lived with his brother and sisters in the Santa María de la Rivera quarter, an area with a strong upper-middle-class flavor.

In contrast with his elder brother, Pablo was an aggressive entrepreneur. His philosophy was to buy: factories, real estate, stores, merchandise, antiques, anything he could afford. He is mentioned by historians of the Cárdenas administration (1934-1940) as one of its most powerful entrepreneurs and "a mainstay of Cardenismo" (González 1979). His connections were not limited to industrialists, bankers, entrepreneurs, and churchmen. He also cultivated the new political and military elite of the time, thus breaking with Gómez family precedents. In 1939 a prominent general was invited to become the godfather of Pablo's daughter, breaking a family tradition that restricted this honor only to close relatives.

His elder brother, Leopoldo Jr., had become a traditional, sedate family elder. His wife came from the old criollo landowner class, and Leopoldo began to cultivate a conservative image through his father's and his wife's relations. While Pablo was busily increasing the family fortune, Leopoldo built up the family prestige. Most of their sisters married impoverished descendants of the old landowner class, except one who married a wealthy Spanish immigrant. Relations among the brothers and sisters (and with the rest of the Gómez kin) remained exceptionally close. Aunt Anita's home was now the social and ritual center of the family; all cousins and nephews met there at least once a week to exchange family gossip and information of an economic and political kind. As an incidental result, five marriages between cousins occurred during this period. Among the male members of the family, all but a very few were working directly or indirectly for either Leopoldo Jr. or Pablo. Uncles Saúl and Roberto worked for them until the end of their lives (both died during the 1930s) and their sons Enrique (III,46) and Alvaro (III,43) remained trusted employees, as were Modesto (II,17), his son (III,59), Bernabé (III,23), and Bernabé's son (IV,73). Agustín Merino y Pacheco (III,e'48), husband of one of Pablo's sisters, became the family architect and builder. As Pablo's business empire spread out and diversified, he mobilized all available kin on behalf of his various enterprises, with the idea that each new concern should have a family member in a position of control.

The exceptions were rare. It seems that the sons of Rosalía and Cecilia worked largely on their own. Two members of the Bañuelos family were employed by foreign-owned firms and had some small investments of their own; one of them owned a small textile shop that did business with Pablo. One of the girls married the owner of a lumber business. Cecilia's son

Pedro Jiménez administered his father's interests and met and befriended Spanish businessmen as well as Mexican politicians, both civilian and military.

Some economic and social differentiation began to take place within the family during this period, as reflected in the gradual formation of four distinct kinship groups: (a) Magdalena (II,18), Rosalía (II,20), Anita (II,22), and their married offspring (including Cecilia's daughter [III,69], married to Ramiro [III,66]), lived in Santa María de la Rivera; (b) Modesto (II,17) and Bernabé (III,23) lived with their families in San Rafael; (c) Roberto (II,14) and Saúl (II,15) lived with their descendants in Popotla; and (d) the group of direct descendants of Leopoldo (II,16) also lived in Santa María de la Rivera.

Because of differentials in power and economic status, the relationships between members of these groups became increasingly asymmetrical, thus leading to the segmentation of the original family network into branches. In some cases these branches were relatively short-lived, either because of lack of offspring (in the case of the Miranda women) or because of voluntary removal or eventual exclusion of descendants who were deemed undesirable by the rest of the family. Leopoldo's descendants mingled with the economic, political, and social elites of the time, but the rest of the family remained typically middle class. Yet all members of the family appeared to share the sense of belonging that was distinctive to the Gómez as a family group.

The evolution of the Gómez fortunes is typical of the way in which the revolution and the postrevolutionary period affected entrepreneurial groups and Mexican middle-class society. Economic and social relations had remained stable during the Porfiriato; the elite was a small group of criollos, foreigners, and church dignitaries. After the Revolution, social and economic relations were in flux; a new class of mestizo politicians and bankers was on the rise. The traditional criollo landowner class, however, managed to retain its social prestige even after much of its original wealth was gone. The changes hint at new sources of capitalization in Mexico: the state and the banks. The Church retained some wealth but was stripped of practically all its power.

Leadership remained a major factor in the evolution of the Gómez family. First Leopoldo (II,16) and then Pablo (III,51) were the trailblazers and visible leaders of the Gómez group. Both were men with strong family instincts who enjoyed strong family support. They broke rules and set up new norms, when necessary, to keep abreast of the times; the group as a whole reaped the benefits. Some social stratification in the family became unavoidable as the kinship group branched out and grew in number. These differences were perpetuated by the laws of inheritance. Essentially, the branch of direct descendants of Leopoldo controlled the major share of the family wealth: they were the family entrepreneurs.

CHAPTER 2

The Gómez in Contemporary Mexico

B ECAUSE of the Second World War, Mexico had privileged access to the American market. Industrialization increased as a result of social and political peace in the country. A great deal of infrastructure had been created in the previous years: power, transportation, roads, irrigation, a central financing and banking apparatus, an educational system, organization of labor in the countryside and in the cities, and the administrative apparatus, as well as a spirit of development and economic progress. Mexico continued to attract foreign investment during the war years, particularly in the chemical, textile, food, and steel industries (Aguilar Zinzer 1978, 5). However, "the accelerated rate of economic growth and the transformation of the economic structure after 1940 are largely the result of Mexican savings and investments. The combination of public and private capital financed development amounting to a technological revolution in agriculture as well as in industry; and, in sharp contrast with the Porfirian regime, these investments had been generated by Mexican savings" (Hansen 1974, 58).

The economy of Mexico grew at a rate of 6.7 percent during 1940-1950, as compared to an annual rate of 1.6 percent during 1925-1940, 5.8 percent during 1950-1960, and 6.4 percent during 1960-1968. The center of gravity of the economy shifted from agriculture to manufacturing. Beginning with the administration of Manuel Avila Camacho (1940-1946), economic policy was directly and openly geared to industrial development. Public investment in industry doubled between 1940 and 1945; in contrast, public investments in the 1930s had been primarily in construction and railroads. The taxes on industry were among the lowest in Latin America. Among the new legislative measures designed to promote industrialization was the "Law of New and Necessary Industry" of May 1941, which granted a five-year tax exemption as well as an exemption from import duties on materials and equipment not manufactured in Mexico to new enterprises. The training of technical personnel for industry also became a primary concern of the state (Cordero 1977, 11; Glade and Anderson 1979, 84-85; Torres 1979, 273-381).

Toward the end of 1945 a new climate of democratization favored the establishment of permanent political parties, as well as the end of the rule of several revolutionary strong men (*caudillos*) in Mexico. The government party changed its name to PRI. The presidency of Avila Camacho had emphasized a search for political unity and compromise between capital and labor, church and state, land reform and land productivity, socialism and capitalism (Medina 1978, 112-34). The new party structure that emerged in 1946 was the work of a new generation of politicians, many of them college graduates, who managed to outline for the first time a clear, coherent nationalistic program. Political democratization, economic modernization, and the institutional neutralization of incipient labor conflicts remained salient features of the new party doctrine.

The administration of the first civilian president, Miguel Alemán (1946-1952), incorporated these principles and provided even more determined support for industry in the form of new tariff barriers designed to protect local industrial growth. This policy was also favored by international events like the Korean War. Exports increased by 23 percent in 1949-1950 and by another 20 percent the next year. The expansion of the traditional industries, particularly the textile industries, now extended to new industries in the fields of steel, cement, paper, and the new capital industries (Derossi 1972b, 17). Under Alemán there was a further increase in state intervention in the economy, to make up for the absence of private enterprise in certain key areas. Mexican industry was almost entirely dependent on foreign technology. Neither the state nor industry was interested in developing technology: rather, their objective was to generate the technical staff capable of using the new foreign technology (Wionczek et al. 1974, 43, 48-49).

Resources generated by agriculture were channeled by the

banks into preferred investments, principally industry. As for the state, its role was not confined to providing the basic infrastructure for industrialization: it also participated directly in production, particularly of capital goods. Mexico again opened its doors to foreign investment. Mixed corporations were organized with the participation of the major prewar entrepreneurs and foreign corporations. A new group of small and medium-sized business entrepreneurs arose under the umbrella of state protection (Aguilar 1978, 7; Barkin 1972; Friedman 1980, 332–33; Hansen 1974, 108; Villaseñor 1976, 185-206; Wilkie 1973, 38). From 1940 to 1950 was also a decade of rapid and accelerating urban growth. The increase in the urban population reached 5.9 percent per year, largely because of rural-urban migration. The population of Mexico City grew from 1,559,782 in 1942 to 2,234,795 in 1950, an increase of 43 percent (Brito 1969, 1; Uniquel 1978, 42-55).

Industrial enterprises rapidly lost their regional and artisanal character and focused themselves on the expanding nationwide market. Industry became polarized around Mexico City, the adjacent industrial areas of the state of Mexico, and Monterrey. The different styles of Mexico City entrepreneurs as opposed to entrepreneurial groups in the provinces, particularly in Monterrey, became more apparent. In Mexico City it was easier to maintain formal and informal contacts with representatives of the political system and with the banking and financial institutions. This was convenient for business, but it made them more dependent on the administration and on political power in general. The Monterrey industrialists, on the other hand, considered themselves rugged individualists and developed an attitude of independence and even defiance of government (Beato and Síndico 1980; Cerutti 1980).

Mexico City industrialists tended to value the outer trappings of economic power, such as luxurious homes where they could lavishly entertain their political associates and friends.[1] One is tempted to revise and amplify Schumpeter's definition

---

[1] The life style of entrepreneurs of the time is illustrated in two well-known novels: *La región más transparente del aire* (Where the Air Is Clear), by Carlos Fuentes, and *Casi el paraiso* (Almost Heaven), by Luis Spota.

of the entrepreneur as a technological innovator in order to incorporate "social technology" as a major characteristic of innovation. In Latin America, changing or broadening the social network to support the process of industrialization and capitalization may have been as important as finding sources of capitalization or finding new markets for industrial production (Barth 1963, 5; Bordieu 1980; de la Peña 1979, 54; Hartman 1958; Márquez and Godau 1980, 46).

The state formally handed over the role of producers to the industrialists, and the latter agreed not to participate directly in politics. This division of labor achieved legal status through the consolidation of the business chambers: CONCANACO and CONCAMIN, in particular, became the organizations recognized by the state as the legal instruments that expressed the points of view of Mexican business (Arriola 1981, 144).

According to Márquez and Godau (1980, 41-49), Latin American entrepreneurs find it indispensable to maintain contacts with the state bureaucracy in order to obtain information. This information allows the enterprise to operate in a hostile, rapidly changing environment. It enables the entrepreneur to neutralize the effects of fluctuating economic policies. In other words, the networks of social relationships with politicians, bureaucrats, and members of the financial and industrial community represent a basic resource that provides access to capital, information, markets, and permits, all of which are essential for capitalization.

Corruption had been endemic since the eighteenth century, but large-scale enrichment of public officials became notorious during and after the Alemán administration. Former bureaucrats turned entrepreneurs catered mostly to the state as contractors and suppliers.

Of all business enterprises that existed in Mexico in 1972, 31.5 percent had been created between 1951 and 1960 (Cordero and Santín 1977, 10). The skewed distribution of income had begun to worsen during the 1940s and became increasingly severe during the 1950s: "between 1950 and 1957 there was a significant drop in the proportion of aggregate individual income earned by the poor 50% of Mexican families"

(Hansen 1974, 74). The relative decrease in the standard of living of the countryside further increased rural-urban migration and eventually became a serious limit on the market for incipient Mexican industrial development.

Political developments after the war, particularly the rise of the United States as a world power, made Mexico increasingly dependent on its northern neighbor. Earlier contacts with European markets were lost. The American market absorbed all Mexican exports, particularly agricultural products, textiles, and shoes. But as American industry began to retool for export after the war, Mexico's hopes of maintaining its lucrative share of the export market soon vanished. By 1952, at the beginning of the Ruiz Cortines administration, it was clear that the situation would soon be reversed and that American goods would invade the Mexican market (Pellicer de Brody and Reyna 1978, 7-16).

The economic policies under Adolfo Ruiz Cortines (1952-1958) were an attempt to stabilize prices, strengthen and broaden the internal market, attain self-sufficiency to feed Mexico's population, and encourage private investments in production. On the political front, Ruiz Cortines attempted to reconcile conflicts between capital and labor by steering a neutral course, thus avoiding a head-on collision with either the unions or the entrepreneurs. He also sought foreign loans to finance the public sector (Pellicer de Brody and Reyna 1978).

The 1960-1980 Period

From 1960 to 1980 Mexico's population grew from 35 to 75 million, one of the highest rates of population growth in the world and one that was reflected in rapid urban growth.

The new urban middle class became an increasingly powerful social and political factor. By 1960 this group had grown so much that it absorbed almost 80 percent of the demand for consumer goods. The broad masses of the peasantry remained poor and backward. Their productivity was extremely low and their purchasing power was practically nil. The widening gap between city and countryside stimulated migration to cities and further increased the population and socioeconomic

45

imbalances between the two (Hansen 1974, 76-77; Márquez and Godau 1980; Pellicer de Brody and Reyna 1978, 236-56; Purcell and Purcell 1977; Shafer 1973; Villarreal 1977, 67-107).

The remedy prescribed by the state was again more industrialization, expanding from basic needs and hard consumer goods to capital goods production. Since private capitalization remained low, the state was drawn into an ever greater involvement in the economy to provide risk capital for new ventures in high-investment, high-technology fields and to make the costly investments that the urban and industrial infrastructure required to meet the demands of the growing number of city dwellers. This model of development implied the growing dependency of the business community on state control. The participation of state agencies as industrial investors was taken for granted and was even welcomed by the entrepreneurs. During the 1953 recession, for example, the industrialists demanded and obtained active state intervention to stimulate the economy; they only came to question such intervention years later.

The state attempted to respond to the new pressures by borrowing money. It also increased its share of industrial investments, particularly in capital goods. It was in this period that large multinational corporations also appeared on the scene. By 1980 the Mexican market was dominated by foreign- and state-owned enterprises. A new class of technocrats became part of the political picture, together with a tendency toward increased centralization and bureaucratization. The growth of the state's participation in the economy was accompanied by an expansion of the state apparatus, which in turn accommodated the large number among the middle class who sought bureaucratic and political jobs.

In order to face the challenge of multinational corporations and state enterprises, private business devised counterstrategies, including the creation of conglomerates or corporations centered around financial groups. A financial group is a group of companies that does business in different markets under a common administrative or financial control (Leff 1978, 663).

Characteristically, the Mexican conglomerates were family enterprises that drew their management from a group of relatives. They appeared in response to both government incentives and the specific economic situation.

Mexican industry thus faced a situation of extremely rapid change. Foreign demand for Mexican products dropped rapidly. The consumer market was altered by the introduction of new products and technologies, in particular plastics, synthetics, and new electrical appliances. These changes meant that more capital was needed for wholesale retooling as well as for new production, management, and marketing techniques. In order for Mexican industry to compete successfully against foreign firms, it became necessary to import capital goods that were not produced locally, in particular new plant machinery.

By 1965 there were slightly more than 630,000 business enterprises in Mexico, but 21,800 firms (3.5 percent) owned 80 percent of the capital (Aguilar and Carmona 1977, 51). These figures indicate the extent to which the conglomerates dominated not only industry but the economy in general.

In spite of sustained government support of small and medium-sized industry, some family enterprises went into bankruptcy (Cordero 1977, 8). On the whole, however, such enterprises survived the challenge and found new ways to prosper. The foreign corporations had technical expertise but lacked experience with the Mexican financial and political system; also, they had little knowledge of the Mexican market. Many Mexican entrepreneurs entered into partnership with foreign firms under favorable conditions that enabled them to make full use of their connections with politicians, financiers, and labor. Others forged partnerships with the state in order to produce capital goods as well as consumer goods. Another strategy was to strengthen the trade and business associations. These associations succeeded in promoting new legislation, for example, a law that regulated and protected the local automobile industry. Some industries succeeded in developing or adapting new kinds of technology and generated their own technicians for this purpose (Bennett and Sharpe 1979; Derossi 1972b; Márquez 1979; Von Bertrab 1979).

47

An expanding consumer market provided further opportunities for industrialists in the area of low-cost consumer goods for the lower-class market. Jobbing and other forms of contract manufacturing became profitable as the industrial operations of the larger corporations became increasingly complex. Many industries of the traditional style were able to maintain low production costs and became wholesale suppliers of large marketing organizations. Finally, many traditional industries geared their production to certain sectors of the market that had been overlooked or neglected by the large corporations: service industries and the manufacture of small objects made of plastic are examples.

It is interesting to point out that Mexican entrepreneurs, despite their growing dependence on government subsidies and related legislation, were always kept at arm's length by the official party. They had no direct participation in the shaping of official policy, except through nationwide associations such as CONCAMIN, CONCANACO, and CANACINTRA. Derossi interviewed a number of industrialists and found no evidence of "direct participation of industrial entrepreneurs in government, in the sense that none of the informants had ever participated in public life, not even at a regional level. Nevertheless, there is unquestionably a constant interaction" (1972b, 45). The exact points and areas of this interaction are not easily identified from the outside. Formally, interaction occurs at the negotiating table, where members of the government confront the representatives of the chambers of commerce and the associations of industrialists. Such interaction "involves large quantities of routine applications and consultations . . . doctrinal assertions or disputes. . . . Protests, bargaining consultations and compromise are to a great degree patterned on institutionalized, functional links between government and business organizations. . . . All these links constitute an effective system of communication between the public and private sectors" (Shafer 1973, 189).

Between 1970 and 1976 the political discourse of the administration of Luis Echeverría was populist and antibusiness, trying to break with what were called "stable development" (*desarrollo estabilizador*) politics. A new generation of young technocrats had come to power and was actively seeking new formulas for a better distribution of income and development on a balanced regional basis. The entrepreneurs saw that they had to change their traditional aloofness, and in 1975 they created the Entrepreneurial Coordinating Council (CCE) as a political action group. The new council published a declaration of principles opposing the encroachments of the state in the economy and demanding that "the political and economic resources of the state . . . support private enterprise" (Arriola 1981, 126). In the course of successive clashes with the administration it soon became clear, however, that the strength of the private sector was purely economic and that it lacked support at the political level. The state apparatus was not about to give up its role as umpire and regulating agency of social and political life in Mexico (ibid., 127).

The Church had been a major source of ideas and inspiration for the entrepreneurial class in Mexico. After Vatican Council II, however, the Church had second thoughts about private property and the social use of capital. Suddenly the Mexican private sector found itself bereft of ideological support. The traditional alliance between business and the Church began to break down; important groups of entrepreneurs, however, remained faithful to the old conservative sector of the Church hierarchy. This alliance remained the hard core of opposition against "authoritarian" and "socialistic" state policies.

In 1976 the new president, José López Portillo, faced a critical situation: "loss of confidence by the business sector, monetary instability, a GNP growth rate that had been steadily eroding since 1973, a paralyzing foreign debt, massive outflows of capital, and a rising rate of inflation" (Friedman 1980, 339-40). The new administration (1976-1982) decided to offer a truce to the business sector and began to invest heavily in capital-intensive industries, particularly the development of the new oil fields. For a short time (1977-1979) the new administration achieved a GNP growth of 5.4 percent, substantially higher than the population growth. But this was attained

49

at the cost of foreign indebtedness and loss of productivity in the agricultural sector (Banca Cremi 1980, 11).

The oil boom produced enormous profits for those Mexican entrepreneurs who did business with the state, including former politicians turned businessmen. The other entrepreneurial groups remained less directly connected with state enterprise but also registered substantial profits. Big enterprises and financial conglomerates directly linked to the government had privileged access to the new sources of wealth.

The social climate of Mexico visibly changed. The middle class affected an air of prosperity and conspicuous consumption; foreign travel became common and nationalism lost ground to their new cosmopolitan tendencies. Those who could afford it began to buy real estate in the United States.

By 1975, 34 percent of the fifty largest firms in Mexico belonged to the state. On the other hand, 25 percent of the five hundred largest firms in Mexico were either foreign-owned or dominated de facto by foreign capital (Banca Cremi 1980, suppl.). The state concentrated its investments in oil, transportation, and capital goods. In addition to oil, there were huge state investments in steel, petrochemicals, mining, and fertilizers. These fields belonged almost entirely to state enterprises. Foreign investments primarily flowed into the chemical industry, the food, industry, and other capital goods.

The oil strategy of the government produced a heavy economic dependence on international oil prices and on the price of money. The foreign debt reached $80 billion in 1982. Mexico's entrance in the international money market generated an outflow of capital of enormous proportions. The lopsided distribution of income became, if possible, even more unbalanced. The world recession and the falling price of oil in the world market finally hit Mexico in 1982 and struck a giant blow at the economy. Inflation went out of control, the currency was devalued three times in a year, workers were laid off, and economic and social panic ensued. The government attempted to brave the storm by nationalizing the banks in September 1982. Businessmen had not waited for this final blow, however, to transfer their capital abroad. The new president,

Miguel de la Madrid, took over in December 1982 in the midst of a climate of uncertainty and deep mistrust.

In summary, it is clear that regional development in Mexico has been unbalanced and the distribution of income has been unfair. Still, the social structure has been changing very rapidly, and the rise of the urban middle class has been particularly impressive. The upper classes, of course, continue to have preferred access to capital and power. Politics, banking, industry, and export agriculture provided the leadership after the Revolution. Beginning in 1940, industry began to dominate owing to sustained state protection.

Mexican entrepreneurs may be classed according to the size of their capital and according to their degree of dependence on the central government. In 1967 around four hundred firms owned nearly all the capital in Mexico; many of them were foreign. At that time, about one thousand families belonged to the group known as "big capital" (gran capital); among these, perhaps one hundred families were prominent and the top twenty dominated the rest (Aguilar and Carmona 1977, 65-74). Ten big families were directly connected with state interests; three dominated the independent Monterrey group; five dominated other parts of the country; and the remaining eighty-two families were located in Mexico City. The other nine hundred entrepreneurial families mentioned in the same source represent what we have called medium-sized entrepreneurs.

Mexican business has increasingly been confined to the more traditional and less dynamic fields of the economy. By 1971 only 46 firms were manufacturing basic intermediate goods (Cordero and Santín 1977, 9). There were 131 conglomerates and groups in Mexico, and the 50 largest groups generated 44.7 percent of the gross national product. Most of these groups were broadly diversified in their production and in their sources of financing. They dominated the industrial structure by means of their financial power and their technological efficiency. They acted as pressure groups and lobbies, and they were less dependent on fluctuations in state policies than the less powerful sectors of the Mexican bourgeoisie.

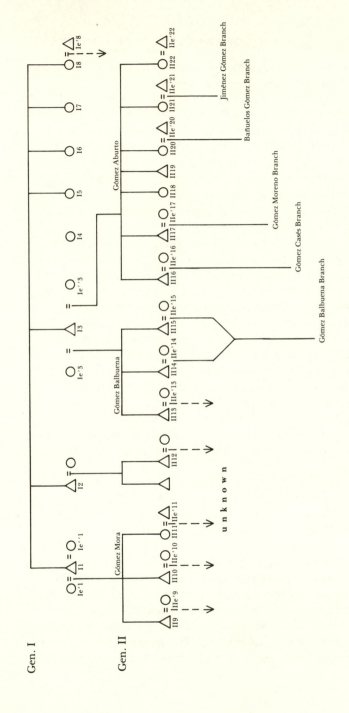

FIG. 1. THE GÓMEZ GENEALOGY
The First Two Generations and Major Branches

The Branches of the Family

By 1978 the Gómez kinship group included 360 individuals, not counting small children and omitting any branches that had become removed from the family or whose existence was unknown to our informants.

Because of the growth in size of the family group, a process of segmentation set in from the third generation on. Five major branches began to be differentiated at that time: (1) the descendants of Leopoldo Gómez (II,16) and his wife Juana Casés (II,e'16), to be called the Gómez Casés branch; (2) the descendants of Saúl (II,15) and Roberto (II,14), or the Gómez Balbuena branch; (3) the descendants of Modesto Gómez (II,17), or the Gomez Moreno branch; (4) the descendants of Rosalía Gómez (II,20), to be called the Bañuelos Gómez branch; and (5) the descendants of Cecilia Gómez (II,21), to be called the Jiménez Gómez branch (see fig. 1 and appendix). Segmentation has introduced profound socioeconomic differences among the five main branches; these differences have entailed interesting cultural distinctions as well. It is true, of course, that most members of the branches consider themselves to belong to the Gómez stock, thus sharing a common kinship allegiance and cultural background. But the differences among the branches extend to nontrivial aspects of economic activity, education, character, life style, and even residential preferences within the urban space of Mexico City.

The Wealthy: The Gómez Casés Branch

The direct descendants of Leopoldo Gómez Aburto (II,16) represent the largest and most powerful branch of the Gómez kinship network. There are 142 blood relatives in the third, fourth, and fifth generations of this branch, or 45.95 percent of all consanguineous relatives in the three generations. These figures do not include relatives by marriage or children born after 1978. At that time there were fifty-two nuclear families in this branch, or 35.13 percent of all nuclear families then existing in the kinship network. A conservative estimate indi-

53

Table 1. Gómez Casés Branch: Demographic Data

Generation (years born)	Men	Women	Sex Unknown	Total Members
III (1894-1906)	2	5	0	7
IV (1912-1952)	13[a]	16	0	29
V (1943-1972)	50	39	17	106
TOTALS	65	60	17	142

	Nuclear Families	Unmarried Members
III (1894-1906)	7[b]	0
IV (1912-1952)	23	3
V (1943-1972)	22[c]	84
TOTALS	52	87

[a] One boy died before reaching adulthood.
[b] One nuclear family disbanded due to death and subsequent adoption.
[c] As of 1977.

cates that their collective worth in 1978 exceeded $100 million, far more than the combined assets of the other branches.

Members of this branch have been prolific (see table 1). We find an average of 3.78 children per nuclear family for the fourth generation. There are unmarried women in the other branches, but not in the Gómez Casés branch. The liberal professions were not represented until the fourth generation; in fact, the branch showed little interest in formal education, particularly for women, up to the fifth generation (see table 2). The men in the fourth generation all married into entrepreneurial families. Some of the wealthiest men married the richest women and became natural leaders of the family network in terms of economic power. Women tended to marry into traditional middle-class Mexican families of professional background. Intentionally or not, this keeps the money in the family, as the husbands often become absorbed into the family business. Nearly all male descendants of Leopoldo Sr. (II,16) and many male in-laws eventually became business entrepreneurs. The branch has at least twenty-one owners of business enterprises of various sizes, including the three most prominent business leaders the Gómez family has produced.

There has been a significant differentiation according to grandfamilies and residential clusters. Nevertheless, there is still considerable interaction among members of the branch. The major entrepreneurs have a great deal of contact through business. They sit on each other's boards of directors, they continuously swap relevant financial information, and they invite each other's cousins into partnerships regardless of their economic standing. Professional services are rendered by relatives to all members of the branch. There are many small cliques among groups of cousins. The female members of the branch, particularly the older women, get together every day if possible and are always in close touch. Sisters have especially frequent contact. Once a year there is a get-together of female cousins, to which female in-laws are also invited.

The branch has produced six centralizing women, who regularly contact both their own branch and members of the other branches (see table 3). There is some downward trend in the number of interactions; nevertheless, these women have been more persistent than their male counterparts in maintaining contacts across branch boundaries. Indeed, the persistence of business contacts and of sporadic financial assistance to members of other branches owes a great deal to the mediation of the centralizing women, whose personal contacts with the Gómez Casés entrepreneurs benefit needy members of other branches.

Gómez Casés has always been the dominant branch of the family because of its size, its capital, and its ideological weight. Its members are the representative core group of the kinship network and are known to outsiders as the Gómez in the restricted sense. Since the death of Leopoldo Sr. in 1925 the branch has generated six grandfamilies.

THE GÓMEZ BENÍTEZ GRANDFAMILY: LEOPOLDO JR. AND HIS DESCENDANTS. Leopoldo Sr. and his wife, Juana Casés, had two sons and five daughters. Both sons married middle-class women without capital; one belonged to the old criollo class

Table 2. *Gómez Casés Branch: Educational Data*

Highest Level of Schooling Attained	Generation							Totals
	III		IV		V			
	Men	Women	Men	Women	Men	Women	Unknown	
Primary (6 years)	0	1	0	1	0	0	0	2
Secondary (7-9 years)	2	4	0	3	1	0	0	10
Junior college or technical high school (10-12 years)	0	0	7	8	3	11	0	29
Professional (13-16 years)	0	0	2	0	19	7	0	28
Postgraduate (over 16 years)	0	0	0	0	3	0	0	3
Unknown or very young	0	0	4	4	24	21	17	70
TOTALS	2	5	13	16	50	39	17	142

Table 3. *Gómez Casés Centralizing Women and Their Contact with Other Branches*

	Gómez Casés	Gómez Moreno	Jiménez Gómez	Bañuelos Gómez	Gómez Balbuena	Totals
Juana G. Casés de Merino y Pacheco (III,48)	23	1	3	1	1	29
María Elisa G. Casés de Aguilar (III,54)	7	1	2	0	0	10
Alicia Merino y Pacheco G. de Benítez (IV,98)	12	0	2	0	0	14
Magdalena G. Benítez de Piña Solórzano (IV,105)	13	1	3	0	0	17
María Guadalupe G. Chacón de Alcocer (IV,112)	6	0	2	3	4	15
Juana G. Chacón de Calvo (IV,113)	6	0	2	0	2	10

NOTE: The data indicate how many individuals in a branch with whom each centralizing woman is in frequent contact.

and the other was related to the new banking groups. Three of the daughters married liberal professionals who belonged to impoverished old criollo families, another daughter married a wealthy Spanish entrepreneur, and the last daughter married a middle-class Mexican without capital.

The character of the Gómez Casés branch can be understood through the personalities of Leopoldo Jr. (III,50) and Pablo (III,51), who were introduced in the previous chapter. Leopoldo Jr., born in 1898, is a conservative with a passion for status. Though successful as a businessman, he has been more interested in aristocratic family values than in economic power. He married into a traditional (though penniless) prerevolutionary family; he insisted on land ownership and cattle ranching as a means of laying claim to legitimacy as a descendant of the landed colonial gentry. His relations with the Church have been equally traditional and devout: he was twice decorated by the Pope and was a lifelong donor to religious causes. He has been involved in Church affairs, including the administration of convents, and is the main patron and benefactor of a Mexican religious order that is concerned with the education of Christian businessmen. One of his grandsons has become a member of the order; other nephews have gone to schools and colleges founded and supervised by it.

A devotee of the Virgin of Guadalupe, Leopoldo Jr. customarily presides over every Catholic ritual celebrated within the family; the apostolic delegate to Mexico is a frequent guest at his home. All his children have married into traditional aristocratic families. One of his daughters married a high executive in a business corporation; another's husband works in one of Leopoldo's enterprises. The other three daughters married men in the liberal professions. They have been extremely prolific: forty-three grandchildren, an average of 6.4 per nuclear family. Leopoldo's descendants tend to be conservative in business and family-oriented to the point of clannishness.

They prefer their homes to be modern and have them designed by reputable architects. Leopoldo's house is large and contains both modern and traditional furniture accented with valuable objects of Mexican colonial art and ninteenth-century Mexican paintings. According to some informants, until about 1950 only Mexican food was served at his table, but his taste has become cosmopolitan due to his frequent trips to Europe. His life style, however, has never changed. He and his descendants retain a taste for bullfights and *charrería*,[2] Mexican culinary traditions, and other habits and lore that hail from the nineteenth-century Mexican hacienda. Decorative objects belonging to the period of the Mexican Empire of Maximilian are displayed and highly prized. It is claimed that these pieces belonged to the imperial family and were bequeathed to Leopoldo Jr. through a close friend of Aunt Anita's who had been lady-in-waiting to Empress Carlotta. This story has been retold many times because it suggests a link between the Gómez and the Empire.

When Leopoldo Jr. inherited the textile concern "El Buen Gusto," it was the major Gómez enterprise. Until 1950 he continued managing it without introducing major changes or developments. He did not branch out into other industrial ventures; rather, he preferred to invest in real estate. Around 1940 he and his brother Pablo (III,51) jointly bought a rural property of about 2,500 acres (larger than the maximum allowable property size in Mexico), which was eventually divided into two separate cattle ranches.

Leopoldo's two sons, Leopoldo III (IV,103) and Ramiro (IV,106), began working for their father at the age of fifteen or sixteen, under the direct supervision of two uncles who had already been trusted employees of the firm under the boys' grandfather, Leopoldo Sr. The two boys never went to college but slowly worked their way up to the executive level. In the 1950s Leopoldo III, having reached the age of thirty, persuaded his father that the administration of the firm was old-fashioned and that he and his younger brother would be better as joint managers. Their father immediately removed their uncles (his cousins, the sons of Uncle Saúl) and remained in sole control with his two sons as administrators. The sons were as-

---

[2] The arts, skills, and traditions connected with the *charro*, or Mexican cowboy.

signed identical positions and their administrative functions were broadly similar; in other words, their father told them what to do. He was open to ideas and suggestions from them, however, and was willing to hire highly qualified technicians and consultants for the organization and conduct of the business. The enterprise grew rapidly and within ten years (by 1960) became the largest of its kind in Mexico. The strategy Leopoldo Jr. and his sons used was to buy up all competitors, beginning with the smaller ones and ending up with the most prominent, until they had secured a virtual monopoly that extended to Central America. The previous owners or administrators were retained as salaried employees and the factories continued to operate as before, except that they were now unified under a single top administration. With this system, neither the local factory administrators nor the technicians were Gómez family members. The board of administration included their managers, advisors, and some uncles and cousins who were not partners. It can be said that the business was becoming a "group" of enterprises linked vertically, with a sort of modern and centralized administration (Cordero and Santín 1977, 20).

This situation continued until 1973, when conflict broke out between the Gómez Benítez brothers. As a result, Leopoldo Jr. divided his estate between the two during his lifetime. Ramiro received his share in capital; Leopoldo III received most of his father's business properties. Each retained a 40 percent interest in his brother's enterprise. The daughters too received their share, in real estate. Leopoldo Jr. and his wife, nevertheless, kept a block of shares in each of the various firms that they had previously owned; thus Leopoldo Jr. continues to be able to overrule Leopoldo III in all business matters, though the same cannot be said of Ramiro. A 1973 law that placed the Mexican automobile industry under state protection (Bennett and Sharpe 1977) stipulated that 80 percent of all parts must be manufactured in the country. Ramiro took advantage of this to begin a brand new industrial venture, using foreign capital and technology (though he also hired an uncle as technical advisor).

Leopoldo III, growing weary of continued dependence on his father, began to diversify and invest in business ventures that he could manage on his own. He became a partner in a farming service business, which he expanded through capital investments. In partnership with a group of Central American investors and using a nephew as a technical advisor, he also created a business of prefabricated components for buildings in Central America. Around 1975 he founded a similar enterprise in Mexico and, in partnership with another nephew, set up an office-cleaning service (a business then new to Mexico). His sons studied engineering and computer science at the university and worked with him later on.

This family invested most of its earnings in real estate and ranching. The large cattle ranch owned by Leopoldo Jr. was sold in 1972 and the proceeds were divided among his sons and daughters; but Leopoldo III immediately invested his share in another cattle ranch in partnership with one of his Gómez Balbuena cousins, who ran the ranch for him and was later bought out. In addition to ranching, investments were placed in foreign bonds (especially after 1970 during the Echeverría administration) and real estate in Mexico and abroad.

In 1979 the Gómez brothers jointly undertook a real estate project in the United States. Following this, in 1980, Ramiro sold his business for $7 million and emigrated to the United States, where he opened a Mexican food business that he runs with the assistance of his son-in-law. His wife and remaining children continue to live in Mexico, primarily so that the children will be educated there, and Ramiro supports them and visits them frequently. The children spend their vacations in the United States.

By 1982 Leopoldo Jr. was the principal figure, with his sons, of the Gómez Casés branch and by extension of the Gómez kinship network. Their social contact with members of the Gómez Casés branch and with the Jiménez branch is extremely intense. To a lesser extent, they are close to the Gómez Balbuena and occasionally the Bañuelos. One of Leopoldo's daughters has become a centralizing woman in the Gómez Casés network.

Because of the fragmentation of their capital and the separation of administrative functions, Leopoldo Jr. and his sons gave up the chance to form a financial group. To survive in a changing political and social situation, they preferred to export part of their capital and keep a low business profile, thus avoiding a head-on collision with the state. Despite fairly close involvement with the United States, Leopoldo Jr. has maintained a life style resembling that of a criollo gentleman of the nineteenth century.

THE GÓMEZ CHACÓN GRANDFAMILY. Leopoldo Junior's younger brother Pablo (III,51), born in 1900, differed from his older brother in many ways. Pablo was a strong nationalist and an innovator; he was a born businessman, and his major objective was economic and political power. He respected family traditions and never sneered at his brother's aristocratic pretensions, which he found convenient. On the other hand, as noted in the previous chapter, he had no misgivings about befriending the new postrevolutionary political elite, which shared his nationalistic and modernizing spirit, and he was broad-minded about his business alliances—he was the partner of bankers, politicians, generals, and relatives. He also had business relations with foreigners. Pablo became a leading Mexican industrialist and the undisputed leader of the Gómez kinship network until his death in the early 1960s. This was due to both his wealth and his consistent employment of family members as administrators and employees in his business interests. To a considerable extent the fortunes of the Gómez family depended on the personal ascendancy of Pablo Gómez Casés. His economic relationships with countless members of the Gómez kin were those of a patron to his clients; but in another and perhaps more lasting sense he acted as a broker between the kinship network and the new political, economic, and social elite of Mexico. In his dealings with what the family described as a "corrupt public administration" or with foreign capitalists, Pablo could count on the large and powerful kinship network behind him.

Pablo's life style differed substantially from that of his older brother. He was not given to low-key, low-profile attitudes. His mansion was right on the Paseo de la Reforma, the main thoroughfare of Lomas de Chapultepec. It was a fifty-room residence complete with chapel, Turkish baths, billiard rooms, and tennis courts, decorated with European furniture, rugs, and other costly articles. He also kept country houses and cattle ranches for raising fighting bulls. On returning from his frequent travels he never failed to bring sumptuous presents for his close relatives and his business associates in and out of government.

Leopoldo Jr. restricted his field of social interaction largely to the family; Pablo, however, eagerly embraced the rising new Mexican upper and middle classes. He favored nonsectarian associations and clubs, secular charities, and political pressure groups such as chambers of commerce and industry. He became famous for his lavish parties, attended by artists, movie stars, bankers, industrialists, politicians (including the president of the Republic), princes of the Church, and visiting personalities who often stayed at his house. No less devout than his brother, he gave generously to Catholic charities, especially for the Basilica of Our Lady of Guadalupe. He sponsored the same religious order his brother did and his grandsons likewise attended the schools and universities of the order.

Pablo had three sons and two daughters. His children did not marry into the traditional Porfirian aristocracy; instead, they preferred entrepreneurial or middle-class professional families, of either Mexican or Spanish descent. All three sons followed the family tradition: they did not go to college but went into their father's business at age fifteen or sixteen.

During the Second World War, Pablo began to diversify: starting out with the textile factory "La Nacional" he had inherited in 1925, he bought a factory of mineral products, a printing firm, and three ready-made garment industries—one in partnership with foreign capital. In 1953 he purchased another very large textile factory in Mexico City, "La Doncella," an enterprise with two factories and about two thousand workers, in partnership with his cousin Pedro Jiménez Gómez, who administered most of his major ventures. These enterprises were closely connected with a Spanish–Mexican financial group of which one of his wife's nephews had become a director.

Pablo's interests included at various times a provincial chain of stores, a chemical products factory, and real estate investments in Mexico City and elsewhere that he continually bought and sold. In general, and particularly as far as real estate was concerned, he preferred buying to selling. When in doubt, he sat on a property in the expectation of better market conditions. During the 1950s he concluded a major real estate operation in partnership with a large firm of land developers, a deal that resulted in one of Mexico City's most elegant new residential neighborhoods. His own sons, plus his cousin Pedro, were brought in as partners in this transaction.

As president of industrial and business chambers, Pablo actively supported the industrialization of Mexico from his position of leadership. His modernization policies coincided with those of the Mexican governments of the day in a framework of progressive nationalism. His business views stressed productivity, which meant an emphasis on innovation and technology; he hired Mexican and foreign technicians and engineers, though he refused to delegate authority to his technical staff. For example, he paid for the technical education abroad of his nephew Enrique Gómez González (IV,88), and the boy returned and went to work for Pablo as a full-fledged engineer. However, Pablo allowed the opinions of his own sons, who had no college education, to prevail over the advice of a "mere technician."

At his death, Pablo was chairman of the board of thirty-one different firms, according to the condolence ads that appeared in the newspapers. This indicated that he was the sole owner or major shareholder in these enterprises. His last will and testament will not be made public until a period of thirty years has passed. According to information from relatives, however, Pablo willed his estate to his widow, allowing his sons to stay on as managers of the industries and businesses that they had administered during his lifetime and that they would eventually inherit.

63

Pablo Jr. (Pablo Gómez Chacón, IV,109), Pablo's eldest son, who was thirty-five at the time of his father's death, gained control of the ready-made garment factories, the printing shop, and the mineral concern. Juan (IV,110), the second son, controlled the textile consortium that had grown around "La Nacional." The youngest son, Leopoldo Jorge (IV,111), took over the real estate operation, urban as well as rural. Pablo's widow and daughters took charge of the administration of the urban properties.

The actual property transfer was completed after the death of Pablo's widow, three years later. It appears that each brother owned shares in the other brothers' enterprises, though the exact percentages are not publicly known. The daughters inherited assorted real estate properties; some ranches were held jointly by all five siblings. Each industry was run independently from then on, but all brothers were members of the boards of directors of the industries formerly owned by their father, as were their uncles Leopoldo Jr. and Pedro Jiménez. Pablo's former personal lawyer (a relative of his widow as well as a representative of his former main financial associates) was also a member of the board in these enterprises.

After Pablo's death, his cousin and former associate, Pedro Jiménez (III,72), was unable to get along with Pablo's sons, and the industrial empire fell apart. Each son administered his holdings and enterprises independently of his two brothers, even though they were partners. The fact that Pablo's enterprises were not considered a financial group put his sons at a disadvantage vis-à-vis the larger corporations.

Sons Juan (IV,110) and Leopoldo Jorge (IV,111) both married into powerful entrepreneurial families during Pablo's lifetime; Pablo Jr. (IV,109) and the two daughters were still unmarried at their father's death. Eventually, Pablo Jr. married a woman without wealth, a fact that placed him at a lower economic level in comparison with his brothers. He is a conservative businessman who lacks his father's aggressive drive, even though he became president of the chamber in his field in the 1970s.

Juan became independent during the 1960s, at the time of the debacle in the Mexican textile industry. His father-in-law, who had no male descendants, died, and it became Juan's responsibility to take over the administration of the estate. He sold some of his own less profitable businesses and delegated the administration of "La Nacional" to his brother Leopoldo Jorge. Juan now manages one of Mexico's most important enterprises, a monopoly. In 1978, his family capital was valued at around $25 million dollars; the capital is largely owned by his wife. An important block of shares has been transferred to his sons. Eventually, upon the death of his mother-in-law, he expects to gain full control of this important industry. He has invested his own capital in other enterprises: real estate and stocks and bonds, especially in the United States. He also presides over a small financial and banking concern. Even so, according to his financial advisor, his enterprises cannot be considered a "group" because of their "old" type of administration. This means his economic and political power vis-à-vis the state is not comparable to that of the big corporations.

Although Juan has grown closer to his wife's family, he also has become a leader among the Gómez. He provides jobs for his relatives. In earlier years he never failed to make an appearance at key family rituals; he continues to do so now. He protects his sisters' interests and is recognized as the economic and social leader of the Gómez Chacón branch. He has served as president of industrial chambers in his field and of service clubs, both nationally and internationally. He has used these positions to bargain with the state and to improve his relations with political leaders. Three cabinet members were present at the wedding of his daughter in 1978.

His sons went to the university and were carefully kept out of the industries and businesses inherited from Pablo Gómez. They are being groomed to take over their mother's financial interests, which are much more important. In the meantime, Juan has provided each of them with small new enterprises, mostly services and real estate of a low-risk nature. His sons' connections on the maternal side (including their powerful maternal cousins) will be decisive in the long run. Nevertheless, they are in very close contact with their paternal cousins of the Gómez Chacón branch. Unlike his father, Juan shows no particular interest in national politics and is mainly concerned with his business interests and those of his close kin.

Leopoldo Jorge (IV,111), the third son of Pablo Gómez, married the only daughter of one of the largest real estate operators in Mexico City. He manages his father's textile factories, the largest of which had fewer than four hundred workers in 1977. He has not created new business ventures; rather, he consistently invests in mutual bonds, stocks, foreign currency, art objects, and so on. His father-in-law willed him considerable capital to invest in real estate. His current worth was estimated at around $40 million dollars in 1978; however, his business style is quite conservative and in direct contrast with that of his father. He is socially more involved with the Gómez family than his brother Juan; he emphasizes his Gómez identity and has become a member of an inner circle or clique with three of his cousins. His sons, who went to the university, are being trained to manage large investments rather than to become industrial entrepreneurs; their contact with the Gómez Chacón grandfamily is extremely strong.

The two Goméz Chacón sisters (IV,112; IV,113) married after their father's death. The husband of the elder unexpectedly inherited a fortune of about $15 million in real estate in 1978. This, together with the real estate holdings inherited from her father, affords her a comfortable income. She is a centralizing woman who is in daily contact with at least ten women of other branches in addition to her brothers and uncles; she is considered a splendid wife and mother. The younger daughter married a man who lacked wealth. Her share of the inheritance was invested in real estate and medium-sized enterprises, which prospered thanks to her keen business sense and to the direct assistance of her brother Juan. She personally manages the garment industry that Pablo Jr. had inherited from his father. After the 1982 crisis, she began organizing groups of churchgoing ladies who dabble in politics and hope to save Mexico from its own government.

On the whole, Pablo's descendants have become real estate

brokers and rentiers rather than the industrialists that the descendants of Leopoldo Jr. have remained. Yet all identify themselves as industrialists. Pablo's sons, following their father's example, are active in the leadership of business associations, chambers of commerce and industry, service clubs, and pressure groups. Socially speaking, the branch keeps its distance from other branches in the kinship network.

THE GRANDFAMILIES OF THE DAUGHTERS OF LEOPOLDO GÓMEZ ABURTO. Leopoldo Sr. (II,16) had five daughters. Juana (III,48), his eldest, married an architect who came from a well-known Porfirian family. She was tall, stout, and red-haired. She always wore black, and she had a chapel in her home where she prayed every evening. In this chapel, it is said, she saw "shadows," or souls of people who were about to die. She became a kind of family oracle. She was strong-willed, and her husband seemed weak in comparison. She had a fierce loyalty to her children and to the Gómez: family pride became the central motivation of her life and that of her descendants. They are considered the haughtiest and least democratic of all the Gómez next to Juan Gómez Chacón, with whom she was very close.

Juana was greatly in demand as an aunt who helped her nephews and nieces; she was both respected and feared. Until her death in the 1970s she was one of the most important centralizing women in the kinship network. She was in daily or near-daily contact with twenty women of different branches in addition to her own children, grandchildren, cousins, nieces, and nephews, and with important clergy and members of Mexican high society as well. Her income came from inherited real estate, which she and her husband spent in high living. Breaking with her father's tradition, she sent her children to American schools; her grandchildren and great-grandchildren have followed the same tradition.

Her sons and daughters, the Merino y Pacheco Gómez, inherited a home: it was all that remained of their mother's real estate holdings. They used their extensive family connections to build up a successful construction business that they have managed as a family enterprise since the 1950s. The firm was based on the partnership of two Merino y Pacheco brothers, one an architect (Agustín IV,97) and the other an administrator who did most of the decision making (Maximiliano, IV, 99). Agustín was often away from the office, hunting for contracts with bankers, politicians, and industrialists as well as with Gómez entrepreneurs. Their employees were often relatives: nephews, sons-in-law, or members of other branches. Agustín's sons went to college abroad; when they returned in 1972, their father and their uncle split the capital. Maximiliano took over the real estate assets, and Agustín with his sons remained in control of the construction firm. Using their managerial skills acquired abroad, Agustín's sons engaged in an ambitious program of modernization, including the participation of hired administrators on the board of directors. Some relatives were replaced by professional managers, who were invited to buy shares and become partners in the enterprise. The youngest son became vice-president of the company and continued to throw his influence behind rationalization, following American corporate models. In 1981 they incorporated as a group with capital of $2 million, but they actually still operate as a family enterprise.

Both Agustín's sons married into extremely wealthy families; their wives are both related to the wife of Juan Gómez Chacón (IV,110), a connection that consolidates family ties and provides financial leverage. Agustín and his sons thus succeeded in overtaking a dominant brother by a combination of skill and family connections. The story is somewhat similar to that of Leopoldo Jr., except that Agustín was content to delegate the management of the company to his sons (though he continued to negotiate contracts, as he used to do under his own brother). Both sons have become extremely powerful businessmen and will inherit considerable capital from both sides. An interesting sidelight is that Pedro Jiménez Gómez (III,72) was associated with the Merino y Pacheco brothers in a large real estate venture. His son, Pedro Jr. (IV,157), associated himself in 1982 with the youngest son of Agustín in a large agricultural enterprise worth a million dollars.

Maximiliano Merino y Pacheco became an important real estate broker. Using his many connections with businessmen and politicians, he created a successful real estate investment firm with his nephews and cousins, sometimes in partnership with foreign corporations. He has specialized in foreign investments since 1975. For the most part, his business is of a speculative nature; he is not interested in industrial ventures. He maintains a grandiose life style and has become the protector of his sisters, daughters, and sons-in-law in the Gómez tradition.

Alicia Merino y Pacheco Gómez (iv,98) married Leopoldo Junior's brother-in-law, an industrial engineer who had been a consultant to many Gómez enterprises. Because his income did not allow his family to keep up with the Gómez life style, Alicia supplemented it with innumerable deals and small business transactions using her family's social relations. Her four sons (all professionals in their thirties) are shrewd businessmen. Two of them are partners in a construction firm, another is associated with his second cousin Leopoldo III in a prefabricated construction business, and the fourth owns a transportation business. Alicia is a centralizing woman who is in contact with all women in her branch and with the Jiménez and Gómez Balbuena women as well. Her daughter is following in her footsteps in the same role.

María de Lourdes Gómez Casés (iii,49), the second daughter of Leopoldo Sr., was a cripple who died in childbirth in 1929. She had inherited some real estate, which eventually came to be owned by her husband Adolfo and their daughter. Adolfo later married Modesta Gómez Moreno (iii,57) thus transferring capital from Leopoldo's heirs to the Gómez Moreno branch and causing a considerable scandal.

María Leticia Gómez de Montalvo (iii,52), Leopoldo Sr.'s third daughter, married a dentist, Genaro, who gave up his profession to join his in-laws in various business ventures. He found himself the owner of a small factory upon Leopoldo's death, basically working under contract for his brother-in-law. The firm did not expand but produced a good living for María Leticia and Genaro. They also inherited their present home as well as a ranch formerly belonging to the Montalvos. They have one son and one daughter: the boy started working in the textile factory at a young age and managed the ranch at the same time. Genaro died, and this son, Genaro Montalvo Gómez (IV,114), now manages all his widowed mother's interests. The younger Genaro is a member of a clique that also includes Leopoldo Jorge Gómez Chacón (IV,111), Maximiliano Merino y Pacheco Gómez (IV,99), and Ramiro Gómez Benítez (IV,106); the close friendship among the four cousins represents a continuing source of business for Genaro. The personal style of this entrepreneur may be inferred from the following anecdote. Finding his ranch unproductive because of poor land and poor access to utilities, he decided to sell it in 1977. Using connections with his cousins' business friends and his membership in a club that has many Gómez members, he invited a large group of acquaintances to a picnic lunch on the ranch. After his friends had been wined and dined in traditional country style, he took them to a hilltop where a large area had been cleared and divided into lots using rocks and whitewash as markers. He gave them a glowing sales talk and sold all the lots at inflated prices on the spot. He has used his persuasive talent and family resources in many similar business ventures. He moved his factory from the city to what was left over of the ranch because he found that the local female population provided a cheap labor source. After much wheeling and dealing, he has finally succeeded in establishing himself at a level that enables him to keep up with the other members of his clique, join them on their trips, keep his wife in elegant clothes and fine jewels, and maintain a high life style. Apparently, he has supplemented his income with successful investments abroad since 1976.

In 1982 Genaro (IV,114) became the leader of the chamber of his industrial branch. He had obtained a bachelor's degree in business administration when he was forty, which made him the only technically educated member of his clique. He became a management consultant to various enterprises owned by his friends, and his sons followed the same career. Each of them went to college and started his own string of business deals, carefully maintaining extremely close ties to the family. To this day, Genaro is the principal source of support for his widowed mother, his sister, and his nephews and nieces.

Elvira (III,53), the fourth daughter of Leopoldo Sr., married a wealthy Spanish industrialist but later eloped with a domestic and was ostracized by the family. She lived off the income of real estate that she had inherited. Her children stayed with their father. One son, a member of the Genaro Montalvo clique, began a business of precious woods in southeastern Mexico, in partnership with a local politician.

María Elisa (III,54), the fifth of Leopoldo's daughters, is famed among family members for her kindness. She is often praised for taking care of her mother in old age and for having raised Luli (IV,101), the daughter of her late sister. She is a blonde, which to the family represents sweetness and similar virtues they value in women. She married a medical doctor, who went to work for his in-laws. Upon her father's death she inherited her parents' home and a small factory that her husband managed. María Elisa's daughter Pilar married an engineer who became administrator of the factory.

The descendants of Leopoldo Gómez Aburto, the Gómez Casés branch, were worth collectively more than $100 million in 1978. They did not make the list of the one hundred top Mexican families (Aguilar and Carmona 1977, 67-74), because their capital was not consolidated under a single business leadership. It was increasingly fragmented by the process of inheritance and by the fact that the Gómez Casés followed the cultural tradition of independent entrepreneurship. Marriage alliances with other wealthy families became an important source of capital and status, enabling Leopoldo's descendants to continue to enjoy a life style that they find necessary to maintain as the principal branch of the Gómez kinship network.

GÓMEZ CASÉS: RESIDENTIAL PATTERNS. In 1917 Leopoldo Sr. (II,16) bought a home in Santa María de la Rivera, then a suburb of Mexico City. This home was surrounded by empty lots that he gave to his sons and daughters as wedding gifts, with the idea of remaining close together in a compact residential unit. Leopoldo's grandchildren grew up together and maintained intense emotional and social relationships at least into the fourth generation (about 1940). Relations with cousins from other branches of the family were also close during the lifetime of Mamá Inés and later depended on families' physical proximity. After 1940 the two brothers of the third generation, Pablo and Leopoldo Jr., moved away from the paternal compound. The oldest daughter, Juana, had also left upon her marriage; she lived downtown, about a 15-minute walk from Leopoldo's (see fig. 2).

By 1940, due to the westward expansion of Mexico City, Santa María de la Rivera had become a middle-class neighborhood that no longer seemed appropriate to powerful captains of industry. Elegant neighborhoods such as Anzures, Polanco, and Las Lomas (see fig. 2) were springing up in that time of prosperity for Mexico, and the Gómez entrepreneurs purchased real estate in the new areas both as a form of investment and as a means of settling their children nearby.

Leopoldo Jr. purchased a large block of property in the Anzures development, where he built his own home and the homes of his sons and daughters as they got married. His sisters María Leticia and Juana and his cousin Enrique Gómez Campos were also invited to purchase neighboring property. The following were living in Anzures by 1970: Leopoldo Jr. himself (III,50); his sisters Juana (III,48), María Leticia (III,52), and Elvira (III,53); his cousins Modesto Gómez Moreno (III,59) and Enrique Gómez Campos (III,46); his children Juana (IV,104), Magdalena (IV,105), Ramiro (IV,106), Lourdes (IV,107), and Lucila (IV,108); his sister Juana's children, Juana (IV, 96), Agustín (IV,97), and Alicia (IV,98); and their cousins Luli Aguirre Gómez (IV,101), Leticia Montalvo Gómez (IV,115), and Carmen Corona Gómez (IV,117). Altogether, there were seventeen Gómez households within five blocks of each other.

Pablo purchased a similar block of real estate in the elegant new development of Lomas de Chapultepec, which remains a favorite area in Mexico City for those with high incomes. By

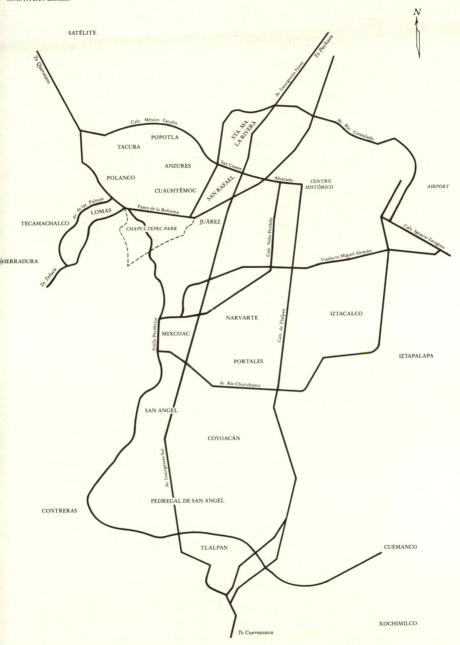

FIG. 2. MEXICO CITY AND ENVIRONS
The distance from the Cuernavaca exit to the Pachuca exit on Av. Insurgentes is 33 km.

1977 his five children still lived on the same block in Lomas de Chapultepec, three on adjacent properties. The Lomas cluster is particularly exclusive because of its personal fortunes, wealthy marriages, and ostentatious life style. Each cluster maintains a considerable social interaction up to the fourth and fifth generations. The wives help each other with their domestic duties; the children play and take lessons together; there are special dinner parties within each cluster; and there is always a great deal of informal visiting as well.

A third family cluster centers around the remaining old households in Santa María de la Rivera. María Elisa (III,54) still lives there. Several relatives have lived in her upstairs apartment at various times: Juana Merino y Pacheco Gómez (IV,96), a daughter of María Elisa's sister Juana, and then Pilar Aguilar Gómez (IV,120), María Elisa's own daughter. Opposite is the former home of Leopoldo Jr., which has been successively occupied by various daughters. Other relatives who have lived there include Alicia Merino y Pacheco Gómez (IV,98, another of Juana's daughers), Aunt Anita (II,22), and Ana María Bañuelos Jiménez (IV,153), a daughter of Ana María Jiménez. It seems that Leopoldo Jr. made this home available at various times to family members who were in economic difficulties.

There is a fourth cluster in the Polanco neighborhood, not far from Anzures, where two married sons of Leopoldo Jr. live. Agustín Merino y Pacheco Gómez (IV,97), a son of Juana (III,48), also moved there during the 1960s. In the fifth generation most family members now live in one of these well-defined clusters, but there is some overflow due to the scarcity of prime real estate in these neighborhoods. Young couples of the fifth generation are found in new developments, such as Tecamachalo and La Herradura (see fig. 2), which had originally been promoted by Pablo and Pedro Jiménez.

The Professionals: The Gómez Balbuena Branch

The descendants of Leopoldo's half brothers Saúl (II,14) and Roberto (II,15) were initially known as the "Popotla branch," because they lived in the Popotla neighborhood of

Table 4. *Gómez Balbuena Branch: Demographic Data*

Generation (years born)	Men	Women	Sex Unknown	Total Members
III (1885-1926)	5	7	0	12
IV (1920-1950)	6	12	6	24
V (1947-1965)	20	20	3	43
TOTALS	31	39	9	79

	Nuclear Families	Unmarried Adults
III (1885-1926)	5[a]	6
IV (1920-1950)	13	3
V (1947-1965)	5[b]	13
TOTALS	23	22

[a] One case of endogamy.
[b] As of 1977.

Mexico City until the late 1940s. Members of this branch are well accepted in the kinship network. Their links are mostly with the wealthy branch of the family: their relationship with the Gómez Moreno and Bañuelos Gómez branches is more distant.

The Gómez Balbuena branch includes seventy-nine consanguineous relatives (see table 4). Descendants of Saúl and Roberto are included in the same branch because of intermarriage between a daughter of Saúl and a son of Roberto. The branch represents 20.06 percent of the total of known consanguineous relatives in the kinship network up to 1978. However, there are only twenty-three nuclear families in the branch (25.67 percent of the total), against twenty-two unmarried men and women (including several nuns). The birth rate of the fourth generation was 4.5 children per nuclear family. The educational level is high (see table 5). Members of the third generation received almost no higher education because of difficult socioeconomic conditions during the Revolution, but most of the fourth generation, born between 1920 and 1950, went to college (men) or finished high school (women). Among

75

Table 5. *Gómez Balbuena Branch: Educational Data*

Highest Level of Schooling Attained	Generation								Totals
	III		IV			V			
	Men	Women	Men	Women	Sex Unknown	Men	Women	Sex Unknown	
Can read and write	1	1	0	0	0	0	0	0	2
Primary (6 years)	1	6	0	0	0	0	0	0	7
Secondary (7–9 years)	0	0	1	2	0	0	0	0	3
Junior college or technical high school (10–12 years)	2	0	0	5	0	2	5	0	14
Professional (13–16 years)	1	0	3	3	0	11	9	0	27
Postgraduate (over 16 years)	0	0	2	2	0	0	0	0	4
Currently studying	0	0	0	0	0	5	3	0	8
Unknown	0	0	0	0	6	2	3	3	14
TOTALS	5	7	6	12	6	20	20	3	79

members of the fifth generation, all the men plus two of the women of the branch were university graduates. This represents the highest educational level in the entire kinship network.

Saúl and Roberto were always very close. As mentioned in chapter 1, Roberto had interrupted his studies in order to enable Saúl to finish law school, even though this meant a lifelong disadvantage for Roberto and a higher social and economic status for Saúl. Theirs was the earliest formal business partnership that has come to our attention: they made joint purchases of urban and rural real estate beginning in the first years of the century.

In terms of physical appearance, Saúl and Roberto came close to the family ideal. Both were tall, blond, "Spanish-looking," and blue-eyed; in addition, both had received an education. Saúl, the lawyer, is remembered as righteous, loyal, honest, and respectful of tradition. His character and personality proved an enduring influence on the Gómez Balbuena branch. In charge of the legal matters of Leopoldo Sr. (11,16), Saúl willingly looked after the interests of widows and underage children. Roberto, on the other hand, was considered an eccentric because of his many love affairs and illegitimate children.

Most men in the branch have been liberal professionals or, more recently, business executives. Three became entrepreneurs; their total capital in 1978 added up to around 10 million dollars, which is less than 10 percent of the aggregate capital of the Gómez Cáses branch. One of them held office as president of a chamber of industry. On the whole, the branch is better known among the Gómez as having produced devoted lifelong employees for the more powerful Gómez entrepreneurs. Saúl's sons, who worked all their lives for Leopoldo and Leopoldo Jr., are often cited as examples of honest men who didn't have what it takes to become entrepreneurs. Their sons and grandsons (generations IV and V) have been upwardly mobile and several daughters married above their status, into entrepreneurial or professional families.

The branch has also produced one of the very few businesswomen in the Gómez kinship network, María del Carmen

Gómez González (IV,87). She owned a fine store specializing in gifts that catered chiefly to the Gómez. This business was also a well-known place of contact for exchanging family gossip. A working woman is still regarded as a deviant among the Gómez, but María del Carmen was highly respected and well thought of, perhaps because she was able to support her parents and provide economic assistance to a less wealthy sister.

A further status symbol among the Gómez Balbuena is religion: members of the branch have been exceptionally devout. Many women of the branch remained unmarried or became nuns. Some of these nuns provided a personal link between the Gómez family and the Catholic church, a connection of great economic importance in the development of the family enterprise.

The married women of the Gómez Balbuena branch tend to pattern their behavior strictly after the Catholic church and "decent" middle-class standards. The only known deviance has occurred in the fifth generation, in which women college graduates have actually worked in their chosen professions. On the whole, the Gómez Balbuena have been the self-appointed guardians of a life style that enables them to socialize on an equal footing with the wealthiest among the Gómez. Their outward appearance, their education, and their preference for good neighborhoods and good manners has made them socially acceptable to the Gómez Casés.

Yet the branch has produced spectacular male deviants. One of Roberto's sons became a flamenco dancer; he was disowned by the family and no particulars are available on him. Another son of Roberto's, Javier (III,39), followed a military career, considered a disreputable calling by the Gómez. He married his own cousin, a daughter (III,42) of Saúl, and later abandoned her. An illegitimate daughter of Roberto's, Carmelita (III,40), was raised by Aunt Anita (II,22) and became her companion until Anita died. She now works as a switchboard operator for one of her cousins and has become an important centralizing woman on behalf of the poorer branches (see table 3). On the whole, though, the Gómez Balbuena show little interest for members of the less affluent branches of the Gómez.

The three Gómez Balbuena entrepreneurs began their careers as salaried assistants in their uncles' business enterprises. Patron-client relations of this type have been quite common, beginning with the founders of the branch, both of whom worked for Leopoldo Jr. An example is the case of Javier Gómez Gómez (IV,80), a grandson of Saúl and Roberto, who came from a broken home and grew up with his maternal aunts. He worked for Pablo Sr. (III,51) as a very young man and became a factory administrator, first for Pablo and then for Pedro Jiménez. Around 1946, still quite young, he married the daughter of a wealthy foreigner who owned a pharmaceutical factory. Twelve years later, Javier left the Gómez enterprises to work for his father-in-law. Little by little he was allowed to take over the administration and to buy shares of the business. When his wife's brother came of age, Javier handed over the administration to him and set up his own company in partnership with his cousin Enrique Gómez González (IV,88), Saúl's grandson, a chemical engineer. They set up a manufacture of plastic containers for bottling his father-in-law's line of cosmetic products. This was successful and Javier bought a ranch in partnership with another cousin, Leopoldo Gómez Benítez (IV,103). Around 1970, Javier's daughter married a foreign technician who had been hired by the cosmetic company; he came from a wealthy family that had close ties with a multinational cosmetics firm. Seeing his chance, Javier withdrew from his partnership with his cousin Enrique, sold his ranch, entered into partnership with his son-in-law, and set up a cosmetics firm in association with the multinational corporation. However, his experience with the foreign firm was disappointing; he found that he was being supplied second-rate materials at a higher price than the locally available product and that he was being used to gain a foothold in the Mexican market. He left the multinational and continued making cosmetics on his own. Javier is now a small but prosperous industrialist who has a prestigious ranch and enjoys the style of life expected of a Gómez entrepreneur. He continually engages in business deals with his uncles and cousins, with whom he maintains frequent contacts. His children went to college and one of them works for his father-in-law, who owns an important enterprise.

Another example is Enrique Gómez González (IV,88), a son of Enrique Gómez Campos (III,46), the trusted manager who faithfully served in turn Leopoldo Sr., Pablo Sr., and Leopoldo Jr. He studied chemical engineering and began working for Pedro Jiménez while still a student, then was sent abroad. When he came back he worked for Pedro Jiménez, first in textiles and later in plastics. With his expertise he entered into partnership with Javier Gómez (IV,80), as described above. By 1966 he was able to afford a comfortable life style, though without ostentation inasmuch as he belonged to the "conservative" branch of the family. He had an elegant home in one of the best neighborhoods, he made yearly trips to Europe, and he owned a valuable collection of antique religious art.

After Javier dissolved their partnership, Enrique (IV,88) remained as sole owner of the container manufacturing firm, which he has continued to build up and manage. He became active in entrepreneurial circles and became a leader of one of the chambers of industry. In 1977 he set up a new plastics factory, with foreign partnership. He has used imported technology and modern administration methods and has given employment to relatives like his younger brother (a graduate in industrial engineering), his sister (who was hired as a secretary), and his brother-in-law (who is also a business manager). His son followed in his footsteps, became an engineer, and works for the firm.

A similar pattern occurred with the third entrepreneur, Enrique Gómez Villa (IV,81), a son of Alvaro's (III,43). He started out as an employee in the textile firm of Pedro Jiménez but continued his studies at the same time and became an engineer. With his own savings and his family connections, he set up a small textile company that did subcontract work for some of his relatives' enterprises. This arrangement worked out well for both parties: for the patron it was a convenient device for increasing production and adding flexibility, while avoiding headaches with administration and labor. For Enrique it solved financial problems in advance. This system is known as *maquila* and is widespread in Mexico. In addition, Enrique developed a construction firm that has grown to a considerable size, making him a wealthy and thriving entrepreneur. He takes care of his sisters, nieces, and nephews, helping them in many ways. His sons have gone to private universities and the eldest, in his twenties, already owns a small construction firm. His father set him up and helps him by providing expertise, tips on contracts, and capital. The other two sons are working as young executives for multinational corporations.

Javier Ortiz Gómez (IV,95), the son of Luz María (III,47) and grandson of Saúl, inherited a small textile factory in a provincial town, where he eventually did subcontracting for the Gómez entrepreneurs. He died early and his widow currently manages the factory and derives an income from it that allows her to remain independent. She has relatively little contact with the Gómez kin.

In the fourth generation, five women had to work for a living due to economic hardship. All of them received assistance—jobs, support, information, and guidance—from their brothers and male cousins. One of them also receives some economic assistance from a female cousin in the Gómez Casés branch.

GÓMEZ BALBUENA: RESIDENTIAL PATTERNS. As mentioned, Saúl and Roberto Gómez Balbuena made their homes in Popotla, a middle-class neighborhood of Mexico City (see fig. 2 above), and the third generation was raised there. During the 1930s, the third generation began to marry and form households in the same neighborhood. The fourth generation grew up in the same area, in close proximity with their grandparents, uncles, and aunts; about that time the members of the second generation died and some families of the third began to move to other parts of the city.

Josefina (III,42), abandoned by her husband and cousin Javier, continued living in Popotla with her sisters into the 1960s. Alvaro (III,43), Saúl's eldest son, inherited his father's home and remained in Popotla. In the 1940s Saúl's second son, Enrique (III,46), purchased a lot in the new Anzures suburb and became the backyard neighbor of his boss and cousin Leopoldo Jr. (III,50). Luz María (III,47), married to a small businessman, moved to the state of Tlaxcala, but was widowed in the 1950s and returned to Mexico City, where she lived alone in the Cuauhtémoc neighborhood, at some distance from the rest of the branch.

Most members of the fourth generation lived closely together in the Popotla neighborhood, went to the same school, and frequented the same social set. Enrique's sons lived close to the sons of Leopoldo Jr. in Anzures and developed particularly close relationships with their rich Gómez Casés cousins. Because Luz María's children grew up in some isolation from the family network, their personalities are less well defined in the minds of their Gómez relatives. Luz María died and her children eventually became estranged from the family.

By the end of the 1940s the members of the fourth generation began to marry. As the neighborhood of Popotla deteriorated, the children of Alvaro and Josefina moved into the southern residential suburbs, a growing area of the capital that had not previously been settled by the Gómez family. On the other hand, Enrique's descendants continued to settle in the Anzures area and eventually expanded into the northern middle-class suburbs, thus producing two differentiated suburban branches of the original Gómez Balbuena branch.

The fourth generation became geographically scattered and economically more diversified, but the business, social relations, and rituals among the cousins remained quite active. Fourth-generation businessmen tended to become partners, and entrepreneurs' wives supported their parents and provided jobs for their sisters. One of the doctors in the branch became the acknowledged physician of the entire kinship network. Many other examples of exchange of goods and services within the family network can be found.

Until 1977, the unmarried daughters of Saúl (Rosalía, III,41; Lucrecia, III,44; and Amalia, III,45) remained the emotional center of the kinship network at large; the entire family gathered around them at Christmas, on birthdays and saint's days, or whenever there was an important family crisis such as

Table 6. *Gómez Moreno Branch: Demographic Data*

Generation (years born)	Men	Women	Total Members
III (1881-1910)	1	5	6
IV (1822-1936)	10	2	12
TOTALS	11	7	18

	Nuclear Families	Unmarried Adults
III (1881-1910)	7[a]	0
IV (1822-1936)	8	4
TOTALS	15	4

NOTE: Data unknown for fifth generation.
[a] Three sororates, one marriage with a widow, and one with a relative.

the death of their brothers Alvaro and Enrique in the 1970s. In the 1980s the families of the northern and the southern sub-branches still meet at family rituals, such as funerals and weddings, but also at a number of informal social occasions.

The Black Sheep: The Gómez Moreno Branch

Members of the Gómez Moreno branch are collectively known among the rest of the Gómez as "los mal vistos," which might be roughly translated as "the ones who are frowned upon or looked askance at." They are the descendants of Modesto Gómez Aburto (II,17), who, as will be recalled, was first associated with his sister Rosalía and their respective spouses in a trading post in the village of Maravatío, Michoacán. After the Revolution both families returned to Mexico City, where they remained close friends and gave rise to separate branches of the Gómez family.

The Gómez Moreno branch includes eighteen consanguineous relatives (5.83 percent of the Gómez kin) among the third, fourth, and fifth generations. This includes Modesto's children, grandchildren, and great-grandchildren. (Those born after 1978 are not counted.) There are fifteen nuclear families in the branch, or 10.13 percent of all Gómez nuclear families (see tables 6 and 7). Their social contact with the rest of the

Table 7. *Gómez Moreno Branch: Educational Data*

Highest Level of Schooling Attained	Generation				Totals
	III		IV		
	Men	Women	Men	Women	
Can read and write	0	0	0	0	0
Primary (6 years)	0	1	1	0	2
Secondary (7–9 years)	1	4	0	0	5
Junior college or technical high school (10–12 years)	0	0	0	1	1
Professional (13–16 years)	0	0	8	0	8
Postgraduate (over 16 years)	0	0	0	0	0
Unknown	0	0	1	1	2
TOTALS	1	5	10	2	18

NOTE: Data unknown for fifth generation.

kinship network is relatively weak. The branch has produced two entrepreneurs, both in the fourth generation.

Modesto (II,17) is remembered by the family as an unremarkable man married to an unremarkable woman. He had one son, Modesto Gómez Moreno (III,59), and five daughters. The eldest daughter, Inés (III,55), married Bernabé Gómez Salinas (III,23), son of a first cousin of Leopoldo's and his chief technical employee. Bernabé and his wife Inés were thus third cousins. Inés died around 1928 while giving birth to her fifth child, and Bernabé next married Inés's sister Amalia (III,56), who died childless some years later. Bernabé then married Celina (III,60), the youngest of the Gómez Moreno sisters. Finally Bernabé died and left his money to his widow Celina, who remarried. Celina had children by both husbands, but her descendants by her second husband drifted away from the family with Bernabé's money, a fact that has not been forgiven. The other two Gómez Moreno sisters also made poor matches, in the family's opinion. When the crippled daughter of Leopoldo Sr. died in 1929, her widower married Modesta (III,57), thus allowing good Gómez Casés money to leak out into an "unreliable" branch. The fourth sister, Susana (III,58), married into a family of postrevolutionary politicians. Her husband was actually a small businessman, yet relatives made him and his wife unwelcome in the family circle.

Modesto Jr. (III,59), the only son of Modesto, married a middle-class woman who was an alcoholic. Their son married a cousin of the Bañuelos branch (IV,130), whom he subsequently abandoned. All these mismatches, sororates, remarriages, and leaks of family money contributed to the bad name of the Gómez Moreno branch among the rest of the family network.

Economically, the branch was considered middle-class with some tendency toward deterioration. Modesto Sr. himself was a small businessman who managed a hotel in downtown Mexico City. Modesto's wife was of low socioeconomic origin. Their children did "fairly well," particularly the daughters, because of the relatively high status of Bernabé and his strong relationship with Leopoldo Sr. Bernabé was largely responsible for the technical development of the Gómez enterprises, but his considerable income was never invested in business enterprises of his own. He remained a close collaborator but was treated as a client and not as an equal; he was not invited to invest in family enterprises. According to family gossip, his income was invested in jewelry rather than in a productive business, like a right-thinking Gómez would do. This made it easy for his widow Celina to dispose of his money through remarriage. Bernabé's three wives and various children enjoyed an upper middle class status. Modesta too had a comfortable economic situation, thanks to her husband's first wife, who had an inheritance from her father Leopoldo Sr.

Modesto Jr. definitely had a lower standard of living than his father. Six of the men in the fourth generation started out working for the Gómez enterprise complex as technicians. Two of them eventually succeeded in setting up a small independent business. The one who married his Bañuelos cousin became a notorious family problem: he had to be bailed out of jail with the assistance of his kin. The other men were businessmen in firms of medium size. The women all married employees working for private companies.

Modesta's two sons were able to go to college and set up their own business enterprises, thanks to Modesta's money and with the support of their fathers-in-law. One makes plastic objects in his backyard; the other owns a car agency. The fifth generation of this branch has become largely indifferent to family rituals and traditions, and they are not seen at family reunions.

As for residential preferences, Modesto Senior's daughters branched out from their parents' home in the downtown section of Mexico City. Bernabé lived near his boss Leopoldo Sr., in the San Cosme neighborhood, upstairs from one of his enterprises, between 1900 and 1935. As a result there was considerable interaction between Bernabé's children and the descendants of Leopoldo.

Modesta has always lived in the San Rafael quarter, in the general vicinity of Leopoldo Sr., Cecilia, and Bernabé. After 1940 Susana moved into the new upper-class neighborhood of

Lomas de Chapultepec and Celina also moved away from downtown, but the exact neighborhood is unknown. These two sisters were geographically removed from the core of the family and their descendants lost contact with the family at large. Modesta was the main contact and go-between with other family branches. The son (IV,125) of Modesto Jr. first lived in the Santa María de la Rivera quarter, near the Bañuelos branch, but after separation from his wife and his stay in jail he became estranged from the family. His former wife and his sons moved to the Portales quarter, a low-income neighborhood where their children were helped out by a Gómez Casés cousin. Modesta's sons lived in different middle-class neighborhoods (Tlalpan and Narvarte), near the families of their wives. Bernabé's children drifted away from the family; one of them became a technician in a family enterprise for a while, but he too was eventually lost to the family core.

This branch is among the least integrated into the kinship network. Its members were not particularly distinguished, either in business or by their moral or educational achievements. Though they formally acknowledged the norms and values of the rest of the family, in practice they tended to infringe them, especially through mismatches in marriage. Yet, Modesta has been a strong link with the family core, a centralizing woman (see table 3). Her presence at family rituals is the primary source of information on that branch available to other family members. It seems likely that all exchange of information will stop with Modesta's death and that her descendants will disappear from the kinship map, as other members of the Gómez Moreno branch already have.

Poor Relatives: The Bañuelos Gómez Branch

Leopoldo's daughter Rosalía (II,20) married a Spanish immigrant, Ramiro Bañuelos, who fathered the least affluent branch of the Gómez kinship network. The female members of this branch, however, are the heirs and guardians of the recipes, traditions, and customs transmitted directly from Mamá Inés.

In the third and fourth generations of the Bañuelos Gómez

Table 8. Bañuelos Gómez Branch: Demographic Data

Generation (years born)	Men	Women	Total Members
III (1909-1916)	4	4	8
IV (1927-1948)	14	14[a]	28
TOTALS	18	18	36[b]

	Nuclear Families	Unmarried Adults
III (1909-1916)	5	3
IV (1927-1948)	21[c]	6
TOTALS	26	9

NOTE: Data unknown for fifth generation.
[a] One girl died before reaching adulthood.
[b] We are counting the Bañuelos Jiménez who also appear in the Jiménez branch.
[c] One case of endogamy.

branch there are thirty-six consanguineous individuals, or 11.65 percent of the total kinship network, not counting affinal members and children born after 1978. The total number of nuclear families is twenty-six, or 17.57 percent of the total (see table 8). There is only one entrepreneur; all others are salaried employees at various levels. The branch produced a key centralizing woman, Anita (II,22). During Anita's lifetime the contact between the branch and rest of the kinship network was extremely intense, but it began to decay after her death in the 1960s. The members of the Bañuelos Gómez now interact mostly with members of the Jiménez Gómez branch. As in the Gómez Moreno branch, information on the fifth generation is lacking because its members have lost touch with the kinship network. The level of schooling rises in the fourth generation but the birth rate also remains high: about four children per nuclear family (see tables 8 and 9).

In the third generation we find two women who never married (III,65; III,68). One of the males, Ramiro (III,66), married a Jiménez cousin. In the fourth generation there were several single women: three spinsters (IV,132; IV,144; and IV,145) and one woman whose husband, her cousin Modesto (IV,125), left her. Another married an Italian craftsman and moved to Italy. One of the males married into a middle-range entrepreneurial family. All others, men as well as women, married into middle-class employee or professional families.

As discussed above, the Gómez sisters of the second generation were extremely close and formed a long-lasting residential cluster with Mamá Inés. This pattern of proximity has been preserved through the years. The Bañuelos Gómez branch maintains a strong sense of family allegiance with a great deal of visiting, partying, exchange of information, mutual assistance, and endogamy in the third and fourth generations. Characteristically, a strong trust exists among the female members of the branch, and five of the most important centralizing women have come from the Bañuelos Gómez.

The branch is middle class, with hardly any capital to speak of. Their relationship with the wealthier branches is maintained through Bañuelos Gómez women regarded as repositories of the Gómez family traditions. The recipes of Mamá Inés are held in secret and are transmitted to daughters only, who derive their authority directly from Mamá Inés, and not to daughters-in-law.

Though married to a Spaniard, Rosalía (11,20) generated the most "Mexican" of all branches. She refused to identify with Europe, unlike some of her richer cousins. The upper-class relatives consider her branch to be typically middle class in appearance, way of life, and tastes, including middle-class Mexican norms of daintiness and propriety. Members of the branch have often sought the patronage of the wealthier branches and have tended to select godfathers from among their members.

Intrabranch solidarity is externalized through a shared ideology with a distinctive middle-class flavor. The social closeness among members of the branch is conditioned by the intensity of reciprocal exchange, whether of an economic nature (particularly among men) or of an informal social nature. In general they cleave to a conservative way of life: they live in musty middle-class homes or, more recently, in tract houses bought with the help of mortgages, unlike the wealthier

89

Table 9. Bañuelos Gómez Branch: Educational Data

Highest Level of Schooling Attained	Generation				Totals
	III		IV		
	Men	Women	Men	Women	
Can read and write	0	4	0	0	4
Primary (6 years)	0	0	0	0	0
Secondary (7–9 years)	3	0	1	7	11
Junior college or technical high school (10–12 years)	0	0	3	4	7
Professional (13–16 years)	0	0	3	1	4
Postgraduate (over 16 years)	0	0	0	0	0
Unknown	1	0	7	2	10
TOTALS	4	4	14	14	36[a]

NOTE: Data unknown for fifth generation.

[a] Includes the Bañuelos Jiménez and one girl who died before reaching adulthood.

branch members, who buy their homes outright. They take pride in the refinements of Mexican traditional cooking, including such delicacies as *buñuelos* and other Mexican desserts. As might be expected, the prescribed role for women in this branch is all a "Gómez woman" should be: homemaker, wife, and mother as well as excellent cook and storehouse of information on everything concerning the family. The women of Bañuelos Gómez never dabble in politics and feel quite at home with their middle-class status. They are religious and participate in the reading of novenas and rosaries but are not fond of the clergy, as the rich are. Their dress is very conservative and they are extremely assertive of their old middle-class status and tradition vis-à-vis recent upstarts, whose neighbors they have become. The older generation cultivates relationships with rich relatives by means of little presents, including samples of their cooking, which is famous throughout the kinship network.

From the point of view of modern middle-class Mexican society, the style of the Bañuelos Gómez branch might be defined as stilted and perhaps somewhat pretentious. According to an upper-class family member, they may be defined as "would-be upper class." Their homes are filled with knickknacks and pseudo-antiques. Unlike the postrevolutionary middle class in Mexico, Bañuelos Gómez respectability is based on a traditional way of life that goes back to the turn of the century. They are not afflicted with legitimacy problems.

Rosalía's (II,20) family is the core of this branch. One of her sons set up a small textile factory that depended on business from Leopoldo Jr.; another, Ramiro Jr. (III,66), became a middle-level employee and married his cousin Ana María Jiménez Gómez (III,69). In the 1960s he set up a hardware retail store. The daughters were employed for years by their cousin Pedro Jiménez (III,72). Eventually they set up a little store with the help of their brother Ramiro Jr., but in the end they were both supported by their nephews. The husband of one of them was a clerk who also worked for Pedro Jiménez.

The two outstanding women of the third generation were Rosalía and Carmelita. Rosalía (III,61) was said to be a fair-skinned, good-looking woman, an excellent cook, and a submissive wife. She was respected as a strong woman, who was able to maintain a posture of great dignity in the face of constant economic difficulties. She married a middle-level businessman who owned a lumber mill. Carmelita (III,40), Roberto's illegitimate daughter, was adopted by her Aunt Anita (II,22) and grew up with the Bañuelos. She inherited Anita's home in Santa María de la Rivera but uses only part of the house and leases the rest. She has become the social link between the Bañuelos branch and the other branches, particularly the Gómez Casés and the Jiménez.

All male members of the fourth generation initially worked, directly or indirectly, for their wealthy uncles. After 1970, when the uncles' sons began to take over their own enterprises in the wealthy branch, the Bañuelos Gómez gradually left and found various jobs in private business. One of the liberal professionals eventually became an executive in a major corporation; two sons of the small entrepreneur followed in their father's business.

The lumber merchant's son (IV,125) inherited his father's firm, went bankrupt, was bailed out by his wealthy uncles, married the daughter of another lumber merchant, and finally built up a successful lumber retail business in a provincial town. He now provides economic assistance to his mother and sisters. Berta (IV,128), the small entrepreneur's daughter, studied chemistry and became the first woman professional in the Gómez family. She was both a successful career woman and a successful homemaker, but she died early. Her widower subsequently married her sister (IV,131). The female members of the fourth generation were mostly secretaries in various Gómez enterprises. The one who was abandoned by her cousin still works as a secretary and receives some additional financial assistance from a wealthy cousin. The male members of the fifth generation are all attending college and have no contact with members of the wealthy branch.

Ramiro Bañuelos and Rosalía Gómez had made their home in downtown Mexico City. Their children grew up and married in this neighborhood. When one of the sons in the third generation married he made his home downtown, not far from his parents' home. During the 1940s he moved near the location of his enterprise in the Río Consulado area (see fig. 2 above). The other descendants of the Bañuelos Gómez branch also gradually moved away from downtown. During the 1930s and 1940s the unmarried daughters moved to Santa María de la Rivera, the old family neighborhood now turned lower middle class.

The generation that lived together in the Santa María neighborhood established a pattern of close personal contact and interaction. They were extremely close to Aunt Anita, who gathered the whole kinship network around her until she died in 1966. Carmelita has continued the relationship and transmits information from this particular branch of the family to the others, but she has not been capable of maintaining the unity that had existed before Anita's death.

In the 1950s, when the fourth generation was grown up and married, the nuclear families began to scatter and established their own households. A widow (III,e′62) and her children moved to Satélite, a new suburban middle-class neighborhood at the northern outskirts of the city. Other nuclear families followed her to the same neighborhood or to adjacent ones such as Cuautitlán-Izcalli.

By 1980 the Bañuelos Gómez branch had become segmented, but members of the third generation who grew up together remain in touch with members of other branches, who are still invited to become godfathers. They attend all family funerals. They have not been denied assistance by the wealthy family members, and the women in particular have been provided for. Members of the fourth generation have become more distant but, as a whole, mutual recognition is maintained.

The Middle Ground: The Jiménez Gómez Branch

Leopoldo's sister Cecilia (II,21) was married to the Spanish immigrant Blas Jiménez; they had one surviving son, Pedro (III,72), and one daughter, Ana María (III,69), who married

Table 10. *Jiménez Gómez Branch: Demographic Data*

Generation (years born)	Men	Women	Total Members
III (1911-1916)	1	1	2
IV (1931-1958)	9	8ª	17
V (1965)	10	22	32
TOTALS	20	31	51

	Nuclear Families	Unmarried Adults
III (1911-1916)	2	0
IV (1931-1958)	15	1
V (1965)	b	
TOTALS	17	1

ª One girl died before reaching adulthood.
b Too young as of 1978 cutoff date.

her cousin Ramiro Bañuelos Jr. (III,66). All their descendants are included in the Jiménez Gómez branch.

Blas Jiménez essentially remained a Spanish peasant all his life. His wife Cecilia was intelligent and devoted to the arts; she always remained extremely close to the Gómez family. She died in the late 1920s. The third, fourth, and fifth generations contain fifty-one consanguineous individuals, 16.5 percent of all the Gómez (see table 10), up to 1978. The number of nuclear families in the network is seventeen, 11.49 percent of the total. This appears to be the most prolific of all branches; the average birth rate is 8.5 children per nuclear family in the fourth generation. The fifth generation, though still incomplete, shows a sharp decrease to about 2.7 children per nuclear family. The branch has five entrepreneurs and a number of liberal professionals. In 1978 the total capital of the branch was around $6 million. By that year more than half the members of the fourth generation were college graduates (see table 11). Even in the second and third generations, when college education for males was not customary, there was a significant percentage of college graduates among the women of the branch. For the most part they married into the middle and upper middle classes.

The third generation had only two members who survived into adulthood: Ana María and Pedro. The personalities of this brother-sister pair dominate the branch: Pedro the entrepreneur-patriarch and Ana María the centralizing and dependent sister. Social closeness is expressed, among other things, by the fact that Ana María is godmother to three of Pedro's sons and Pedro is godfather to three of Ana María's children. There is a great deal of formal and informal exchange, both social and economic, between members of the third and fourth generation. On the whole, there has been a kind of patron-client relationship between Pedro and Ana María that extends to their children. Among members of the fourth generation the relationship tends to be more symmetrical. There one notices the formation of friendships between cousins that lend internal cohesion to the branch.

Pedro Jiménez (III,72) was molded by two contrasting influences: the sturdy immigrant values of his father, stressing honesty, hard work, and a certain anti-intellectual bias; and the imprint of his elder cousin Pablo Sr. (III,51), who introduced Pedro to the business world and to the Mexican upper class. Pedro owed to Pablo his restless business style, always looking for new ventures but ever mindful of his obligations to the family.

The homes of members of Pedro's grandfamily tend to be stylish, bearing a touch of Mexican baroque, with modern paintings, Persian rugs, and quality furniture. Pedro has enriched the Gómez life style with his preference for international cuisine as well as the usual fine automobiles, expensive clothing and jewelry, trips abroad, and so on. Pedro's children were sent to expensive private schools but later attended the National University of Mexico instead of going to private universities, as do members of the Gómez Casés branch.

Pedro's ideology, which has largely been transmitted to the Jiménez Gómez branch, represents a fusion of Mexican bourgeois nationalism with European immigrant elements. Perhaps because of this fact, and also because of multiple relationships

Table 11. Jiménez Gómez Branch: Educational Data

Highest Level of Schooling Attained	Generation						Totals
	III		IV		V		
	Men	Women	Men	Women	Men	Women	
Primary (6 years)	0	0	0	0	0	0	0
Secondary (7-9 years)	1	1	3	0	0	0	5
Junior college or technical high school (10-12 years)	0	0	0	3	0	0	3
Professional (13-16 years)	0	0	4	2	0	0	6
Postgraduate (over 16 years)	0	0	2	2	0	0	4
Unknown or very young	0	0	0	1	10	22	33
TOTALS	1	1	9	8	10	22	51

with the poor and wealthy branches of the family, the Jiménez Gómez branch occupies a central position in the kinship network. It has served as a bridge and a unifying element between the family's various branches.

Ana María is a strong-willed woman who is supportive of relatives and widely admired and beloved. She is the perfect link between the poorer and wealthier branches of the family (see table 3). Though a devout Catholic, she tends to mistrust priests and nuns. After marriage she forsook what were considered girlish frivolities (such as playing the piano) and became a full-time wife and mother. She has known tragedy: two of her children died. Her home is conventional in an early twentieth-century Mexican way: French furniture, crystal, and porcelain. Her cooking is famous for the old-style Mexican recipes she uses, inherited from her mother and grandmother. She will share these recipes with none but her own daughters.

As a conservative businessman and an entrepreneurial innovator, Pedro might be placed somewhere between Pablo and Leopoldo Jr. He began the trend of sending his sons and daughters to college. His wife, of Spanish origin, is strong-willed but submissive to her husband; she has become fully accepted as a Gómez by the rest of the kinship network. Her tastes and attitudes are copied by other members of the family, but she is sometimes thought to be a bit distant in her behavior.

From the point of view of capital accumulation the Jiménez branch is independent of the main branch of the Gómez family, at least in its origins. Blas Jiménez had his own businesses in the traditional style: his centralized administration was run with the help of relatives and trusted friends from the old country, most of them kinsmen as well.[3]

His son Pedro (III,72) was the youngest member of the third Gómez generation. He started working on the ranch at the age of twelve. When he turned seventeen he officially took charge of his father's business, including the ranch and some bath houses in Mexico City, while his father retired to Spain. In his

[3] This style seems to have been characteristic among Spanish immigrants in Mexico, according to García Acosta 1979 and Suárez 1979.

97

new role, Pedro met postrevolutionary politicians who became his lifelong friends.

Upon his father's death in 1945, Pedro inherited most of his business concerns; Ana María was provided with real estate. Pedro had already been in charge of his father's business interests for about twenty years, and his cousin Pablo (III,51), whom he saw daily at Aunt Anita's home, was in the process of building and expanding his economic empire. Pablo's sons were too young to assist in the development of these enterprises; Pedro, however, had business flair, relationships with politicians and members of the Spanish business community, and some money of his own. He was the logical choice to administer Pablo's largest textile enterprise.

Over the years Pedro became his cousin's closest associate, and upon Pablo's death Pedro was appointed tutor of Pablo's youngest children. He became the director of a textile consortium that included investments by bankers and industrialists as well as Pedro's own money. The administration of Pedro's own business interests, including the ranch and the public baths, was entrusted to Ana María's sons who were of age, to a Spanish cousin on the Jiménez side, and to some Bañuelos relatives.

Ana María allowed herself to be guided by her brother's advice in investing her inheritance. Her husband, Ramiro Bañuelos (III,66), remained an employee almost to the end of his life, though finally, as mentioned above, he bought a hardware store, which he managed until he died in the 1970s. His wife's investments were managed, in practice, by her brother. By 1950 Pedro had become a prominent industrialist, a partner in Pablo's industrial holdings, which he also administered. He had bought another ranch, and had made it productive; a few years later he sold his father's ranch in order to share the proceeds with his sister (as a joint inheritance). His share of the money was used to purchase, in association with Pablo, a large textile mill. He then withdrew from the administration of Pablo's broader interests and concentrated on the new acquisition, which he modernized and built up within a few years to the point where, at the height of the boom, the factory had a labor force of two thousand workers. At this time, again in partnership with Pablo, Pedro invested in a plastics factory and in urban real estate for housing developments. He was considered a technically advanced entrepreneur for his time: he imported German and Swiss technicians for his textile mill and offered a partnership to a Swiss engineer in his plastics factory. As mentioned above, one of his nephews, Enrique Gómez González (IV,88, of the Gómez Balbuena branch), who had studied chemical engineering, was jointly sponsored by Pedro and Pablo to take a course in Germany, so that their Swiss technician could be replaced by a trusted relative. In spite of their technical innovations, Pedro and Pablo never changed their administrative style. They continued to favor centralization of decisions, autocratic management, and the hiring of relatives. The only outsiders permitted to work in administration were lawyers and accountants. Nonrelatives did, however, participate on boards of directors.

When Pablo died, Pedro seemed the natural leader of the business consortium; but Pablo's widow and her sons refused to accept Pedro's leadership because he was not a member of their grandfamily and because he had less capital than they did. Since Pedro was reluctant to bow to his younger and less experienced nephews, the consortium was partitioned and Pedro developed his own textile enterprise in partnership with some Spaniards. He also created one of the first self-service supermarket chains in Mexico. To administer this business he again selected mostly relatives.

By the end of the 1950s Pedro Jiménez was worth around $20 million in industrial and commercial enterprises. He was a prominent leader of the Mexican business community and of several clubs and other prestigious organizations. His ideology emphasized exports in order to generate foreign currency and to improve the standards of the population. After 1960, with the textile crash and the introduction of new technologies, he had economic trouble. In the period when family enterprise in Mexico was giving way to large corporations as a more efficient way of organization, Pedro, following the nationalistic discourse of the time, tried his hand at the export business.

But, partly because of his outdated technology and old-style administration, he was unable to compete in foreign markets. His creditors attached most of his possessions.

In order to pay off his outstanding debts and to continue his expensive life style, Pedro joined his Merino y Pacheco cousins in a real estate venture and also developed his ranch with an eye on the urban food market. He hired technical managers but never relinquished the personal direction of his business affairs to anyone except relatives. Key administrative posts were managed by his own sons as well as the sons of his sister, his cousins, and his aunts. He also hired some of his nephews from the Bañuelos and Gómez Balbuena branches and eventually helped them to set up small business enterprises, generally linked with his own. In the 1960s, despite continuing economic problems, he was powerful enough to invite the president of Mexico as well as members of the cabinet to be witnesses at a daughter's wedding.

Due to shortage of capital and serious technological lags, Pedro's food business was beset with continuing financial difficulties. Finally he decided to enter into partnership with a large multinational corporation, though he had long opposed this merger because of his nationalistic and family-oriented ideology. When, he gave in, he lost control of the administration and kept only 33 percent of the shares. The new management immediately overhauled the business from top to bottom. With liberal injections of foreign capital, they introduced new products that lost money for a while but then became profitable. Pedro was ideologically incapable of playing the minority shareholder in his own enterprise and never agreed with the policies of the new management. He sold out, even though he was drawing a good income. He then decided to sell part of his ranch to a housing developer. He has stated that he had created more than five thousand jobs in Mexico and that his real estate operations were indirectly providing jobs for at least three thousand more. He holds up this record as an example to other Mexican businessmen.

Eventually, his sons graduated from college and returned to find fault with Pedro's traditional style of management and his reluctance to delegate responsibilities. At first they worked with their father, but eventually, one after another, they went their own ways. The eldest bought a ranch in partnership with a Merino y Pacheco cousin and moved to the country with his family. He runs the ranch using new technology. Pedro was disappointed about his moving away but nevertheless helped him to get settled.

The second son moved to a multinational corporation that he got to know through his father's enterprise; he eventually became associated with the husband of one of his sisters and an entrepreneur, patronized by one of the corporation executives. Part of his initial capital was provided by his father. The other two sons are professionals: one is a lawyer, and the other went abroad to do graduate work. On returning to Mexico the latter turned down work in the private sector and is now a well-placed technocrat in the public sector. Members of the family occasionally rebuke him for working for the government.

One of Pedro's daughters married a big entrepreneur, two daughters married liberal professionals, and the fourth married a middle-class employee, who decided to live in the United States, partly in order to get away from the domination of the Jiménez Gómez family. Their withdrawal from the family was far from successful. Several sisters have bought properties near them, and on one occasion a planeload of fifty-one Jiménez Gómez relatives arrived to spend Christmas with the would-be loners.

Ana María's five sons worked for Pedro during different periods, managing some of his businesses. Eventually, one of them became a partner with him in his *maquila* enterprise. Another is now working with the Merino y Pacheco construction industry: he is an architect. The third is an employee in a corporation and the fourth eventually became an executive in a large international corporation. The fifth died young. The eldest daughter, Lupita (IV,148), married a well-known physician who has since become the family surgeon. She is a strong centralizing woman and has contacts throughout the kinship network. The youngest daughter married a middle-range entrepreneur.

The homes of the Jiménez Gómez are scattered over a large area of Mexico City, but initially they clustered in a relatively small area. Ana María married in 1929 and moved into a home near her Aunt Anita and her parents-in-law in the Santa María de la Rivera neighborhood. Around 1950 she moved downtown into the home she had just inherited. Shortly afterward, using the money from her inheritance, she bought a home in the upper middle class area of Cuauhtémoc, not far from her brother Pedro and her cousin Leopoldo Jr. (see fig. 2).

Pedro lived in Colonia Júarez, an upper middle class area. A few years later, about 1945, he moved to Polanco, then a brand new upper-class European-style development. Though the city was spreading out toward the suburbs, Polanco was close to the other branches of the family: Leopoldo's family in Anzures, Ana María's family in Cuauhtémoc, and Pablo's family in Las Lomas de Chapultepec.

When Ana María's sons began to marry, the eldest son first made his home in his parents' neighborhood and later in Polanco. Her remaining sons and daughters married mostly during the 1960s and established their homes together, on the same street of the expensive development of Tecamachalco, a joint real estate venture of Pablo and Pedro. Most of Pedro's children married during the 1970s and also settled in the Tecamachalco–La Herradura development, on lots provided for them by their father.

Pedro relies on Ana María and on his own wife for his contacts with the kinship network. The Jiménez branch is highly sociable and maintains frequent and lively contact with the Gómez Casés and Bañuelos branches in particular but also with the rest of the kinship network, more so than do members of the Gómez Casés branch. In the 1970s they were still invited to be godparents of members of other branches, including the Gómez Casés. Pedro continues to socialize with politicians, bankers, and entrepreneurs. These social resources have been highly useful to members of the fourth generation of the Jiménez Gómez branch.

Conclusions

When the Gómez talk about "the rich," "the poor," "the professionals," and so on, they acknowledge the effects of a process of segmentation that has been taking place from the second generation on. This is a natural development in any kinship group. What is more unusual is the extent of social cohesion found among the Gómez despite the centrifugal forces of life in a large twentieth-century metropolis.

Three factors have contributed to the continuing family solidarity of the Gómez: (1) family enterprise as a source of patron-client relations and generalized economic exchange; (2) the presence of dominant males in the family who take their role seriously, both as prominent public figures and as employers and protectors of their relatives; (3) the influence of centralizing women who gather and disseminate information about their branches both within the branch and with centralizing women of other branches.

These three reasons are not independent. Most of the network's dominant male figures (but not all) have been family entrepreneurs as well. Most of them have interacted closely with centralizing women, providing jobs and assistance as needed. There has always been at least one centralizing woman in every generation of each family branch. Family life has been organized around the homes of these women, and the ideology of family enterprise has been transmitted in family gatherings.

We may identify what amounts to a fourth reason for the continuance of family cohesion in the urban industrial environment: the preservation of the Gómez family subculture through ideology and ritual. At the intersection between family business and family socialization is the ritual family gathering, an arena for circulating information and for reaffirming the distinctive identity of membership in the Gómez family.

CHAPTER 3

Family and Enterprise

GENERAL patterns of economic behavior have developed over time and have become characteristic features both of the Gómez family and of a significant sector of Mexican society. There is an important relationship between family and enterprise, in particular, and between social relations and economic life in general. Some aspects of this have remained constant, yet economic behavior has changed in response to new conditions and trends in the national and world economy. Family enterprise is the focus of economic activity in the Gómez family. Most males have been trained in family enterprises and have worked in various positions in them. Family enterprise is the basis of an entrepreneur's action group (the group with whom the entrepreneur organizes his work), and its internal structure reflects the family structure.

Social relations are an essential resource for Mexican entrepreneurs and for Mexicans in general. This resource may be thought of as social capital in the sense of Bourdieu: "Social capital is the set of actual or potential resources related to the possession of an enduring network of relations of intercognition and interrecognition, which are more or less institutionalized; in other words, which are related to belonging to a group" (1980, 2-4). Each member of an entrepreneurial group has a network of kinship and friendship that extends in the direction of different social groups and different sectors of society. However, the core of this social network is the kinship group, with the grandfamily as its center.

The Development of Gómez Family Enterprises

To review family history from an economic perspective, it will be recalled that the Gómez were originally small country gentry and small-town traders. Leopoldo Sr. (11,16) began his career as store clerk, working for a relative. Over the years he learned the trade and acquired valuable urban contacts. At a time when industrialization was barely beginning in Mexico, he cautiously invested in textile manufacturing in association with foreigners who had the necessary expertise; some capital from the Church was apparently also involved. For the sake of security, Leopoldo's savings were largely invested in urban real estate. By his death in 1925, he had established a pattern for others to follow. Among the rent-producing enterprises he left to his sons were four textile mills, all located outside Mexico City.

In the reconstruction period that followed the Revolution, the Gómez benefited from official government support of industrial development. Gómez investments were still basically in textiles and in urban real estate, though there was some diversification in other profitable directions, such as the food industry. At this stage, the increasing reliance on government support encouraged the Gómez to cultivate personal relations with top government officials, industrialists, and bankers. After 1960 the Gómez became increasingly displaced by large industrial corporations financed by foreign multinational groups or by the Mexican state. Old-style family entrepreneurs were faced with a difficult choice: to find new resources of capital for overhauling or modernizing their industries, or to learn to live with the new economic realities by finding a suitable niche in middle-range industrial development. Especially during the 1970s, the Gómez have preferred the latter alternative and have concentrated their efforts on survival in an increasingly hostile political climate. They became associated with foreign capital; they concentrated in specialized fields of the textile industry; they went into construction, into agro-business, into jobbing for other industries, and into real estate development. As a concession to the increasing importance of technology they began sending their own sons to college, thus opening the possibility that a Gómez could eventually occupy a position as a technocrat in the civil service, which indeed occurred in the Jiménez Gómez branch.

Economic Activities

The economic activities of male members of the Gómez family (including in-laws who joined the Gómez kinship network)

Table 12. *Economic Activities*

Generation	Agriculture	Commerce	Industry Small	Industry Medium	Industry Large	Investment	Liberal/Technical Professions	White-Collar Employee
Gómez men								
Up to 1850	1	1	0	0	0	1	0	0
1853–1874	0	1	0	0	1	0	2	1
1880–1916	0	0	1	0	3	0	2	5
1914–1958	2	2	7	5	10	0	10	2
1940–present	0	3	1	5	12	4	17	0
TOTALS	3	7	9	10	26	5	31	8
In-laws married to Gómez women								
Up to 1850	0	0	0	0	0	0	0	0
1853–1874	1	1	0	0	0	0	0	2
1880–1916	0	1	0	5	1	0	2	0
1914–1958	0	2	0	6	3	0	13	5
1940–present	0	1	0	0	3	0	20	2
TOTALS	1	5	0	11	7	0	35	9

NOTE: Individuals were counted more than once if they changed jobs, held more than one job at a time, or if their economic activity spanned more than one period. See text for definition of small, medium, and large industry and for discussion of source.

have changed over time. The data of table 12 register the occupations of individuals in the prime of life. It should be remembered that most industrialists and other businessmen started out as salaried employees in some relative's business and later became their own bosses. This is true of every entrepreneur in the Gómez family. Many individuals also changed economic activities during their lifetime, deriving their main income first from commerce and later from industry or investments. A family member whose economic activity changed or spanned more than one period may be counted twice in the same or different columns of table 12.

The classification of industries (or enterprises) as "small," "medium," and "large" in table 12 is to some extent arbitrary since the data spans different historical eras. Particularly for the earlier years, information about the amount of capital investment is not always available. After 1940, we define "large" industry as an industrial enterprise with more than five hundred workers and a capital in excess of one million dollars. "Medium" industries are those with a work force of 100–200 workers and a capital of $350,000–1,000,000; and "small" industries are those that fall below these figures. In a few cases, we have classified an entrepreneur as a "large" industrialist because the aggregate capital of his various industrial concerns significantly exceeded one million dollars, even though no single enterprise was large enough to qualify as such. This was notably the case with Pablo Gómez, who owned medium-sized industries with a total capital of $30 million dollars in 1951 (NAFINSA 1982, 15). His enterprises were never incorporated as a holding company.[1]

---

[1] In 1967 about four hundred firms dominated nearly all the capital in Mexico; many of them were foreign. At that time, about one thousand families belonged to the group known as "big capital"; among these, perhaps one hundred families were prominent and the top twenty dominated the rest (Aguilar and Carmona 1977, 65-74). Three families dominated the independent Monterrey group, five families dominated other parts of the country; and the remaining eighty-two families were located in Mexico City. The Gómez were not listed in these references. The other nine hundred entrepreneurial families mentioned in the same source represent Mexican businesses increasingly confined to the more traditional and less dynamic fields of the economy. Conglomerates and financial groups supported by state and foreign capital

The data for periods prior to 1940 have largely been estimated from information supplied by informants. We have found that legal documents are generally unreliable, particularly regarding the true size of industrial enterprises. Wills are somewhat more reliable than property deeds, but verification on the basis of information supplied by family members has been most useful.

Forty-five percent of the male members of the Gómez family can be described as deriving their main income from industry. Beginning with the second generation, an increasing number of Gómez men have been active in the liberal and technical professions; this is true particularly after 1940. After that year as well there were no more lifelong employees in the family. In all, only eight Gómez men have been employed by relatives all their lives; they mostly belonged to the third generation, prior to the advent of the liberal professions as a viable livelihood.

Of the thirteen Gómez in-laws who became industrialists, five began working for their fathers-in-law, from whom they then inherited part of their industrial properties. Most in-laws were in the liberal or technical professions. Overall, about 75 percent of all Gómez males and male affines of the Gómez family were entrepreneurs or independent professionals.

The Entrepreneurs

In Mexico a person who owns and manages his own business is known as an entrepreneur (*empresario*). Some informants speak of "true entrepreneurs," meaning the more creative breed of businessmen who are not satisfied with managing enterprises that they inherited but who create new sources of capitalization. In this restricted sense, an entrepreneur is a businessman who is also an innovator (Schumpeter 1961). The innovations usually involve introducing new technology, developing new products, or opening new markets; in the case of

---

dominated big business. Only forty-six firms were manufacturing basic intermediate goods (Cordero and Santín 1977, 9). By 1971 there were 131 conglomerates and groups in Mexico, and the fifty largest generated 44.7 percent of the gross national product. Most of these groups were broadly diversified in their production and in their sources of financing.

Mexican entrepreneurs like the Gómez, the most remarkable innovation has been the development and use of social networks for tapping economic resources.

According to Belshaw (1955, 147), an entrepreneur may be defined as "someone who takes the initiative in administering resources and who pursues an expansive economic policy." The attributes of an entrepreneur include management of a business, profit making, business innovation, and bearing uncertainty: "these characteristics imply that the entrepreneur must initiate and coordinate a number of interpersonal relationships in a supervisory capacity to carry out his enterprise. In other words, around the entrepreneur there arises a corporate group, new in terms of its particular membership and function and perhaps also an innovation in terms of its composition and structure" (Barth 1963, 5).

The Gómez talent for tapping social resources for economic purposes began with Leopoldo Sr., whose contacts with members of the hierarchy of the Catholic church were probably crucial in the rapid expansion of his industrial enterprises. Pablo Gómez is considered the most innovative entrepreneur among the family. In openly associating with "politicos," as well as with foreign industrialists and bankers, he broke new ground in terms of the existing family ideology. Because he was the most powerful member of the kinship network at the time he could affort to defy traditions that had grown obsolete, thus finding fresh social resources that provided financing, contracts, permits, markets, and new technology. Starting out with only two inherited industrial concerns, he ended up with a complex of thirty-six factories, some of them geared for the export market.

Size cannot necessarily be equated with creativity. Some of the Gómez entrepreneurs with smaller businesses have been noted for their creative use of social relations. Entrepreneurs at any level enjoy the highest prestige in the family. Administrators and employees in private business are also accepted, especially if they are young aspiring entrepreneurs. Eventually every male member of the family is expected to become an independent businessman, but the family commiserates with those who fail to attain independence rather than rejecting them.

On the other hand, politicians, civil servants, bureaucrats, and academics are generally rejected. Independent professionals are well regarded and respected, especially when their income is high enough to allow them to make substantial investments. The family counts among its more prestigious members prominent doctors, engineers, architects, and accountants. These individuals often provide services to family members and may end up as partners of family entrepreneurs: for example, the engineers Enrique Gómez González (IV,88) and Alvaro Gómez Villa (IV,83), Modesta's sons, and the architects of the Merino y Pacheco branch. Ramiro Bañuelos (IV,150), an accountant, is a partner in a major accounting firm. All of them enjoy prestige in the family.

Many family members are patients of Gómez (or Gómez in-law) physicians, who socialize on an equal footing with the big family entrepreneurs. The latter are usually not billed. The family doctor plays an important role as an all-purpose counselor, even if quite young. At family reunions people wait for the doctor's arrival to start eating.

Daughters of upper-class families tend to marry professional men or administrators who are eventually absorbed into the family. Should they marry a wealthy entrepreneur, they risk being pulled away from the Gómez kin by their husband's family. Eventually the in-laws invest in the family business or become associated in one way or another. Those in-laws who are neither independently wealthy nor active in a profession become employed in the family business or are set up in business by the father of the bride.

Family Enterprises

Two basic organizational patterns are common to all Gómez industrial organizations, irrespective of their size.

First, they have centralized management. The entrepreneur is the owner and manager of the industry; he rules his enterprise much like his own family. His authoritarian control extends not only to his sons and relatives but also, as far as possible, to his workers and employees, including technical experts. This has also been found in other Mexican and Latin American family enterprises (David 1972b; Derossi 1972a; Llano Cifuentes n.d.a, n.d.b).

The entrepreneur is the paterfamilias of the industry; he expects to make all decisions and to be respected and consulted in all matters. He feels responsible for the personal welfare of his subordinates. Gómez entrepreneurs retain full authority over their enterprises even if the sons who are working under them are middle-aged. They are invariably the chairmen of the board of directors. They retain control of the shares of the enterprise during their lifetime and they distribute second-ranking posts in the enterprise according to their own criteria.

In this paternalistic role, a Gómez entrepreneur feels entitled to make use of his subordinates' services at any time of the day or night. He expects them to be available on call; he personally controls their work and checks into their working hours; he discusses and criticizes their attire, their progress in study or advancement, their personal friends, and their way of spending leisure time or vacations. Usually he allows no objections and his will must be unconditionally obeyed. He feels entitled to the same respect from his subordinates that as a father he expects from his sons. As a result the administrative apparatus of the enterprise is largely fictitious, because the actual authority is vested in one man; there is often no administration to speak of, in fact. Other studies in Mexico confirm this pattern (Davis 1972b, 295; García Acosta 1979; Hunt 1969; Suárez 1979). The only relevant structural change occurs at the death of the entrepreneur.

A Gómez entrepreneur cannot renounce his position as head of the enterprise during his lifetime any more than he can resign his duties as head of the family. This situation may lead to an undercurrent of tension in the enterprise, particularly between a father and his sons.

Second, if an entrepreneur has no sons (or if his sons are not yet of age), he will use other relatives to fill key management positions. These are often brothers, nephews, or cousins from poor branches, but affines who have married into the Gómez family are preferred. Such relatives are retained in positions of trust until the heirs grow up to take their place.

Sons of an entrepreneur start working for their father's business as early as possible, often before finishing high school. They start out at a low level and work their way up, dislodging people who may have held positions in the firm for years. Other relatives may be asked to join the enterprise if their technical abilities are required, their capital and connections are useful, they have been recommended by relatives, or simply because of their own needy situation. Young relatives are often hired so that they will be taught a trade with which to make a living. This also happens with the sons of trusted workers and employees who have been with the family for many years.

In general the tendency is for members of the owner's grandfamily to occupy key positions. The ranking of sons and others relatives in the enterprise will usually reflect their age and place in the succession. At death the enterprises will be transmitted to the owner's sons; there is correlation between the age of a son and the importance of the share he inherits.

The relatives who are displaced by the owner's sons usually set up independent businesses with the assistance of their former boss. They tend to remain in the same branch of business and to do business with their former employer; often they become subcontractors, jobbers, providers of services (e.g., transportation), or subsidiary producers of parts and materials for the industry that they originally served. Thus each major industry generates a network of subsidiaries or client enterprises, each of which is fully owned by a client relative. This pattern implies continuing patron-client relations between an entrepreneur and his relatives. Patron-client relations are very important within the Gómez kinship network (see table 13). The business relationship between patron and client usually follows the pattern described between employer and employee.

Patterns of Inheritance

The Gómez family assets are transmitted from father to son in a pattern that reflects the structure of the grandfamily.

Table 13. Patron-Client Relationships within the Kinship Network

Entrepreneurs	No. of Client Relatives
Juan Miranda (II,e′11)	1
Leopoldo Gómez Aburto (II,16)	21
Leopoldo Gómez Casés (III,50)	27
Pablo Gómez Casés (III,51)	35
Pedro Jiménez Gómez (III,72)	54
Javier Gómez Gómez (IV,80)	16
María del Carmen Gómez González (IV,87)[a]	8
Enrique Gómez González (IV,88)	15
Agustín Merino y Pacheco Gómez (IV,97)	11
Maximiliano Merino y Pacheco Gómez (IV,99)	19
Leopoldo Gómez Benítez (IV,103)	11
Ramiro Gómez Benítez (IV,106)	16
Pablo Gómez Chacón (IV,109)	9
Juan Gómez Chacón (IV,110)	10
Leopoldo Jorge Gómez Chacón (IV,111)	6
TOTAL	259

SOURCE: Data calculated from information provided by our informants.
[a] The only woman entrepreneur of the family.

When an entrepreneur dies, his widow remains at the center of the social and emotional life of the grandfamily: she also retains economic control of the enterprises even if she does not interfere in their management. Actual partition of the legacy only occurs after the mother's death.

Occasionally, sons have taken over their father's enterprise or investment at his death or even before, either as administrators or as legal owners if their father so decides in his lifetime. To avoid legal and financial complications, business firms may be nominally transferred to a son, but this does not mean that the son can exercise the privileges of ownership before his father's death (see Hunt 1969 for a similar case in Mexico).

Daughters do not normally inherit enterprises unless their husbands happen to be in charge of a particular business. A daughter's share of the inheritance is not necessarily smaller than that of her brother, but it normally consists of real estate, antiques, works of art, jewelry, and other investments. Women may also inherit shares in enterprises that are expected to be managed by their brothers. Since a daughter's descendants have no direct access to her father's industrial enterprises, the less wealthy branches of the family are descended through female lines. Males in these descent groups typically work under their uncles and will be dislodged by their less experienced cousins belonging to the male lines of descent. Here family ideology overrules rationality in business decisions.

In most cases the inheritance of a son consists of one or more independent enterprises. When a business concern is inherited jointly by two brothers, conflict may arise over control of the enterprise. Each descendant will feel entitled to be the boss and to enjoy total control of the enterprise, much as he controls his own family. In the case of brothers working in the same concern, the split may develop at an earlier stage when they share management responsibilities under their father's direction. The rivalry between brothers may lead to conflict, but the two continue to share the same social circle and the same social resources.

The process of economic segmentation caused by the inheritance pattern has effectively prevented the Gómez from consolidating their holdings into financial groups. Since 1960, due to rising economic pressures of big corporations and of the state, the relative status of Gómez enterprises has declined. They now occupy a second-level position in the ranking of Mexican industry.

Technology

Technical ability has been underappreciated since the early days of the family, under Leopoldo Sr. This was particularly true for accountants and people with expertise in the process of production. Such people were never awarded positions as "trustworthy personnel" (*personal de confianza*) unless they also happened to be relatives. In any case, the decision-making process, including technical decisions, is ultimately the privilege of the boss.

More recently, some young Gómez businessmen with college degrees have acquired technical qualifications in addition to qualifying as relatives. But technology is still given a low priority in terms of investment. The smallest possible share of the profits is reinvested in technology. If a choice exists, used equipment and machinery are purchased in preference to new ones. This policy is consistent with the Gómez propensity for buying up old, ailing industries in financial trouble. Such industries are floated with the barest minimum investment needed to make them profitable. Until the 1980s there was no record of any specific technological development financed by a Gómez enterprise. Whenever a new technology became necessary, it was purchased ready-made and a technician was hired to introduce the required changes.[2]

Attitudes toward Profit and Risk

As a rule, Gómez entrepreneurs prefer short-term profit making over long-term investments. A Gómez expects his business to pay off from the start. He will say that "business is good" if the profits are high enough to maintain his family's life style. Dividends are reinvested in the enterprise only if they are likely to produce quick and safe returns. Though additional enterprises may be purchased, the favorite reinvestment is in real estate in Mexico and, since the 1970s, abroad. Rural properties are safe investments that also generate prestige, although there are four cases in which Gómez ranching has become a profitable enterprise.

The stock market generates little interest among the Gómez. This attitude is rooted in the reality of an unstable economy, where the currency is subject to devaluation. Rapid urban growth guarantees that real estate investments are relatively inflation-proof and, though they have a lower yield than industrial investments, they represent a source of security. Since 1970 investments have increasingly been made in American

[2] Since the 1982 devaluation of the peso, there have been two cases of Gómez entrepreneurs investing in technological developments in their enterprises.

currency, replacing, to a certain extent, land investments as a source of security.

In terms of risk management, an owner-controlled enterprise may have a definite edge over other kinds of enterprises that exist in the early stages of a country's development. Administrative roles are assigned in a more natural fashion as a company grows, and the firm presents a monolithic front to the outside world. The same man who makes the decisions assumes the financial risk. Troubles arise when the enterprise grows beyond a certain size: this size depends on the historical and market conditions. Eventually, large centralized family enterprises become cumbersome and difficult to control. The history of the Gómez enterprises suggests that family enterprise served a useful purpose during the period of export substitution in Mexico, particularly in the fields of consumer goods: the era of the "Mexican miracle," when Pablo, Leopoldo Jr., and Pedro rose to the top of the entrepreneurial elite. Eventually the family business strategy became a liability, as competition and state policy forced enterprises to modernize their internal organization. Only the smaller and less technically advanced companies survived with a family-sized administration.

If Gómez entrepreneurs continue to insist on sole ownership and control of their enterprises, they have their reasons. Total control means, among other things, total freedom for the owner to withdraw capital for his private use. It also means that he can hand out jobs and positions freely, thus creating an entourage of relatives and clients that symbolizes family unity and bolsters his personal prestige. An example is the common practice of featherbedding. *Aviadores* (flyers) are people on the payroll who do not perform any visible function in the business. They are often close relatives (daughters, aunts, sons-in-law, and so on), who are supported by the entrepreneur with little or no effect on his income after taxes. Benefits of this kind are only possible when the entrepreneur retains total control over his enterprise.

For these reasons, Gómez entrepreneurs dislike the idea of going public or of entering into partnerships with foreign corporations. Actual experience with such partnerships has been disappointing to the family. The Mexican partner is often shouldered aside or used as a local promoter until a foreign product has gained a foothold on the market. Administrative controls are seen as demeaning, as they interfere in the freedom to conduct business affairs in the family style. The business approach of foreign corporations is alien to Gómez needs: foreign businessmen are rarely flexible on matters such as providing jobs for relatives, handling expense accounts, arranging for convenient work schedules, allowing for cash withdrawals, and safeguarding personal prestige. The Gómez say the foreigners "cannot understand our mentality."

Family and Business

A fundamental feature of the enterprise is its degree of integration with family life. It might be said that business among the Gómez can largely be understood in terms of family circumstances and family events. The family serves the enterprise; the power, prestige, and money derived from the enterprise revert to the family. Needless to say, there are other personal gratifications that an entrepreneur obtains from his work; yet family reasons appear to be dominant in terms of business decisions.

The Gómez industries do not function as institutions separate from their owner and his family. Kinship interest often overrules the interest of the enterprise, as Derossi pointed out in her study of Mexican entrepreneurs (1972b, 25). A few Gómez enterprises are organized along more impersonal lines and do not follow the family pattern, but they appear to be the exception.

Business is more than just a source of income. It means power and prestige and hence emotional identification. Family members refuse to buy brands or patronize establishments belonging to the competition. Even after a family enterprise has been sold, its products are still preferred by the family for sentimental reasons, as an original family creation. Such attitudes tend to spread to the entire kinship network: relatives in one branch will favor the other branches' products.

The whole grandfamily promotes the enterprise. Consider the grandfamily of the entrepreneur, and the entrepreneur's wife in particular. All close relatives are public relations agents of the entrepreneur, but his most dedicated publicity agent is his wife. She is in charge of hospitality for business relations and visiting business friends, and she makes all necessary social arrangements. She will not require any instructions for this; rather, she takes the initiative whenever she meets anyone whose connections may be useful to her husband's business. She regularly visits with friends and relatives, purchasing appropriate gifts and making plans for attendance at important family rituals. At each of these occasions she gathers and transmits to her husband all information that may be useful to his business. If an entrepreneur is a member of a club or a service association, his wife and children eagerly participate in club activities and try to make a good impression.

The wife's role is demanding: she should be fashionable, well dressed for every occasion, well groomed and bejewelled, versed in business affairs, and conversationally adept at sorting important information from irrelevant gossip. At home she manages her servants efficiently, plays the gracious hostess, and is a good cook. Gómez entrepreneurs are fully aware of the importance of their wives in the success of their enterprises, though this might not be gathered from their conversation, in which the official posture is that wives have nothing to do with economic matters and that their business role is irrelevant.

All Gómez family members, from childhood on, are groomed as promoters of the family interests. The availability of such a large network of volunteer agents is no small advantage. Perhaps the most relevant quality of Gómez entrepreneurs is their skill in manipulating social connections and their ability to transform social connections into economic assets. An entrepreneur is always ready to drop everything and give priority to family matters. He will not hesitate to leave an important meeting if a relative is ill or has a problem. It is his privilege: he is the owner and not a hired executive.

Social Networks

One way of understanding social resources in a Mexican family enterprise is through network analysis. Three kinds of networks may be distinguished in the economy of a Mexican family enterprise: action groups, social networks for the circulation of information, and power networks for access to economic and bureaucratic resources.

An *action group* for economic purposes is a group of trusted relatives organized around an entrepreneur, who acts as a broker on their behalf toward the rest of society. Depending on the resources of the entrepreneur, such an action group may be more or less permanent. Action groups grow around an entrepreneur as his business ventures grow and diversify. Positions of trust (*confianza*) are filled from the available pool of relatives as vacancies develop. *Confianza*[3] is thus a basic element of economic interaction in business. The entrepreneur requires a circle of persons, each connected to him through a relationship of trust. In the kind of enterprise described here, business and money matters are delicate and require the kind of trust and interpersonal loyalty one expects to find in relatives. The entrepreneur also sees himself as a provider of jobs for his relatives, and he is forever branching out into new ventures to create suitable openings for them.

As a rule, relatives are hired at a young age; eventually they are expected to outgrow their stage as employees and become independent businessmen. There is a rotation in the composition of the action group as older relatives set up their own business enterprises and younger relatives of the next generation come in. It is also true, however, that newly independent entrepreneurs who graduate from the action group remain connected to their former boss by business relationships. The resulting pattern of patron-client relationships may be seen as the end result of a complex history of membership in action groups formed around individual entrepreneurs. An individual initiates his economic life as a member of an action group and eventually outgrows it to become an independent entrepreneur, ultimately becoming part of a network of related and complementary enterprises.

---

[3] Some attention has been given to the relationship between *confianza* and economic behavior in Latin America; see, e.g., Aubey 1979; Gilbert 1977; Greenfield and Strickon 1979; Long 1977.

Social networks, as informal sources of information, are a prime resource in Latin American business (Aubey 1979). The markets are usually thin and public information is scarce and unreliable. Networks of relatives and friends represent the main source of business intelligence. Family parties and gatherings among the Gómez are remarkable in that business conversation is quite active, among women as well as men.

The grandfamily is the center of the information network. Family rituals, beginning with the weekly family dinner and continuing across the spectrum of ritual family interaction, are the medium in which these networks develop and grow. Different networks intertwine as information is shared with other relatives. The intensity of exchange of information is related to the closeness of kin. Information involves business opportunities (e.g., properties and businesses for sale), availability of personnel and expertise, political information, information on money markets, legal and bureaucratic leads, and so forth.

Power networks, for access to economic resources and bureaucratic influence, are also important. Each entrepreneur has a network of contacts among nonrelatives that includes the state and federal bureaucracy, financial and banking circles, business and labor circles, and the hierarchy of the Catholic church. Personal relations are essential here as well.

Considerable time and expense are devoted to the cultivation of these networks of business relations. To friends in the banking world, for example, it is essential to demonstrate that one can support an expensive life style. In the past it was possible for a top Gómez entrepreneur to go directly to the president of Mexico or to the owner of the largest bank in order to solve most of his problems. More recently the network of necessary and useful friends among the bureaucracy and the financial community has grown enormously; specific problems require the intervention of friends at many levels. Contacts at the top are still essential but have become increasingly difficult to obtain. In addition, an increasing number of day-to-day problems require the intervention of officials of lesser rank.

The cultivation of a network of business and power relations requires ingenuity and tact. Top-level politicians and bankers are entertained in the grandest possible style, but minor bureaucrats may be reached through younger or less wealthy relatives. An entrepreneur's young son-in-law who works, say, as an architect in a project for a state-owned concern may become an asset when problems arise in connection with building permits. The power network is built on mutual exchange and mutual dependence, as network participants large and small trade favors and consolidate mutual interests. Such a network is nurtured not only among government and company officials and friends of relatives but also among the entrepreneur's vast social network of acquaintances from school, play (leisure, travel, clubs, sports), and the normal course of business activity.

To the extent that family business has become displaced by large corporations, social relationships have undergone certain changes. Before 1950 the major industrialists had personal access to top officials, because they themselves were the chief representatives of the business community. Ease of access has now become a prerogative of the top executives of the large corporations, and the former captains of Mexican industry are referred to second-rank or third-rank officials.

Trade Associations, Clubs, and Charities

The Gómez are joiners. Some have been national leaders of industrial chambers, and members of the family are prominent on the rosters of service clubs, alumni associations, industrial and trade associations, and so on. The Gómez believe that it is important to belong to at least one such association and to become a leading member if possible. Fathers usually register their sons as members at the earliest possible age, and sons remind them if they do not. Women, too, without losing sight of their primary role as housewives, participate in associations and enthusiastically support charities and artistic activities, through which they feel they are actively serving society.

Entrepreneurs are well aware that such societies and clubs are forums for ideas, meeting places for the economically powerful, and generators of class consciousness (Domhoff n.d.; Holzberg 1977; Mills 1975; Ratcliff 1974). They are convenient political vehicles of the private sector, through which the government and the general public can be reached. As one informant said, "it's a good idea because you meet people and you make connections." Such clubs represent ideal arenas for introductions, business deals, and display of prestige and wealth. Many business deals originate in such arenas.

Membership in charitable societies is regarded as socially and morally beneficial, and this too has its economic and political advantages. The Gómez have taken turns on charity boards for years. In this capacity they have dealings with government authorities and with important provincial delegates. Alumni associations are also important; college acquaintances can be useful in many ways. For example, a young Gómez who went to the same high school as a top government official was able to revive their old school friendship when he had a problem involving this friend's agency.

At least five family members have been presidents of national chambers of commerce or chambers of industry. Gaining such a position testifies to a long business career, starting out as a member of a local chapter and rising through the ranks step by step. Others have been officers of the various confederations of chambers or have been presidents of specific industrial sectors. These chambers and confederations are extremely important political organizations (see e.g. Alcaraz 1977; Arriola 1981; Brandenburg 1972; Derossi 1972; González Casanova 1965; Vernon 1977). Officers are national figures who represent the private sector in negotiations with the government. Their speeches often make front-page news in the press and are carefully scrutinized by newspaper columnists, the public, and of course by the cabinet. Statements also may be taped and shown on television. Such comments range over the entire field of politics: agriculture, education, budget policies, and the state of the economy in general.

In the 1950s during the postwar economic boom in Mexico, industry leaders were treated almost like cabinet ministers and enjoyed official rank as ambassadors when they traveled. Those days are gone. The heads of the chambers and federations today are educated and technically sophisticated businessmen rather than self-made men. Though Gómez family members are still prominent in the chambers, they are no longer national figures. Possibly they are being displaced by modern-style entrepreneurs. Hired executives have become presidents of federations lately, a fact deplored by the Gómez entrepreneurs, who resent the trend away from traditional business styles and family values.

Conclusions

Family enterprise has been a common feature of the early stages of industrial development (Benedict 1968; Kempner, Macmillan, and Haukins 1976, 21-49). In Latin America it has been unusually persistent.

Social networks have played a key role in securing the smooth transition of Gómez family fortunes over historical crises such as the liberal reform, the Revolution, and the present situation, in which family enterprise is increasingly isolated and is holding out against the invasion of national and foreign corporations and the encroachment of the Mexican state. Social networks cannot solve every problem. The family enterprise embodies a basic weakness in that it tends to put loyalty above performance. Eventually, some of the major Gómez companies have proved no match against the superior efficiency of modern corporations using hired professional management.

Social networks can absorb the shocks of a bumpy historical road, but they cannot replace technology or mobilize resources on a scale comparable with large multinational corporations or the state. In other words, family businesses have limitations on their growth. Paternalistic structures adapt poorly to the corporate organization of modern business. However, social resources continue to be a source of security and adaptability to deal with the repeated periods of economic instability that characterize the Mexican and Latin American economies. In an entirely different social setting, the Mexican shantytown people too use kinship networks as a form of social security, but networks are no substitute for full participation in the market economy (Lomnitz 1977). Economic decisions are often guided by symbolic-cultural or ideological rationales rather than by strictly economic motives.

Four characteristics of the business style represented by the Gómez family in Mexico may be singled out.

First, the principal characteristic of Gómez business is its integration with the family. Both family and business find their raison d'être in each other. There is no clear-cut separation between family interest and business interest, or between the person of the owner and the legal personality of the firm. Kinship social distance is reflected in the structure of the enterprise. Nephews are supposed to leave eventually, while sons carry on management duties until their father's death. In its ideal form, the social unit (the grandfamily) becomes identical to the economic unit.

Second, the process of capital accumulation is disrupted every thirty years or so by the death of the entrepreneur, when his inheritance is partitioned among his sons, who inherit the means of production, and his daughters, who receive passive capital.

Third, for the sake of family harmony, entrepreneurs prefer several medium-sized enterprises to one or two large, modern companies. This makes it easier to leave each son the owner of an independent enterprise (see chapter 6 on ideology). Medium-sized enterprises are also easier to manage than large ones, which are too complex and technology-laden to be managed by a single owner and would require a change in life style and the sacrifice of values connected with family life and leisure.

Fourth, the reluctance of the older Gómez entrepreneurs to enter into partnerships has prevented them from establishing large and more powerful enterprises. They missed the opportunity to become a family conglomerate during the 1950-1960 period, for example. Some Mexican family groups did take this option (e.g. the Monterrey group), which enabled them to face the impending changes in the socioeconomic structure of Mexico successfully (Derossi 1972b, 64-74). However, the Gómez have maintained the basic family structure that they hold to be all-important.

CHAPTER 4

Kinship

THE SYMBOLIC system that underlies the social actions of the Gómez family can be abstracted from our data. We propose that the basic unit of solidarity in the culture of Mexico is the grandfamily, or three-generation descent group. This implies that in Mexico, the cultural symbol "family" means a well-defined group comprising one's parents, siblings, spouse, and children. Firth, Hubert, and Forge (1970, 285) define the grandfamily as "the extension of the simple family prolongation of a second generation," carrying a strong set of obligations and expectations of ritual, economic, and social support.

In cultural terms, the grandfamily represents a *value ideal* as the fundamental element of solidarity: the basic building block of society. This ideal is shared by members of the culture who attempt to conform to it in their lives through repeated acts of ritual, exchange, and ideological commitment, although its actual realization in terms of action is subject to variations resulting from class differences.

The Mexican family can be contrasted with the family in the United States and England (see Berger and Berger 1982; Firth, Hubert, and Forge 1970; Macfarlane 1979; Schneider 1968; Schneider and Smith 1973). The most salient differences between the two kinship systems are the following: (a) the two-generation nuclear family that prevails in England and the United States ideally disbands after the marriage of offspring, if not before; in the three-generation grandfamily the bond between parents and children continues through life and is carried over to grandchildren; (b) in the two-generation nuclear family the affinal bond (husband-wife) has priority, in terms of solidarity, over the consanguinity bond (parent-child); in the three-generation grandfamily the consanguinity bond (parent-child-grandchild) has priority over the affinal bond (husband-wife) and, moreover, direct descent has priority over lateral de-

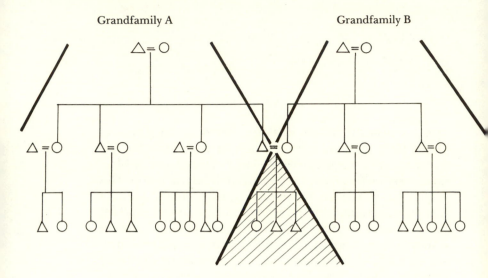

FIG. 3. GRANDFAMILY SEGMENTATION

scent; (c) in the two-generation nuclear family each individual is a member of one family at a time: first that of his parents and siblings, then that of his spouse and children. In the three-generation grandfamily an individual is simultaneously and permanently a member of two grandfamilies: that of his father and that of his mother (see fig. 3). An individual is not unconditionally considered a member of his spouse's grandfamily, but his children are.

A further difference between the two kinship systems is the large number of bonds and the diversity of relationships in the three-generation grandfamily. When they assemble for a ritual, the members of a Gómez grandfamily may include ten to twenty adults and perhaps ten to forty children, all of them siblings or first cousins. This is the basic unit of solidarity (outside the grandfamily): among more distant relatives the solidarity is conditioned by social and emotional closeness.

Finally, there is an important difference in the lifespan or duration of a basic family unit in the two systems. In the two-generation nuclear family each son or daughter forms his or her own family unit at marriage: hence the nuclear family is only operational for twenty to thirty years. In the three-generation grandfamily the operational lifespan of the family is the lifespan of the grandparents. As long as one grandparent is alive, the family exists as an effective unit of solidarity. After both grandparents are deceased, each son or daughter becomes the head of a grandfamily. This means that grandfamilies remain operational during the entire life of the individual, since there is no switch of allegiance at marriage, nor do children "leave the home" in a final sense in their parents' lifetime.

Solidarity is expressed in different forms, depending on social position, economic resources, geographical location of members, and historical or individual circumstances. In general, economic resources facilitate the expression of family solidarity and the lack of them tends to impede such expression to a greater or lesser degree. In all cases, however, unconditional solidarity is the ideal among members of a grandfamily: this implies shared rituals and ideology, close social interaction, economic assistance, and emotional support.

Grandfamily Solidarity

Consider the intersection of two grandfamilies (see fig. 3). The intersection occurs in the third generation: the children in the shaded area owe allegiance to both grandfamilies at once. Similarly, individuals of the second generation owe allegiance to both their father's and their mother's grandfamilies. The formal naming system in Mexico as well as in all Latin America and Spain sanctions this by prescribing the use of both family names (the father's and the mother's, in that order).

Among the Gómez, kin solidarity is expressed in four domains: social life, rituals, economic relations, and ideology. Beginning with social interactions, we have found that members of the Gómez kinship network express their social closeness within the three-generation grandfamily in a number of ways. They are always fully informed of each other's health and activities. This implies frequent (often daily) telephone contact, as well as mutual visiting. Even when a member of the grandfamily lives permanently abroad, there are frequent telephone calls as well as visits as often as possible. Centralizing women often initiate these contacts and spread the news to the rest of family.

Social resources are shared among members of the grandfamily. Anyone who has access to friends or connections of potential use to someone in the family is expected to provide the relevant information and, if requested, facilitate the needed personal contact.

Rituals among the Gómez, to be discussed further in the next chapter, recognize the grandfamily as the basic unit of participation. Perhaps the most obvious example is the weekly family dinner, an institution that has priority over other social engagements. It is held at the home of the head of the grandfamily on a fixed day of the week, and it assembles all members of a grandfamily, their spouses, and their children. For a married Gómez who is not himself the head of a grandfamily, two evenings a week will normally be devoted to these dinners: one with his own grandfamily and one with his spouse's.

In ritual events such as christenings, weddings, and birthday parties, all members of the grandfamily participate. This includes brothers, sisters, uncles, aunts, nephews, nieces, and first cousins in addition to parents and children. No invitation is really necessary but no one can be omitted. All must be considered welcome, and all are expected to attend. Members of the larger kin group will be invited according to social closeness.

In terms of economic cooperation, we find that there is generalized exchange among all members of a grandfamily. Prior to 1960, all Gómez entrepreneurs took their sons into the business; many had also invited nephews to join the enterprise, as described in chapter 3. Sons usually continued working under their father's direction after they got married. Although outwardly resembling a patron-client relationship, the obligation between father and sons is actually mutual. If a son appears to be unsuited for business, his father still feels required to provide an appropriate job for him in his enterprise. Conversely, even if a father is authoritarian and old-fashioned in his approach to business, a grown-up son will follow his directions. Male heads of a grandfamily seldom retire; if incapacitated by old age they may divide their industrial assets and properties among their children, but they retain their authority to the end.[1]

Business deals between brothers are continued, as a rule, despite the economic rivalry that ensues after a father's death. Brothers are enjoined by their parents to take care of their sisters, and this responsibility is not automatically transferred to the husband at a sister's marriage. A Gómez woman can always count on her brothers for economic support for herself and her children, regardless of whether her husband is a good provider.

When Leopoldo Sr. became a wealthy entrepreneur in the 1890s, his relationship with his brothers and sisters changed from one of reciprocity to one of patron and client. Ever since, wealthy Gómez entrepreneurs have provided economic assistance to their siblings or nieces and nephews in return for loyalty and service. The record shows that patron-client relations can endure within the structure of the grandfamily and that the social solidarity they engender can be as durable and as intense as that produced by reciprocity (see table 13, p. 113).

The new wealth of Leopoldo Sr. merely strengthened his allegiance to his grandfamily. His ambitions to be recognized as a member of criollo high society did not stand in the way of his devotion to his mother, a pure Indian, who remained head of the grandfamily and the center of family life until her death. Leopoldo did not shun family rituals. He never stopped providing assistance to his sisters; he never turned down a relative. He became godfather to most of his nephews and nieces. This tradition of economic cooperation within the grandfamily was continued by the heads of the Gómez branches and can be found today at all levels of the kinship network.

In the Gómez ideology, to be examined in chapter 6, there is considerable emphasis on kinship. The cultural ideal of the

---

[1] Similar patterns of solidarity are found by García Acosta (1979) and Suárez (1979) among Spanish migrant entrepreneurs and their descendants and by Hunt (1969) among Oaxaca provincial entrepreneurs.

grandfamily translates into countless instances in which the family myths encourage and glorify assistance between rich uncles and poor nephews or between close kin in general. Examples of filial piety and grandfamily solidarity are by no means limited to Mamá Inés, Leopoldo, and his sons and grandsons. As transmitted from grandfather to grandchild at countless family reunions, these embellished stories become ideological patterns that influence and guide the conduct of kin relations.

Patterns of Residence

For the last hundred years or more the dominant type of household among the Gómez kinship network has been nuclear and neolocal. By this we mean that the social group that shares a residential unit and the associated domestic functions is the nuclear or elementary family, consisting of a married couple and their children. Newlywed couples begin their married life in a separate dwelling and become a complete nuclear family after the first child is born.

However, neolocality among the Gómez is more apparent than real. A pattern of residential clustering was established as early as the second generation. Leopoldo Sr. and his mother and sisters lived with their descendants in one neighborhood, and his half brothers Saúl and Roberto set up their residence in another. For decades relatives lived on the same block and their children went to the same schools. After 1950 some of these neighborhoods, such as Popotla, began to deteriorate and members of the fourth generation moved to Anzures, San Angel, and other middle-class and upper middle-class neighborhoods of Mexico City. The residential pattern among the wealthy branches of the family was described in some detail in chapter 2. Residential clustering meant that members of the third generation of the Gómez family grew up in close personal contact with their first cousins. During the lifetime of Mamá Inés, all relatives met frequently in her home. As social differentiation developed among the wealthier branches of the family, Leopoldo Jr. and Pablo bought large lots of real estate in new residential developments. The Jiménez and the Merino y

Pachecos imitated them and bought lots as wedding presents for their sons and daughters in the newer developments.

When a Gómez grandfamily decided to move it was usually because of urban deterioration, rising status of the family, or the availability of real estate transmitted through the inheritance of an in-law, usually a spouse. As a result, there is now a highly nonrandom distribution of Gómez residences in the Mexico City urban area. Localized clusters of kin occurred initially in Santa María de la Rivera or in San Rafael, or in the downtown area of Popotla; today they are found in Anzures, San Angel, Lomas, Tecamachalco, and other middle-class neighborhoods (see fig. 2). Purchases of large sections of real estate ensure that the offspring will remain in close proximity to their parents after marriage. Middle-class relatives have followed the lead of the wealthy as far as their resources permit. The lower middle-class family members have either stayed behind in the old neighborhoods or have been the last to move out.

Centrifugal tendencies coincide with the process of branch segmentation. As time goes on, each paterfamilias increasingly feels the urge to head a grandfamily of his own. Affine members may occasionally wish to move away in order to escape the dominating influence of the Gómez kin. Grandfamilies are less likely to scatter if the daughters marry slightly below their economic status.

Since about 1960, a wider residential dispersion is observed among middle-class family members, due to the greater availability of housing developments that are competitively marketed with payment arranged in installments. However, the pattern of living next to kin prevails.

Of 133 Gómez couples, only twenty-five (19 percent) initially chose neolocal residence, a choice frequently determined by job or other external requirements (see table 14); all others known (108 couples, 81 percent) made their homes in the vicinity of one or both sets of parents (see tables 15 and 16). Thirty-four (19.21 percent) never changed their residential pattern, and most changes of residence that did occur involved improvements in housing or location that did not alter the cou-

Table 14. Reasons for Neolocality among Gómez Children

Reasons	Men	Women	Totals
Jobs outside the community	6	5	11
Improvement of economic level of nuclear family	3	1	4
Without family in Mexico City (first generation)	0	3	3
Break of norms	0	1	1
Physical convenience (no place near, land expensive, etc.)	2	2	4
Unknown	0	2	2
TOTALS	11	14	25

ple's proximity to one set of parents. Usually the Gómez won the contest over which set of parents would prove more attractive to the new couple: this is less surprising when the Gómez partner is male, since virilocality seems to be the cultural ideal (Foster 1972; Nutini and Bell 1980). However, uxorilocality among Gómez women is even more prominent, if anything, than is virilocality among Gómez men. Thus, of the known choices of initial residence (133 cases), 86 (65 percent) were either ambilocal (near both sets of parents) or located in the vicinity of a Gómez parent. The strength of a family is demonstrated by the fact that it is able to draw affine women into its own sphere of influence while at the same time retaining most of its own women (Lomnitz-Adler 1982; Olivera 1976). However, the bilaterality of the system implies that both men and women may pull their nuclear families to the neighborhood of their own grandfamilies.

Since a couple's offspring belong to both parents' consanguineous kin at once, there is an intrinsic competition between husband and wife over whose side the grandfamily will identify with more closely. The issue of residence is of paramount importance, because residential closeness affords more intimate interaction and eventually a much closer social and emotional identification between the offspring and a particular lineage. In the urban milieu the competition is a tug-of-war

Table 15. Residential Patterns of the Gómez: Tendency to Live Near the Family

	Initial Residence	Only Initial Residence	Final Residence
Gómez men			
Neolocal	10 (14)[a]	1	13 (25)
Virilocal	29 (42)	2	19 (37)
Uxorilocal	14 (20)	4	9 (17)
Ambilocal	16 (23)	5	11 (21)
TOTAL KNOWN	69 (99)	12	52 (100)
Unknown	18	2	21
TOTAL	87	14	73
Gómez women			
Neolocal	15 (23)	6	11 (21)
Virilocal	8 (13)	3	8 (15)
Uxorilocal	37 (58)	8	29 (56)
Ambilocal	4 (6)	2	4 (8)
TOTAL KNOWN	64 (100)	19	52 (100)
Unknown	26	8	11
TOTAL	90	27	63
Combined			
Neolocal	25 (19)	7	24 (23)
Virilocal	37 (28)	5	27 (26)
Uxorilocal	51 (38)	12	38 (37)
Ambilocal	20 (15)	7	15 (14)
TOTAL KNOWN	133 (100)	31	104 (100)
Unknown	44	10	32
GRAND TOTAL	177	41	136

SOURCE: Data from informants' account of residence.
NOTE: Initial residence is the first residence of a couple after marriage; final residence may also mean final residence known. Recently married couples were asked only of their first residence. (There were 41 cases of married couples who were still living in their first residence as of 1977.) The concept of non-neolocal residence means that the couple lives near the parents' home, not in the same residential unit.
[a] Numbers in parentheses are percentages, based on totals known. Not all totals add to 100% due to rounding.

Table 16. Changes in Location of Residence of Gómez Couples

Type of change	Couples with Gómez husband	Couples with Gómez wife	Total
Neolocal to neolocal	2	8	10
to virilocal	2	0	2
to uxorilocal	0	2	2
to ambilocal	3	1	4
Virilocal to neolocal	8	0	8
to virilocal	12	4	16
to uxorilocal	3	2	5
to ambilocal	0	0	0
Uxorilocal to neolocal	2	1	3
to virilocal	4	4	8
to uxorilocal	6	22	28
to ambilocal	6	3	9
Ambilocal to neolocal	1	0	1
to virilocal	0	0	0
to uxorilocal	0	0	0
to ambilocal	8	2	10
TOTALS	57	49	106

NOTE: Data based on lists of residences of one or both sets of the couple's parents. Unknown cases were not counted, nor were cases of couples who had only one residence at the time of the study. Some couples had moved more than once, and each move is counted separately.

between affines that starts before marriage and involves many factors: opportunity or availability of residences in a given neighborhood; relative economic power of the grandfamilies of husband and wife; relative prestige, bondedness, and ideological aggressiveness of grandfamilies; and degree of harmony or conflict within each grandfamily. Sometimes the competition is settled at marriage; more often, it may linger for a number of years or until the couple heads a grandfamily of its own. The pattern of residential closeness to kin persists among middle-class families, both for ideological reasons and for the practical convenience of using relatives to care for children or elder members of the family.

Affinal Relations

There are no formal norms that prescribe the choice of a mate among the Gómez. On the contrary, marriage is supposed to be the result of free choice based on love between the partners.[2] However, there are many factors that influence the selection of a spouse in an urban, socially stratified environment, where young people are apt to meet potential marriage partners of varied backgrounds. In general, there is some social pressure to conform to certain social, occupational, and religious criteria. The individual actors may not be conscious of such restrictions and may continue to believe in love as the guiding principle of mate selection unless they happen to transgress the unspoken norms, in which case they may find themselves subjected to considerable social pressure.

The mating norms are expressed in informal ways, such as in advice given to the young by their elders, for example, "Find someone of your own educational background." People of working-class background or belonging to a different religion are excluded. The prime requisite for a mate is to belong to a Catholic and "honorable" family, in the sense described by Pitt-Rivers (1974) in studying Mediterranean families. From their migration to Mexico City until 1975, the Gómez married into families living in the city; all spouses have been Roman Catholics; only 13 out of 172 were foreign-born (mostly Spaniards, plus 2 Mexicans born of Spanish parents). The vast majority (145) were Mexicans of middle-class origin.

During the first generation, one out of seven men married below his socioeconomic level; the women, on the other hand, tended to marry at least their social equals (see table 17). This trend is found even more clearly in the second generation: none of the men married above their status and none of the women married below theirs. The family still belonged at this time to the rising middle class. Spanish immigrants were considered desirable marriage partners even if they came from

[2] The same attitude prevails in rural Mexico. Foster (1972, 73-75) points out that any interference in the free choice of a mate would be considered gross meddling.

Table 17. Socioeconomic Level of Affines by Branch, Relative to Gómez Spouse's Grandfamily

	Female Affines			
	Higher	Equal	Lower	Total
Prior to 1900	1	2	4	7
Gómez Casés branch	5	11	8	24
Gómez Balbuena branch	9	9	4	22
Gómez Moreno branch	2	7	0	9
Bañuelos Gómez branch	3	6	0	9
Jiménez Gómez branch	1	7	2	10
TOTAL	21	42	18	81
%	26%	52%	22%	100%

	Male Affines			
	Higher	Equal	Lower	Total
Prior to 1900	2	1	0	3
Gómez Casés branch	3	18	15	36
Gómez Balbuena branch	8	12	7	27
Gómez Moreno branch	5	2	1	8
Bañuelos Gómez branch	1	6	2	9
Jiménez Gómez branch	2	3	3	8
TOTAL	21	42	28	91
%	23%	46%	31%	100%

NOTE: Levels were rated by economic, social, and ethnic status.

peasant backgrounds. What counted were their "racial" characteristics and the high status of Spaniards in Latin America.

In the third and fourth generations, the middle-class branches have married among their own class; in the wealthy families, men might select partners of inferior status (although a superior status is considered desirable), while women have not. By the fourth generation a new pattern seems to emerge: most women of the entrepreneurial branches marry *below* their own economic status, mostly "acceptable" young professional men of "decent" middle-class origins.

Matrimony institutionalizes the union between two marriage partners: it also institutes a structural conflict between the spouses and between their respective in-laws. Most conflicts relate to kin solidarity. Each spouse is expected to continue fulfilling his or her obligations toward parents and siblings, in addition to the new set of formal obligations contracted toward the parents and siblings of the spouse. Female affines are merged, as far as possible, into the Gómez kin; yet a woman will not be fully accepted as kin until she has given birth to Gómez children. As she grows older she tends to become totally absorbed into the Gómez family; and if she survives her husband she retains full spiritual and emotional authority over her Gómez grandfamily. In principle, relations between the two affine branches are symmetrical; often, however, the Gómez kin exert a stronger pull than the other family, because of their ability to draw sons-in-law into Gómez enterprises and Gómez daughters into residential units.

Beginning with the wedding, a couple finds itself to be the focal point of competition between the two affinal families. Open or undeclared, this rivalry is nearly always present. It takes place on all levels: social, economic, moral, ritual, residential, and so on. Sometimes the affinal kin live outside Mexico City, or the parents are both deceased or belong to an inferior social stratum; in these cases there is no contest. Otherwise, the ascendancy of one kin group over the other emerges gradually. Loyalties and obligations toward consanguineous kin are recognized by both sides; but the final test of ascendancy is probably to be found in which life style is more closely adopted by the new nuclear family. Both sets of kin usually realize this and attempt to win the new household over to their own patterns, particularly regarding the education and world view of the grandchildren. The stronger families (economically and ideologically) exert a firmer pull over their descendants and emerge stronger after each successful contest. In the long run, this generates family groups that may become dominant in the social system, especially vis-à-vis their affinal relations.

Open conflict is averted through ritualization of affinal relations. For example, in the area that represents the most important source of potential friction, namely the raising of grandchildren, conflict is diluted through the institution of godparenthood, to be discussed in chapter 5. In other areas, such as ritual celebrations, Christmas presents, and the like, the relations between the two sets of parents tend to be formal and ritually correct. There is an avoidance of giving or taking offense, but one keeps one's distance. We know of no instance of mothers-in-law becoming intimate with each other to the point of requesting assistance in household matters or going out shopping together.

On the other hand, there is a definite tendency toward solidarity among siblings-in-law, particularly brothers-in-law. There are frequent instances of partnerships, deals, and personal friendships as expressed in mutual visiting and joint trips abroad. There are many cases of sons-in-law employed by Gómez entrepreneurs: job-giving also extends to the brothers of affinal women. It is not easy to decide to what extent such arrangements can be attributed to personal affection or to the desire of the Gómez kin to consolidate their ascendancy over an affine kinship group.

Alliance Strategies

The strategy of alliances between grandfamilies and branches changes, depending on the social status or on the socioeconomic situation that prevails in the country. At times the strategy has been one of complementarity; or as in the case of the Porfiriato period, marriage may be used as a means of social legitimization, through which a family could become identified with the old criollo life style within a generation. Thus, new money may acquire social prestige by marrying an old name. As we have seen, marriage partners of European origin were often the most acceptable choice in the period when the Gómez were still unknown in Mexican society. Much later, when the aristocratic leanings of the family became a political liability, Pablo, the leader, took a middle-class wife and eventually allied himself with the new mestizo power elite. At this time the Gómez developed a split personality: one brother built the bridge of access to economic power and the other,

Leopoldo, remained aloof and raised the citadel of social prestige. Today, after several stages of segmentation and economic stratification, the family reunions comprise a remarkably wide social spectrum, including foreigners, descendants of the old class of landowners, industrialists, and members of the middle class. Yet all of them present a seamless front as members of a well-established entrepreneurial family with old criollo roots.

The fourth generation produced separate branches of industrialists as a result of segmentation, with the bulk of the family remaining in the middle class. At this point the entrepreneurs began to marry into the bourgeoisie. Their sons tended to marry the daughters of wealthy entrepreneurs belonging to their own social group and economic rank. On the other hand, the daughters married upwardly mobile middle-class professional men. This strategy has as much to do with family and class interests as with access to desirable partners.

As long as the Gómez were a young entrepreneurial family on the rise, they refused to entertain the possibility of any social contacts with the postrevolutionary political leadership. They consistently minimized their own Indian origins. Eventually, however, the grandchildren of the mestizo leaders have become politically dominant and socially acceptable as members of the ruling establishment of administrators and technocrats. Their rejection by the Gómez as possible marriage partners is no longer as firm as it once was. Every change in strategy opens up new social resources, as each new affinal member contributes his or her own share to the pool of connections that enables the Gómez to stay on, or find their way to, the upper levels of the social pyramid of Mexico.

Segmentation and Evolution

Each individual belongs to two grandfamilies, those of his father and of his mother. Eventually he or she forms a nuclear family and later becomes the head of a grandfamily himself or herself. An individual continues to belong to the remnants of his two original grandfamilies after the death of both parents: these remnants include siblings, aunts, uncles, cousins, and nieces and nephews.

139

The children of one set of parents grow up with the experience of solidarity with uncles, aunts, and first cousins who, because of their more remote kinship, do not belong to the children's grandfamily yet require a prescribed amount of loyalty and affection.

How and when are the limits of kin solidarity defined? Clearly, solidarity relations and obligations are created first between children and their parents and siblings; later, they extend to both parents' consanguineous kin, to one's spouse, one's children, and eventually to one's grandchildren. Linear relations have priority over collateral relations: this rule is reflected in the inheritance laws.[3] The next highest order of solidarity in the kinship system is logically found in the four-generation descendance group, namely the group of all linear descendants of a common great-grandfather. We call such a group a "branch." The level of solidarity among members of a branch is lower than among members of a grandfamily, but it is still considerably higher than among members of the Gómez kinship network from different branches.

It is also helpful to use the concept of a "stock," defined as "all the descendants of a man and his wife, counting descent through females as well as males" (Freeman 1961, 199). Thus, all descendants of don Carlos Gómez are members of the Gómez stock, regardless of the interactions that may exist between them. Membership in a stock is a genealogical fact that is analogous to lineage, in that two individuals can be located in terms of relative genealogical position without their mutual knowledge of each other or the existence of exchange between them. In a kinship system based on the grandfamily, individu-

---

[3] The priority of inheritance specified by Mexican law is as follows: first, sons and daughters share equally in the inheritance; second, the share of the surviving spouse equals that of any one of the offspring; third, the right of parents of the deceased is limited to an alimentary pension if there are surviving children; and finally, all collateral kin (uncles, nephews, and so on) inherit on the basis of equal shares. Sons and daughters have priority over the surviving spouse, who is merely an affine: by virtue of the marriage contract, the surviving spouse receives the same share as a child. Widows will thus frequently be dependent on their consanguineous males, particularly their sons and brothers, for support (Rojina Villegas, 1976, 255-60; Salas-Lizaur n.d., 83).

als who are members of the same stock are more likely to meet and have significant social interactions than, for example, in a kinship system based on the two-generation nuclear family. Each individual is considered to belong to four stocks, those of his or her four paternal and maternal grandparents. The four corresponding family names are known to each member, and members of any of the four stocks are recognized as potential relatives: they are the members of the kindred of a given individual.

In theory, a stock may extend in time through an unlimited number of generations. In practice, the stock is bounded because the cognitive map of each member (even of the more kin-conscious members) is limited to those with whom any kind of personal relationship exists or has been transmitted through family lore (Mitchell 1976, 400-401). According to Firth (1964) and Schneider (1968), members of the English and American middle class can remember up to four generations of descendants. Among the Gómez most members of the stock are aware of at least five or six generations of ancestors.

During the third generation there were five cases of endogamy in the Gómez kinship group; this made for a particularly compact stock and more extensive sharing of information among relatives. It should also be remembered that practically all members of the stock live in Mexico City and that there has been a pronounced tendency for residential clustering within the city.

In conclusion, the segmentation and evolution of stocks are based primarily on the principle of linear descent and secondarily on solidarity between descendants of a common ancestor. The more distant the common ancestor, the less intense is the solidarity: from the nuclear family (two generations), to the grandfamily (three generations), to the branch (four generations), to members who acknowledge belonging to a common stock, to the boundaries of the cognitive map of one's kindred.

Spanish kinship terminology, as used in Mexico, reflects the kinship structure. There are special terms for the nine generations of consanguinity, from great-great-grandparent to great-great-grandson or -daughter. Cousins from the same grandparents are called "primos hermanos"; second cousins are called "primos" for short. Members of the Gómez stock refer to Leopoldo's mother as "Mamá Inés," because in Mexico grandmothers and grandfathers were traditionally called "Mamá" and "Papá" as a term of endearment.

A well-known Mexican institution is the so-called *casa chica*, which refers to permanent or long-term extramarital affairs of males, generally with unattached women of lower social status than the males' wives. Among the Gómez we found six cases of such illegitimate unions, three with offspring. Generally there is a great effort to hide such relationships, but when the offspring is known, he or she is not considered a relative by the family. Only in Carmelita's case (III,40) was an illegitimate child recognized as a member of the kindred due to the fact that her Aunt Anita adopted her; still, she has never acquired full kinship membership. In one case, a Gómez woman of the second generation had a son out of wedlock. That son is known to be a Gómez, but is a "second-class" member of the kindred. His mother, however, was erased from the genealogy and is not considered part of the family. No one talks about her and her identity is unknown to the fourth generation. This contrasts with lower-class situations in which half brothers and sisters born of different unions are recognized as siblings if they have knowledge of each other (O. Lewis, 1959, 197-268). The upper classes see both having a "casa chica" and/or illegitimate children as a shameful black spot on the family name and as a drain to their economic resources. Probably for the lower classes it is an expansion of their social networks needed for survival.[4]

Kindred

A stock is composed of all the descendants of a man and his wife; a kindred consists of all one's bilateral consanguineous relations (Murdock 1965, 3-4). Since the kindred is a cognitive category that takes the individuals as a point of reference

[4] See Carol Stock's description of poor American black families in the United States (1974).

(Campbell 1976; Freeman 1961, 19; Keesing 1975; Peranio 1961), it is in practice defined by the individuals.

In order to understand the processes of kinship in nonunilineal societies, meaning the actual behavior as opposed to the formal structure, the theory of social networks is useful. Firth has pointed out that a kindred in a modern complex society is not a true social group, since its membership is based on recognition by the individuals. But the criteria of inclusion and exclusion are not entirely governed by personal whim; rather, the development of exchange relations plays a major role in the constitution of the kindred (Firth 1971, 386; Gulliver 1971). The main forms of exchange among kin are exchange of information and exchange of goods and services.

Reciprocal flow of information between Gómez relatives contributes toward the construction of a cognitive kinship map that is wholly or partly shared by members of the kinship group. The information a member has typically includes: genealogical connection with oneself, name and outstanding physical or personality traits of each kinsman, names of spouse and children, and relevant biographical details. Personal acquaintance is not a prerequisite; much information, for example, involves deceased ancestors.

The membership of one's kindred depends on the information at one's disposal. Gómez siblings' kindred (theoretically expected to be identical) have significantly different compositions because of individual variations in kin recognition and the amount of information received or lost. Some relatives are unaware of entire families of the stock included by others.

One's kindred grows through personal contact with members of the kindred or shrinks through lack of information and loss of contact. The flow of information is largely transmitted in social encounters, both formal and informal. The information is updated in an institutionalized arena—ritual family get-togethers at which attendance becomes tantamount to a mutual acknowledgment of family affiliation. A prolonged absence from family rituals, however involuntary, may mean a weakening of family links and the eventual estrangement of the individual concerned.

CHAPTER 4

In the case of distant relatives, the social acknowledgment of kinship is conditioned by criteria like prestige, class, politics, social behavior, and personal preference. Relatives who have sunk below a "decent" middle-class socioeconomic level or who have committed some misdemeanor or social breach of the norm are ignored or deliberately excluded from the kinship network. They are no longer invited to family reunions, with the result that such individuals disappear from the kinship map of younger family members.

Business and family interests are inextricably interwoven. It may be said that the system of economic exchange is imbedded in a matrix of family recognition. There are countless transactions between relatives of equal or comparable economic status. These transactions include business deals, partnerships, mutual referrals between professionals, free consultations on family business, political and administrative backing, loans, business tips, and similar services. In addition there is an intricate pattern of present-giving and the extension of small favors among relatives that occurs continuously.

The factors that determine the intensity of exchange between members of the kindred are: (a) physical distance: people who have moved abroad or to the provinces tend to get lost from the cognitive map of members of the Mexico City family network; those living in close proximity have an opportunity to share experiences and exchange communications, goods, and services; (b) genealogical distance: the ideal model of kinship relations, as internalized by the members of the culture, implies a set of rights and obligations that depend on the specific degree of kinship; (c) economic distance, which may be of two kinds: differences in the type of economic activity and differences in the amount of capital (the latter implies patron-client relations that in the long run separate the stock into "poor" and "rich" branches, producing a class differentiation that affects the quality and intensity of exchange of information); (d) age difference: generation gaps imply changing view points, interests, and ideologies, and these tend to increase social distance; and (e) ideological distance: shadings of ideological differences within the kinship network increase the social distance among its members. This is produced by the influence of the official political doctrines, particularly through education.

All these factors determine the degree of *confianza* (or personal trust) that expresses and measures the capacity and disposition to exchange information and favors between two particular individuals (Lomnitz 1971, 100; 1977, 209). Physical, socioeconomic, ideological, and generational closeness promote a level of confianza that in turn determines the intensity of exchange between members of the kinship network (Simmel 1964, 213).

The intensity of exchange between kin is not random. It is conditioned by a set of factors, as well as by the implementation of exchange relations themselves. The existence of an exchange relation not only places a relative on one's cognitive map of kindred; it also situates the relative at a greater or lesser social distance in relation to oneself. Exchange may be carried on beyond one's death through the bequeathing of legacies as well as indirectly through the incorporation of deceased members into family lore.

The Grandfamily and Society

The kinship system we have described has the following features: (a) it is bilateral with, ideally, a tendency toward patrilineality; (b) it distinguishes between the "family" as a basic unit of solidarity and the household as a residential economic unit; (c) the "family" is the three-generation grandfamily based on consanguinity: collateral bonds are strong but ultimately subordinated to lineal bonds; (d) the household may contain one nuclear family, but nuclear families belonging to the same grandfamily try to locate themselves in residential proximity to each other.

Many features of a society can be traced to a particular kinship structure. The fact that the grandfamily is the basic unit of solidarity has deep implications for Mexican society. In fact, we claim that the grandfamily is the metaphor for the way Mexican society is organized.

A child is usually born into a large social group. Due to the demographic characteristics of Mexico, the total membership of an individual's two grandfamilies may easily number fifty to seventy people. In addition, there is the immediate kindred beyond the grandfamily, for example, parents' uncles and aunts, second cousins, and so on, bringing the total of significant relatives to a hundred or more.

The size of this human group tends to grow in time, as children are born to members of both grandfamilies and in-laws are acquired. This is the reference group of the individual for life: it determines social status, it provides basic social networks, and it supplies social controls and economic and emotional support.

This situation may be contrasted with the one described, for example, by Macfarlane (1979) for individualistic Western societies such as Britain. The dominant impression that emerges from the comparison is that the three-generation grandfamily produces societies in which an individual enjoys more social support at all times and particularly in critical life situations; but this support also results in limitations on personal freedom. Individuals are born into a social group that controls them through life. They cannot escape this control except, perhaps, by migration. To a considerable extent, social and economic life is determined at birth. And the greater the security (economic and emotional) that a kin group can provide, the heavier are the restrictions imposed on a member's personal freedom.

In an individualistic society the individual lacks such a protective social cocoon; society must provide reasonable substitutes in the form of laws and institutions that control and protect the individual (Macfarlane 1979,193–200). As Ianni and Reuss-Ianni (1973) and Blok (1974) have pointed out, Mediterranean societies have not developed effective institutions of this kind. In Sicily the government institutions are ineffectual in solving people's problems, and only the Mafia (a family-based informal organization) is effective.

Although the family is generally recognized as important in Mexican and Latin American life, the notion of the three-generation grandfamily as the basic unit of solidarity in the society has not been explicitly discussed. The grandfamily may be hidden, however, behind terminologies such as "extended family," "kinship network," "nepotism," and so on. We believe that in most cases described in the literature the existence of the three-generation grandfamily system can be inferred from the ethnographic context.

Carlos and Sellers, in their review of research on the family in Latin America, show that family ties are not breaking down under modernization, because family networks continue to provide essential support to individuals for adapting to the socioeconomic and cultural environment: "two concepts need to be separated and clarified—the nuclear family . . . and . . . the network of kin, both cognatic and affinal, described by various writers as critical to an understanding of Latin American society" (1972, 95).

In a study of the agro-exporting elite in Paraiba, Brazil, Lewin points out that "colloquially, the elite extended family or parentela was simply referred to as 'the family' (a família) . . . as it still is everywhere in Brazil today. . . . Family at one extreme could embrace only the nuclear family . . . of parental couple and offspring, but it most commonly was applied to the enormous extended family . . . whose several generations of lineal and collateral members were distributed over a number of extended households on separate estates and could be counted in the hundreds. The Brazilian extended family was circumscribed by a given individual's bilateral descent group which embraced both maternal and paternal ascendants and collateral consanguineal together with lineal descendants of several generations" (1979b, 276). In practice this means only three generations, due to the limited normal lifespan.

Elite families in modern Brazil closely resemble the Gómez family: "These great groups do not form a residential unit, but the conjugal families that comprise them often live in the same apartment buildings, thus maintaining cohesiveness and facilitating contacts in large cities. Solidarity and the power regime are structured around the oldest and most respected member of the old line, who is shown deference and is consulted when circumstances require. He symbolizes the unity of the entire

147

group. . . . Among the rural aristocracy [we find] . . . still large extended families. . . . These large networks of relatives still maintain constant contact by telephone, by visits, by 'family reunions' . . . neatly distinguishing 'the strangers' from the relatives by many means. A member of one of these families is capable of identifying more than 200—perhaps as many as 500—close and distant relatives, recalling their names and histories. . . . In such families godparents may have the function of reinforcing blood ties. . . . Some family 'reunions'—for a wedding, a baptism, or a graduation—may gather together seventy, eighty or 100 relatives and a similar proportion of friends" (Azevedo 1965, 292-93).[5]

Among the so-called oligarchy of Peru, a "clan" is defined as "a number of households related by descent from a common ancestor and committed to each other through mutual rights and obligations. . . . The founder of the clan is typically a late 19th-century countryside figure who organized an enterprise with which his descendants continue to be identified. The clan may be differentiated internally into several lineages defined by their individual descent lines from the founder" (Gilbert 1977, 63-68).

Among the rural elite of the Peruvian highlands (1885-1950), the extended family operates as a corporative unit in the sense that property stays in the family group. One son inherits, but all members of the family share in the benefits. This system runs counter to the logic of capitalist efficiency (Wilson 1970), but the logic of the kinship system overrules such economic considerations, as it does among the Gómez.

Also similar to the Gómez family is the urban middle-class family of provincial Peru, as described by Escobar, who says that "the extended family consist normally of married sons and daughters living relatively close to each other. The unity of an extended family is based on one or two recognized ancestors, usually a great-grandfather or great-great-grandfather; on recognition of elderly parents as 'heads' or 'trunks' of the

---

[5] Oliven (n.d.), Wagley (1959), and Greenfield (1969) also describe similar upper- and middle-class cases in Brazil.

family: and on the sons' obligation to provide for their parents' sustenance. . . . Relationships within the extended family exist chiefly in terms of assistance to parents and to some adult and younger relatives, of reciprocal assistance among brothers, and, because of the annual round of family rituals. . . . the extended family enforces considerable social control over its individual members (1980, 686-88).

The difficulty in sorting out what the authors mean by "extended families" or "clans" may lie in the linguistic ambiguity that the word *family* has in Spanish as used in Latin America. "Family" can refer to anything from the conjugal pair to any wider group of people. When one says *mi familia*, the real meaning of the word has to be inferred from the context. As Lisón-Tolosana describes in Spain: "It may be equivalent to the nuclear family, composed initially of the spouses, and later of the spouses with offspring. . . . In the second place family is synonymous with kinship. Kinship is the bond which, in respect to an individual, unites each one of the ancestors, descendants, and co-laterals of his family by consanguinity or affinity. Taking 'ego' as a basis in practice kinship embraces these two zones: a) from the grandparents to the grandchildren through its line, i.e., five generations on the one hand, and on the other, collaterally to second cousins and the sons and daughters of uncles and aunts in second degree. b) Kinship by affinity is more restricted. It includes the family of orientation of the husband and wife. The remaining members who constitute kin of the husband or wife of 'ego' in the sense first defined fall into the category of 'the family of my wife' or 'of my husband'. . . . Another meaning of the family . . . refers in a wide sense to a constellation which encloses three nuclear families together with the spouses of all the married members: the families of orientation and procreation of 'ego' and the family of orientation of his or her spouse. . . . It refers to the family of orientation and procreation of 'ego,' but as 'ego' is married, his or her spouse includes another social cell, i.e., her or his family of orientation, in the nuclear family sphere" (1970, 164-65).

In Mexico, Hunt (1969, 41) defined three different meanings of the term *familia*: "la mera familia" or nuclear family, "la familia cercana" or near kin, and the far remote kin or "parientes lejanos." She is less specific than Lisón-Tolosana about the precise meaning of the intermediate-sized group, which she does not define.

The Grandfamily and Class Structure

In the preceding section we have suggested that the ideal kinship structure based on the three-generation grandfamily may be common to Latin America and that this structure may explain certain features of society. The active expression of this cultural ideal, however, will depend on the class position of the families. This will determine the actual forms of solidarity and residential arrangements.

In a Mexico City shantytown a residential pattern is found (Lomnitz 1977) in which each household either contained a three-generation extended family, or two or more adjoining households were occupied by members of a three-generation extended family. Only 15 percent of the households in the shantytown fit the model of the nuclear-family household: most of these cases were found to be irregular (young couples without relatives in the city, elderly childless couples, or incomplete families with numerous children).

In spite of the disruption caused by migration, there was a tendency to reconstruct extended family groups with any available kin: parents, fraternal extended families, and cousins' extended families, for example. Each migrant moved in with relatives and tried to get the members of his grandfamily to join him as soon as feasible. The enactment of solidarity required close physical proximity under shantytown conditions.

Whenever a settler was asked a question about his relatives he tended to name first the members of his nuclear family of orientation and procreation—his grandfamily. Next he mentioned any relatives who lived close by. If his parents lived with other relatives elsewhere in Mexico City, the relatives might be counted as part of his close-kin group. After both parents died, the relationship with these relatives tended to fade if they were distant cousins or uncles and aunts. Surviving ties with relatives in the rural area of origin also depended on the degree of kinship. If they were members of the grandfamily of the migrant, a significant relationship was maintained. The significant unit of solidarity invariably included the parents and siblings of the individual beyond marriage and beyond migration.

Social interaction in shantytowns took place within and through a network of reciprocal assistance. This network was the unit of survival; it was recruited from among kin or neighbors. Shadings and gradations of solidarity were expressed by the intensity, frequency, and generalization of the exchange within networks: the three-generation grandfamily was the pole of strongest solidarity. Households living together and sharing expenses and domestic functions were also households in which a parental figure (a mother, usually) headed a three-generation family. In the absence of the centralizing elder parent the extended family might often form a jointed household, where exchange was still intense but where each nuclear family had its own separate household economy. The pole of lowest solidarity was found among mixed networks that included non-kin neighbors. Solidarity is a function of social distance, residential distance, economic distance, and "confianza." On all four counts, the grandfamily household ranked highest in solidarity (Lomnitz 1977, 133-35).

Solidarity was expressed through economic assistance during and after migration, involving housing of recent migrants, loans of money, clothing, food, tools, and services such as connecting newcomers with a potential employer, training them in an urban skill, looking after the children of working mothers, and so on; and moral support, including care for the sick, care of the aged, and participation in rituals. All available members of a grandfamily were expected to be present at rites of passage involving any member. To a lesser extent, cooperation was also expected of other relatives, depending on their degree of consanguinity.

Other case studies among the urban poor of Mexico also suggest that family solidarity goes beyond the nuclear family. For example, Kemper (1976, 84) found that nuclear families related through kinship tended to share important and domestic functions. He talks about "extended family enclaves." Oscar Lewis described three different slums in Mexico City. In the first slum: "nine of twelve households are related through kinship, representing three extended families . . . but in only one case they live together as a true extended family consisting in a married couple with their married daughter and their grandchildren" (1959, 27). In the second slum . . . "more than one third of the residential units had people with kin in the same slum" (1959, 25). Similar results about marginal populations in Mexico City were reported by Alonso and others (1980).

Butterworth (1962) found that migrants from Tilaltongo settled in Mexico City as extended-family groups, rather than as nuclear families. He stressed the fact that close relatives assisted each other in finding lodging, work, and emotional support. Members of an "extended family" tended to live in close residential proximity and often had identical occupations. Arizpe (1978, 60) reported similar findings about Mazahua migrants to Mexico City.

If we compare this pattern of kin interaction with the pattern described for the Gómez family, we find that the differences can be accounted for by class-related circumstances. The cultural ideal of the kinship system is the same. In the shantytown, the realization of this cultural ideal is contingent upon physical proximity, migratory history, and availability of resources. In response to the extreme hardships of shantytown life, the social resources of the three-generation grandfamily are mobilized for survival.

Among the Gómez, its is sufficient for members of the grandfamily to live in the same neighborhood or on the same street. The contact between grandfamily members is as intense as it would be in the shantytown, thanks to the telephone and the automobile. Solidarity is expressed in the ritual life of the family and in its economic interaction. Each social class develops its own responses to the practical problems posed by the ideal of the grandfamily. For example, García Acosta (1979) and Suárez (1979) discuss the phenomenon of three-generational solidarity among Spanish migrants to Mexico. A business or store exists for the sake of one's children and grandchildren: in return, sons and daughters are expected to remain under parental authority as long as their parents live. It is immaterial whether a son or daughter is married or not; his or her filial duties remain unchanged.

The features characterizing the grandfamily found in urban Mexico are also found among mestizo peasants and Indian communities. Foster (1972) notes that in Tzintzuntzán, the solidarity between parents and their children persists until the parents die and is not altered by marriage. Oscar Lewis (1976) initially thought that the nuclear family was the basis of social and economic life in Tepoztlán, but he later contradicted his early interpretations. For example, he says that the closest kinship tie is with a grandmother but also with uncles and aunts, and with first cousins who may treat each other as siblings (1976, 145).

In 1978, Lomnitz-Adler (1982) restudied the village of Tepoztlán and found "barrio families" that dominated a given barrio or quarter. Sons as well as daughters of these families usually succeeded in persuading their spouses to live in close residential proximity to their family home, as occurs among the wealthy branches of the Gómez family. Such residential trends are best explained as expressions of the grandfamily as a unit of solidarity. This agrees with Olivera's findings (1976) in Cholula.

In Hueyapan, Friedlander (1974) described a three-generation household in some detail. She provided a portrait of a strong grandmother and her role in maintaining the economic, social, and ritual aspects of solidarity within the family. De la Peña (1979, 181-89) described a peasant community in Jalisco. He found that each unit of production tended to correspond to an extended family, though not necessarily to a single household.

The grandfamily as a unit of solidarity exists also among several indigenous cultures of Mexico. Taggart (1975) studied a Náhuatl community of Puebla and noted that networks between close households exist everywhere in Mexico and Central America: they were variously termed "joint homes," "joint families," and "multiple-family homes" by different authors. Similar results were obtained by Pérez-Lizaur (1970) in a study of a Náhuatl-speaking group near Texcoco.

Among the Tzoltzil, "the kinship and residence group which exceeds the nuclear family has important corporative functions in Zinacatán, Uruapan" (Vogt 1964). The group constituted by all brothers (sons of a given couple) represents the basic ritual unit and unit of solidarity (Cancian 1976, 136). In cases of conflict the community cites not the plaintiff and the accused party but their respective parents (Guiteras Holmes 1965, 85). The three-generation family remains the responsible legal unit for life. Even after the parents have died, the surviving sons must agree once a year whether they will invite their souls jointly or separately on the Day of the Death (ibid., 132).

Among the Mayas of Yucatan, "three-generation extended families are common." However, "there were no cases of married brothers sharing a household after both parents had died" (Littlefield 1976, 157). This does not necessarily mean that the feeling of solidarity between two brothers will decrease; only that the composition of the unit of solidarity necessarily changes after both parents die.

Romney and Romney explain the methodological problems they faced when trying to define the type of family prevailing among the Mixtecs of Juxtlahuaca: "the question arises as to whether to count adjacent families who are related and interact frequently as nuclear or extended. If we count them as nuclear families, we find that one third of the barrio would be classed as nuclear families. On the other hand, if we count on the basis of interaction, relationships and adjacency . . . only 3 of the 22 intensively studied families would be counted as nuclear families" (1966, 43).

The prevalence of the three-generation grandfamily is clearly summarized by Nutini in his study of Nahua-speaking communities of San Bernardino, Contla: "the extended family is the most important single social unit in the total social structure; in it the individual finds the greatest degree of economic, social, and religious cooperation" (1968, 227). He finds that "independent nuclear family households are never economically, socially, or religiously self-sufficient" (ibid., 241). He emphasizes the distinction between household and kinship units. A given kinship unit may share the same household or may live in separate households, without noticeable differences in the relations of solidarity between kin: "there appeared to be two different structural units with the same functions: the residential extended family, and the nonresidential extended family" (ibid., 242).

Finally, historians who studied the eighteenth and nineteenth centuries in Mexico (Brading 1978; Chance 1978; Harris 1975; Kicza 1983; Ladd 1976) tell us about the predominance of the lineal extended family among merchants, miners, landed gentry, and urban entrepreneurial families. Harris, Ladd, and Brading described three-generation notable families in northern Mexico during the nineteenth century, showing how through family solidarity, alliances, and networks they rose to regional and national power. They also describe such cases for Guatemala and Buenos Aires and present a review of the historical literature on this point.

We conclude that the kinship system is based on the three-generation grandfamily as a unit of economic, social, and ritual solidarity; that the outward expressions of this cultural ideal depend on the circumstances and needs determined by social class and historical context; and that the grandfamily is a widespread cultural ideal that probably occurs throughout Latin America and possibly in Spain and in other Mediterranean societies.

It is true that the cultural ideal of the grandfamily and large extended families is better expressed among the affluent classes, where there are the resources required to maintain rituals, economic solidarity, favorable residential arrangements, power to support the patriarchal ideals, and geographical stability. It might be objected that the Gómez are dominated by their upper-class branches and that middle-class members have adopted an upper-class ideology and upper-class values. But the values pertaining to the three-generation grandfamily existed 150 years ago, when the Gómez were impoverished farmers in a provincial backwater. Through all socioeconomic changes of the Gómez and in spite of segmentation into wealthy and poor branches, the ideal of the grandfamily has been resilient. We submit that this persistence is due to the fact that the three-generational kinship structure is a basic feature of the culture that permeates all areas of social interaction and affects all major aspects of human life.

CHAPTER 5

Rituals as a Way of Life

To be a Gómez means, among other things, participating in a complex interlinking system of symbolic actions that amounts to a way of life. Not a single week goes by for a Gómez but that the family lays claim to his or her presence at some kind of gathering: a dinner party, a wedding, a call on an aunt on her birthday or saint's day, a christening, a Sunday on the ranch, or a visit to a niece and her new baby. These ritual occasions are prescribed by family custom. They convey messages at many interlocking levels: solidarity status, pride, allegiance, reaffirmation of self, belonging, and obedience to the call of the blood.

Within the prescribed forms, these rituals allow for endless personal variations. Going to the hospital to pay a visit to a sick relative is an obligation: going more than once is a mark of personal esteem and affection. Congratulating a relative on a birthday or promotion is a ritual act that may be performed in several different and nonequivalent ways: by telephone, at the office, or through a personal house call and a present. Each of these forms carries messages that correlate with status, personal closeness, competition, or conflict. A big Gómez party is more than an occasion for merriment: it is an arena of ostentation and power, aspirations to leadership, loyalty and spite, solidarity and discrimination.

Participation in such rituals provides a great deal of inside information. This is circulated and updated at every formal or informal gathering among family members; it refers to individuals, nuclear families, grandfamilies, cliques, branches, and to the Gómez kin as a whole. However, the three-generation grandfamily remains the basic social unit, as far as participation in ritual is concerned.

The Gómez family is more than a kinship network that has created its own system of rituals. It is a political group that belongs to the socioeconomic sector known in Mexico as "iniciativa privada" (private initiative) as opposed to "el sector publico" (the area of socioeconomic activity dominated by the state). It becomes necessary for any member of the group to share not only the norms and ideological constructs but also the life style and rituals that have become incorporated into its world view (Cohen 1974, 23). Patterns of symbolic behavior become institutionalized; they express the essence of the group, its meaning. Durkheim's idea that "enduring symbols were needed to give continuity to memories of social experience" (1965, 131) applies clearly to the case of the Gómez family, in which it can easily be argued that family ritual is needed to embody family sentiment across the generations; after all, the difference between a kinship relation and one of friendship may be found precisely in the endurance through time of such ritual symbols.

Rituals are also arenas of communication through which the world view or ideology of a group is transmitted. Leach perceived ritual as a symbolic statement about the social order. "The participants in a ritual are sharing communicative experiences through many different sensory channels simultaneously. . . . Verbal, musical, choreographic and ritual aesthetic dimensions are likely to form components of the total message. When we participate in such a ritual, we pick up all messages at the same time and condense them into a single experience" (1976, 41).

The upbringing of a Gómez includes weekly family dinners, traditional dishes served on special occasions, and a sequence of experiences and events connected with rituals such as weddings, christenings, funerals, and other rites of passage. The Gómez share a meaningful symbolic structure that amounts to a common language that reinforces their Mexican identity and sets them apart from the rest of society much as a totemic religion does a primitive clan. Consecration of family rites through the Catholic liturgy represents a further important element of the total ritual experience.

The Gómez rituals contain a strong element of polarization between those who are included and those who are excluded.

Religious rituals serve to distinguish between the sacred and the profane: similarly, Gómez family rituals set aside members from nonmembers—not only of the kinship network as a whole but also of different branches within the family. Distinctions of status and situations of competition or conflict are enacted at regular intervals. Status is reflected in ritual gestures: the seat of honor at the dinner table or the number of godsons consecrates the position of the entrepreneur in the family hierarchy. When individuals lose their economic or social status, they withdraw from regular gatherings outside the immediate grandfamily.

The primary ritual occasions celebrated by the Gómez include rites of passage, often religious ceremonies celebrated with a specific flavor by each family, and secular rituals, institutionalized customs that are not related to religious occasions or rites of passage but that feature a repetitive formal behavior specific to the family tradition.

Rites of Passage

Like 94 percent of all Mexicans, the Gómez are Catholics. Religious observance among the Gómez has taken specific ideological forms that are consistent with class position and family values. A number of rituals that coincide with the rites of passage[1] are prescribed by the Catholic religion, but the extent to which the Gómez ritual conforms to the prescribed canon or deviates from it is not of concern here. Rather, the Gómez case expresses the degree to which religion and family values are entwined and how the family ideology seeks mutual reinforcement and fuller realization through ritual.

[1] In 1908 Van Gennep defined rite of passage as follows: "A man's life comes to be made up of a succession of stages with similar ends and beginnings: birth, social puberty, marriage, fatherhood, advancements to a higher class, occupational specialization and death. For every one of these events there are ceremonies whose essential purpose is to enable the individual to pass from one defined position to another which is equally well defined. . . . In this respect, man's life resembles nature, from which neither the individual nor the society stands independent. The universe itself is governed by a periodicity which has repercussions on human life, with stages and transitions, moves forward, and periods of relative inactivity" (1977, 3).

CHILDBIRTH. Preparations for childbirth in the Gómez family include, in addition to readying all the things a new baby may require, making a list of names and telephone numbers of friends of the mother and wives of friends of her husband who will receive a birth announcement. Female relatives are included as a matter of course; similar lists are compiled by the expectant mother's mother and mother-in-law. The husband's secretary compiles a similar list of important business relations. The length and composition of these lists varies a great deal, depending on the importance of the child's parents or grandparents; if the family is of relatively low social standing, the list may contain only some of the closer relatives and the patron or patrons of the husband. This custom is observed among many members of the Mexican upper and middle classes; the Gómez kin use it as an indicator of status. They keep track of the number of visitors to the hospital and of the flowers and other presents that are delivered and that are more or less on display in the hospital room. Such gifts carry an obligation of reciprocity and are carefully noted by the new mother and the grandmothers. The recipient of a birth announcement feels obligated to include the sender in her own list for the next baby she may have. Relatives only visit the new mother if they have been officially notified; otherwise they abstain and, if they have been purposely snubbed, they take offense. Members of the rich branches normally notify all the wealthy relatives and some selected members of the middle-class branches. Thus, members of the Jiménez Gómez branch customarily mail birth announcements to members of their own branch and the Gómez Casés branch, some of the Bañuelos (because of endogamy), and a few of the Gómez Balbuena branch; the latter usually includes María del Carmen (IV,87), the owner of the gift shop that caters to all Gómez, rich or poor. Carmelita Gómez (III,40), the illegitimate daughter of Roberto who is employed as Pedro Jiménez's telephone operator, is also included because she will transmit the news of the birth to the more remote branches of the family. Such indirect notifications do not amount to an invitation and relatives will not normally visit the new mother unless they have been explicitly and directly invited. The number of relatives informed on the occasion of a birth is smaller than the number of relatives invited to a wedding; childbirth is an occasion reserved for a narrower circle of relatives.

A more elaborate ceremony is customary on the occasion of the birth of the first son or grandson; as in the Spanish tradition of *mayorazgo*, the first born rates a major celebration and the number of people informed is usually much larger. Any birth is an occasion of utmost importance to the grandfamily: parents and siblings of the parents participate with their children. If possible, they will be present at the hospital during labor and delivery. Those who are unable to be present are in continual telephone contact with the hospital. Even young children are excited about the event.

The Gómez have their babies in private clinics, but the wealthiest family members rent elegant hospital suites with adequate rooms for receiving visitors and for displaying gifts and flowers. Fine bedspreads and bed coverlets are used to conceal or replace the hospital linen. One Gómez woman married to a middle-class man had a set of sheets made especially for her stay at the clinic: most of these sheets were made of ordinary material but the visible outer parts were of expensive monogrammed linen. This detail was promptly noticed and ridiculed among visiting relatives.

CHRISTENINGS. Among the Gómez family it is customary to christen a baby in the clinic, three or four days after birth. In every clinic there is a chapel where christenings take place. The position in the religious hierarchy of the priest at a ceremony is a status symbol. Among the wealthy, an archbishop, bishop, or the superior of a religious order will perform the baptism.

Christenings are held in the morning; it is customary to serve champagne and canapés afterward. The expense is borne by the parents of the child, though sometimes a rich godfather or grandfather may insist on paying the bill. The number of invitations to a christening is more restricted than the list of people informed of the birth. It always includes the grandfamilies of both husband and wife, the rich uncles and aunts, and selected cousins and friends, with their spouses. Among the middle class there are usually no more than sixty guests; among the more wealthy or prominent members of the family they may be more numerous. Young couples invited to a christening also usually take their small children along.

The name selected for a newborn child is of great importance. Formerly firstborn sons and daughters were named after their parents, but this is no longer customary. The parents ultimately decide on a child's name, but all members of the grandfamily have their say. The discussion may begin months before birth. Some names are avoided for class reasons (e.g., Petra is a "cook's name"); others are preferred by certain branches of the family or by the family as a whole (e.g., Inés, Cecilia, Alvaro, Carlos, Enrique). Among the Gómez, Castilian-sounding names are preferred, and names of Anglo-Saxon or Náhuatl origin are taboo. The peasant custom of christening a child by the calendar saint corresponding to its birthday is also shunned.

There is magic in a name. Pedro's older brothers, who died in infancy, were both named Blas after their father. When Pedro was born, it was decided that his second name be Joaquín, thus placing him under the protection of St. Joachim, so that he might live. All Jiménez sons now use the second name of Joaquín.

Every branch of the Gómez family usually owns a *ropón*, the white shift that an infant wears during christening. It is of some significance whether the ropón belongs to the grandfamily of the husband or of the wife: this decision may be the outcome of a test of strength or tradition between the two grandfamilies. An ancient ropón carries prestige and is normally preferred. The garment is handed down from mother to daughter; in each family one daughter keeps the ropón and lends it to her sisters or cousins as needed. Some families do not own a ropón; in this case it is customary to make a new one from the material of mother's or grandmother's wedding gown. Among the poorer Gómez branches the ropón is a gift of the godfather and godmother, as is usual among the Mexican middle and lower classes.

Table 18. Baptismal Godparents' Relation to Godchild: Jiménez Gómez Branch

Chosen as Godparent	Number	Percent
Sibling	3	3%
Mother's sibling	24	25
Father's sibling	14	15
Mother's parents	20	21
Father's parents	18	19
Other relative	3	3
Friends	4	4
Unknown	10	10
TOTAL	96	100%

Godparents are normally members of the grandfamily of the infant: grandparents, uncles and aunts, or brothers and sisters, by order of age and precedence. Godparents are not selected to broaden the kinship group, as is the case among the Mexican peasantry (Forbes 1971; Nutini and Bell 1980; Nutini n.d. and 1984). Compadrazgo (fictive kinship) and less often kindred relations are rather used to strengthen the grandfamily solidarity. Normally the godfather and godmother belong to different grandfamilies. The godfather is a member of the child's father's grandfamily and the godmother of the child's mother's, or vice versa. A tally of godparents in the Jiménez Gómez branch shows the working of the system (see table 18).

The normal procedure is to have a mixed pair of grandparents as godparents for a first christening. The other pair of grandparents will follow for the second child, and so on. This enhances the acceptance of the bilaterality of the system. If no grandparents are alive, one calls upon uncles, aunts, brothers, or sisters of the baby. No godfather or godmother is asked twice in the same nuclear family, as might be the case among the lower class of Mexico (Lomnitz 1977, 159-74). Rich relatives are frequently called upon to be godfathers or godmothers, particularly by the less wealthy family members. We did not find any case of a poor relative being asked to be a godparent to the rich.

Godfatherhood or godmotherhood is a special honor that is sometimes conferred upon elderly entrepreneurs or centralizing women even though their kinship ties may be remote. The godfather-godson relationship is acknowledged as one of personal closeness, which may be reinforced by other rituals: for example, a godfather may be asked to be best man at his godson's wedding. The participation of godfather and godmother in the christening involves carrying the infant, ordering a special commemorative card that is printed for distribution among the guests, paying for the "bolos" (bags of coins that are thrown for children to catch), and giving a present to the child. Sometimes the godfather pays for the ceremony and for the party that follows. Otherwise no special importance is attached to godparenthood; few of our informants recalled the names of their siblings' godfathers, and occasionally they could not recall their own. In many instances only the more prestigious godfathers or godsons were recalled with ease. The term "compadre" is not used as a form of address when the compadres are members of the same kinship group, but it is used in the rare occasions when the compadre is not a member of the family group.

Compadrazgo is an institution known for its flexibility, in which different types of social relations are enlarged or strengthened and conflicts are avoided. Among the Gómez it is used as a means of strengthening existing family ties, for expressing or consecrating relations between different branches of the kinship network, both among equals or between the rich and the poor. There is only one known case in which a politician—not a member of the family—was invited to become a baptism godfather; the family accepts it reluctantly and only because it was done by Pablo.

FIRST COMMUNION. First communion is the ritual that marks the occasion on which a child first receives the Host. It implies the religious initiation of the child into the community of responsible adult Christians and requires a prior indoctrination of the child, called catechization. Until the 1960s the catechization of all Gómez children was the duty of Amalia Miranda

Gómez (III,30), spinster daughter of doña María Guadalupe Gómez de Miranda (II,11). The old lady earned her living in this fashion. Once a week, the families of wealthy would send for Miss Amalia in a chauffeured car. When she arrived from her home downtown, a group of children aged four to seven was waiting for her. The class took one hour and was imparted jointly to children of different ages; it consisted of committing catechism to memory. Amalia also used to bring picture books along that contained illustrations of Bible stories and the Holy Mysteries. After class she distributed sweets to the children; she was then paid and driven back home. All boys and girls of the third, fourth, and fifth generations—at least 100 to 150 members of the Gómez family—underwent preparation for their first communion under her supervision. This not only reinforced kinship relations but represented a powerful mechanism of ideological socialization. When Amalia died, the question of her replacement became a major issue. Young children are now being instructed in catechism by their own mothers.

Children take first communion at an early age, usually after they are five and before they are ten. Prior to the ceremony they are sent to stay with nuns in Mexico City for a "retiro," a one-day period of withdrawal during which they make confession and meditate on their "sins." The ritual is usually held the following day. During the religious persecution in 1926-1928, first communions were normally held in private homes, especially at Mamá Inés' or Saúl's. Leopoldo's sons, Pablo and Leopoldo Jr., had their own chapels in their homes, and other members of the Gómez family used a small church hidden away in the Santa María neighborhood where most of them lived in the early years. This chapel was built during the persecution with the financial assistance of the Gómez family; for years it was regarded as *the* Gómez church and a large number of Gómez family rituals were held there.

The ceremony itself consists of a morning mass officiated by the highest-ranking priest available. Girls wear a white dress of lace and embroidery and are veiled; they carry a rosary and a missal. The entire outfit must be new and as expensive and fashionable as possible: the parents' prestige is at stake. Boys wear a white formal suit or a sailor suit, depending on the fashion of the day.

Invitations to a first communion are meant to include both the early mass and the breakfast that is served immediately afterward. The child is led to the ceremony by his or her communion godparents. They are not the same as the christening godparents; they may be selected from among close relatives, friends, or business associates. A communion godfather has no obligation except to give a present to the child and to assist the child in receiving communion for the first time. After mass, breakfast is served at the parents' home or in a rented hall. The guests of honor are the child's grandparents, granduncles and grandaunts, brothers and sisters, and other important relatives, particularly those who have a patronage relationship with the family. Among some of the Gómez it has become customary to invite the eldest sons or daughters only, as representatives of each nuclear family in the kinship network. The total number of guests is normally larger at a first communion than at a christening, because friends of the parents and of the child (or children) are also invited. The wealthy usually invite client relatives to a first communion.

The breakfast is of the traditional Mexican variety and may include a fruit cocktail, hot tamales, sweet brioches (*pan de dulce*), and hot chocolate. There are no formal seating arrangements. Presents are customary, and may be either toys or religious objects such as medals, crucifixes, and religious books.

THE FIFTEENTH-BIRTHDAY CELEBRATION. A girl's fifteenth birthday is celebrated throughout Mexico as a social coming-out party. Although girls now go to dances before they are fifteen, this was not done among the Gómez until about 1960. Because they have been widely adopted among the lower classes of Mexico, however, fifteenth-birthday parties are considered affected and vulgar by most branches of the Gómez; among the richer branches they no longer occur. Instead, a girl's fifteenth birthday is marked by special presents, family parties, and sometimes a trip abroad.

Formerly, however, a girl would participate at a special Te Deum on her fifteenth birthday and would later give a ball, where she would wear her first evening gown. It was an important occasion and eligible young bachelors from among relatives and friends were selected as *chambelanes* or squires by the girl's parents. She danced the opening waltz with her father, and not until after that was she allowed to entertain social invitations from young men. The ceremony connected with this ritual was elaborate and included a guard of honor of specially selected and splendidly dressed young women as well as a set of godparents.

We have not personally observed this celebration among the Gómez though the older women still talk about parties of the past. Males never had an equivalent ceremony marking the transition between childhood and adolescence; the boys were considered to be on their own as soon as they earned money or were given an allowance by their parents. After this they might freely invite and otherwise court eligible young women of their acquaintance.

THE ENGAGEMENT. The engagement is a formal occasion involving the groom and the parents of the bride, which occurs when the groom's economic situation is such that he can support a family. The bride's dowry or her eventual income cannot be counted as a part of the wedding plans, no matter how wealthy the bride's family may be relative to that of the bridegroom.

Once the prospective husband's income is judged adequate, he has a preliminary conversation with the bride's parents in order to discuss the marriage prospects. If the parents raise no objection they will set a day for the *petición de mano*, or formal marriage request. At this point the outcome of such a formal request is assured; otherwise the parents would discourage the match and no engagement would take place.

The bride's mother then calls the bridegroom's mother and invites the groom's grandfamily to her home for the day of the petition. This event takes the form of a dinner party; brothers and sisters as well as any living grandparents of both bride and groom are normally invited as well. The formality of the petition varies greatly among the Gómez, depending on how traditional each family happens to be and what the previous relationship between the families has been.

After the groom has formally asked for the bride's hand, the couple is free to select the date of the wedding, though consultation with both sets of parents is customary. Chaperoning of engaged young people has now practically disappeared, but no premarital sex is allowed. The time interval between the engagement and the wedding varies and involves complicated negotiations between the couple and their parents. The outcome depends on the relative strength of their respective grandfamilies. The issues at stake involve the style and details of the wedding ritual and where the new couple will live (i.e., how near their grandfamilies they will locate).

Normally the bridegroom is expected to pay for all expenses connected with the wedding itself (invitations, dress, church costs, and so on). The bride's family pays for the reception, if one is planned. A very important set of decisions concerns the wedding ceremony: the choice of a church, the type of reception or party to be held after the ceremony, and the important matter of the guest list and the printing and distribution of invitations. In addition, the bridal trousseau must be selected and all details of the ceremony and reception attended to. An important social activity during the weeks and months preceding a wedding is attendance at a considerable number of bridal showers and stag parties given in honor of the bride and groom by their male and female friends.

The marriage of the daughter of one of the wealthier Gómez entrepreneurs to a middle-class professional man during the late 1960s may serve to illustrate what can be involved. The bride, a college-educated woman, had expressed a preference for a simple and informal wedding. Eventually, at the insistence of both sets of parents, a traditional wedding was agreed upon, this being "the last chance to please one's parents before becoming independent." The bride's mother suggested that the wedding be held in a private chapel belonging to an extremely wealthy individual associated with her husband in business. An open-air cocktail party would then be held on the grounds of the park surrounding the chapel. Once the couple had agreed, the proposal was forwarded to the groom's parents for acceptance. The chapel was secured and two guest lists were prepared, one for the bride and one for the groom. The bride's list was compiled by her parents, based on their set of relatives and family friends. All wedding invitations received during the previous three years, which had been carefully filed away by the bride's mother, were taken into account. The bridegroom's list of guests was similarly drawn up by his parents. The length of the groom's list is often the cause of some argument with the parents of the bride, since they bear the cost of the wedding reception. In this case, however, no limits were set and no objections were raised.

The cost of the engraved invitations is an expense customarily borne by the future husband. The bride's father insisted upon a very expensive kind of invitation, in keeping with his social prestige, and some argument with his daughter ensued. It was finally decided that the invitations should be highly presentable but not unduly expensive. A total of 1,100 invitations were distributed, more than 700 for the list of the bride's family. Only about 100 invitations went to personal friends of the bride and groom. Practically all those invited lived in Mexico City; the invitations were all hand-carried by personal messengers, as is still the custom in the city despite the enormous growth of the metropolitan area. The father of the bride made his business cars and drivers available for this purpose.

The young couple, in close consultation with the mother of the bride, began to plan the details of the ceremony. Special wedding decorations for the chapel were catered by a Gómez cousin. Though the groom pays, the bride's family makes the arrangements; Mexican custom is very strict about excluding the groom's family from all such matters unless requested by the bride. In the period preceding the wedding there were twenty-three farewell parties: ten bridal showers organized for the bride by her female relatives and friends, two stag parties organized for the groom by his own relatives and male friends, and eleven mixed parties in honor of the couple and their parents, brothers, and sisters. It is significant that sixteen such parties were organized by relatives of the bride; three were organized by relatives of the groom; and four were organized by friends of the bride and groom.

The system of preliminary parties is important because it affords an opportunity for the families of the bride and groom to get to know each other and to get a feeling for their respective status and social resources. It is customary for each guest at these showers to bring a present for the engaged couple, in addition to the wedding present that will eventually be due. Gifts for showers usually include kitchenware and crockery, luggage, linens, canned goods, wines, and more recently American currency.

All wedding gifts are delivered to the bride's or groom's home before the ceremony. Keeping track of wedding presents is extremely important. The father of the bride made a daily tally of gifts received, listing the name of the sender and the estimated value of each gift. If unfamiliar with the cost of a gift, he would make an inquiry. It is essential to evaluate whether guests are responding adequately to earlier favors and what the next reciprocal step ought to be. The financial worth of the sender is taken into account in such an evaluation; gifts from poorer branches are particularly appreciated as a public recognition of clientelism. In this marriage, the entrepreneurial branches of the family sent costly gifts such as silverware, television sets, and record players, as they usually did on such occasions. Gifts from the nonrelatives were also carefully evaluated, but relatives were expected to be more generous than acquaintances of comparable economic position. Expensive gifts from outsiders were expected when the giver owed the family some special favor: a wedding present from one nonrelative was held to be skimpy because the giver owed his high-level job to the father of the bride and was, furthermore, related through marriage to the groom's family. It was an expensive gift but, according to the bride's parents, not expensive enough. Presents sent by people on the groom's list were similarly evaluated by the groom's parents. In addition to the gifts received during the showers, more than six hundred wedding presents were received.

THE WEDDING. In Mexico there are two wedding ceremonies: the civil or legal wedding, consisting of an official contract signed before a local public official, and the church wedding, which is more widely recognized from a social point of view. The marriage contract is signed first; this ceremony is normally held at the home of the bride in the presence of a small group of relatives and friends. The presence of second cousins and more distant relatives is no longer required, unless there is a special personal relationship.

A special role in this ceremony is reserved for those guests who have been asked to witness the marriage contract on behalf of the bride and groom. Witnessing a marriage certificate is regarded as an honor that strengthens the witness's bonds with the new couple and their parents. The law requires a minimum of two witnesses for the bride and two for the groom, but there are usually at least five on each side. The order in which the witnesses are called denotes their rank and their closeness to the family. They are usually selected by the parents, although the bride and groom may designate a special friend. Among the Gómez it is customary for all witnesses to be males. Witnessing a marriage contract is a secular act and may be used to confer special honors on politicians, business acquaintances, and other associates outside the family.

At the wedding of an entrepreneur's daughter in the early 1960s, the president of Mexico, the secretary of the Treasury, Uncle Leopoldo Jr., three wealthy Spanish industrialists, an important banker who was a business associate, the entrepreneur's sister's husband and his wife's two brothers, and other nephews and cousins of the wealthy Gómez families were selected as witnesses. The bride was not consulted. The rank of the political witnesses was important to the entrepreneur as a show of status; the presence of these powerful personages helped consolidate his prestige in front of the other businessmen and wealthy relatives who had been invited. As wedding gifts, the president sent a set of enormous silver candelabra and the secretary of the Treasury sent eighteen sterling silver place settings.

It is interesting to note that politicians have been gradually excluded in the 1970s because of the strain that has developed between the business community and the public administration since the Echeverría presidency. In certain instances (not necessarily connected with the Gómez family) President Echeverría and members of his administration have been known to turn down invitations from important business entrepreneurs, and these refusals have been judged discourteous.

The main patriarchs of the family are normally asked to witness most weddings of the Gómez kinship network: they are apt to take offense if they are not invited. Important business associates are also normally included. Witnesses from the less wealthy branches of the Gómez family are only selected in the event of a special relationship or for some other reason. Close relatives from within the branch would of course also be invited to witness the marriage contract, as would some select family friends. The judge performing the ceremony is paid by the bridegroom. There is some status involved in the selection of a judge; some are more fashionable than others. After the signing of the contract the judge recites a hortatory text known as the "Epistle of Melchor Ocampo," a secular sermon written in 1855 that reflects traditional Mexican ideas concerning the ideal marriage. Once the formal ceremony is concluded, a cocktail party begins: among the wealthy, this normally includes French champagne and caviar. It is sometimes followed by dinner, depending on the day and time of the ceremony. If held on the same day as the church wedding, only cocktails are served. The expenses are borne by the family of the bride. The customary dress also varies according to the timing of the ceremony: when held before the day of the church wedding, the bride wears a formal dress but not a bridal gown. The other ladies dress according to the time of day, but always with elegance and wearing their finest jewelry.

A church wedding is a much more momentous affair and a much more expensive one on all accounts. The expenses of the religious ceremony, borne by the bridegroom, can be considerable. Some churches are more fashionable than others, and their selection depends on the taste and status consciousness of the couple and their parents. Some are colonial, others are modern; size, architecture, and geographical location vary greatly. For example, all the sons and daughters of Leopoldo Jr. and Pablo were married in the Basilica of Our Lady of Guadalupe; this was the most prestigious church for weddings at the time and it expressed the "guadalupismo" of the family. But a modern church in an upper-class residential area has now become more fashionable for upper-class weddings.

Selecting the priest is also an important decision. Formerly the priest was invariably selected by the Gómez parents; he was always a high-ranking prelate in the Catholic hierarchy. The wealthier Gómez were married by the archbishop himself. Rich or poor, every Gómez tried to get the highest-ranking priest possible to officiate. It has become more common among the fourth and fifth generations of the Gómez for the couple to be married by a priest who is a personal friend. Younger couples often select a member of the religious order favored and protected by the Gómez family.

The appointment of godfathers and godmothers for performing specific functions at the wedding has become customary in the middle and lower strata of Mexican society: the "madrina de misa" pays for the mass, the "madrina de pastel" brings the wedding cake, and so on. Among the Gómez family only parents of the bride or groom are invited to be godfather and godmother at a wedding, and there are no specific obligations. Mexican custom requires the designation by the bride of special godmothers such as *madrina de lazo, madrina de arras,* and *madrina de ramo.* The first is the most important; she symbolically binds the bride and bridegroom to each other at the height of the church ceremony by tying them with two long rosaries on end. The bride usually asks a sister, close cousin, or friend to perform this special task. The madrina de arras carries the box containing the wedding rings and the *arras,* gold coins presented by the groom to the bride as a symbol that he can support her. This is also usually a sister or close friend of the bride or groom. The madrina de ramo carries the bridal spray.

The maids of honor are usually sisters of the groom or the bride; they are identically dressed in gowns selected by the bride. According to tradition, the three special godmothers should also consult the bride regarding their dress, but this is no longer compulsory. The pages are small boys (less than eight years old) selected by the bride from among her cousins or nephews; they might also be relatives of the groom or of friends. They are identically dressed, but their parents must buy the suit for the occasion.

The bride is dressed entirely in white, considered a symbol of chastity. No color is allowed, not even in the bridal spray: anything other than white would reflect on her virginity. The groom and the father of the bride are both dressed in a formal morning coat or jacket if the wedding is in the morning, a tuxedo if it is in the evening. The bride's and groom's mothers and the bride's godmothers are dressed in new gowns, as elegant and expensive as possible. This is an occasion to display one's status, and the women are expected to wear their best. Diamond and pearl necklaces are produced from safe-deposit boxes and other hiding places; for those who don't own such jewelry, a wealthy aunt may be willing to lend something she is not wearing herself that day. Among the wealthy branches of the Gómez family, it is customary for the bride's parents to give her a present of costly jewelry to wear.

Weddings were formerly held only during the day; but fifteen years ago the Church began to allow weddings to be held in the evening, and these are now considered more elegant. This is a decision left to the couple. Naturally, the time of the wedding has some bearing on the time of the ball that follows. The bride begins from her parents' home, in her father's best car (or in a car borrowed from a rich uncle if her father does not own an elegant limousine). The bride's limousine is adorned with white ribbons and flowers. She is alone with her father; the remaining members of the family travel to the church in other cars. There are no similar rules for the groom except that he should be waiting at the church when the bride arrives. The entrance of the bride is dramatic: first the little pages, then the bridesmaids, then the godmothers, followed by the groom's father leading the bride's mother, then the bridegroom with his mother, and finally the bride herself on the arm of her father. If the bride's father is deceased, his place is taken by her eldest brother. Women always walk on the left and men on the right.

The officiating priest in full regalia awaits the bridal party at the door of the church and leads the procession toward the altar, to the accompaniment of solemn music. Once in front of the altar, the mothers of the bride and groom flank the bride on the left, and similarly the two fathers flank the groom on the right. The remaining members of the bridal party stand behind the kneeling pair. Formerly it was customary to have the wedding performed before the mass, but according to new Church reforms the wedding is now performed during the mass. After the Gospel reading, a sermon is given, usually containing personal allusions to the bridal pair. This is followed by the wedding ceremony; the priest formally asks the groom and bride whether they accept each other as husband and wife and the public whether there is any impediment to the union. Then there is the exchange of rings, and the bride receives the arras from the groom. Now the priest proclaims them man and wife, and they are symbolically tied together with the lazo. This may later be hung above the bridal bed. Quite often, the same lazo is handed down from fathers to sons in a family.

The mass then proceeds, normally ending with communion. The more people from among the congregation who take communion, the higher the prestige of the wedding, because it means that most of the public are good Catholics. After mass, some brides deposit the bridal spray at the feet of the statue of the Virgin.

The bridal procession forms again, headed by the bride and groom. They are followed by the parents of the bride, the parents of the groom, the godmothers, the bridesmaids, and the pages. Solemn music is heard once again as they walk down the aisle of the church. Once outside, the procession disbands and the public lines up to embrace and congratulate the couple and their parents and relatives. When there is a party, those invited go immediately to the place where it is held. Drinks are served; among the rich, only champagne is served right after the ceremony. In recent times some couples have requested that there be no wedding ball and that the money be given to them instead for their own use, to be spent on some special purchase or for travel. Among the rich, however, wedding balls are traditional and are only omitted in the event of recent mourning. Expensive food and drink are served in abundance; after dinner there is dancing to live music. Relatives may be in the minority among the guests, but they are expected to stay after everyone else has left.

The newlyweds retire early. Sometimes they spend the night at an elegant hotel in Mexico City, and the following morning they leave for their honeymoon. Among the wealthier Gómez it has been customary to spend the honeymoon in Europe or in the United States; less wealthy relatives go to fashionable Mexican resorts. They return to their new home, which is ready and waiting for them. They are immediately incorporated into Gómez family life as a full-fledged couple: they are invited to all normal family rituals, and their relationships with relatives (including their own parents) becomes more relaxed. One of their first duties as a couple is to send printed thank-you notes, prominently displaying their new address, to all those who have sent a present or a card.

THE FUNERAL. A grandfamily never leaves the patient's bedside in cases of grave illness. In the event of a death, the entire kinship network knows the details, including the arrangements for the funeral, within a matter of hours, because relatives spontaneously phone each other in no particular order, without worrying whether others may already have done so. More distant relatives or those who are difficult to reach find out the next morning from the newspapers; it is a Mexican custom to insert paid notices in the daily press on the death of a relative. Notices are also inserted by institutions or business concerns with which the deceased was associated; for example, a business firm will often put in a black-rimmed ad when one of its directors or executives is in mourning for a close relative. This is mandatory when the deceased worked directly for the firm. The number of paid insertions that appear at the death of an entrepreneur is a measure of his economic power and the diversity of his investments. Thirty-one notices appeared in one issue of a Mexico City daily when Pablo Gómez died. When a poor relative dies, on the other hand, a single family notice may be published.

Until about ten years ago the wake was held at the home of the deceased: it was a family gathering that included friends of the deceased. Coffee, food, and wine were served. More recently funeral parlors have become fashionable, though some older members still request that, in the event of their death, a wake be held at their homes. In general, black dress is mandatory at a wake or funeral, though younger men are now seen on such occasions in grey or dark-colored business suits. By Mexican law the wake must last a minimum of 24 hours; large numbers of relatives and friends come to pay their last respects to the dead. The members of the bereaved grandfamily are expected to stay at the wake until burial; this includes men as well as women. Other relatives spend various amounts of time at the wake, depending on the degree of kinship. Distant relatives come in, present their condolences and leave, but clients and other relatives who wish to make a favorable impression on the family of the deceased often stay until late or may even remain all night at the wake. Wakes and funerals are open to all. Because the notice has appeared in the daily press, no invitation is expected. Funerals are the largest kinship arenas, and relatives who have not seen each other for years meet and renew their acquaintance on such occasions. It is common to get together once or twice with distant relatives after a funeral. People find out about the economic situation of the widow and whether she will need assistance; a great deal of information about other relatives is also passed around. Relatives take the opportunity to talk freely about their intimate concerns; if someone needs an operation he will be referred to a good doctor, or if he needs a job he may be given tips for the right opening. New business opportunities are often discussed. Such contacts are all the more apt to occur because wakes and funerals take time and there is nothing else to do. It is considered appropriate to talk about old times, whether or not the memories are connected with the deceased.

A dead man's status or that of his family may be measured by the number attending the funeral. Whenever a major entrepreneur or a close relative of an entrepreneur dies, all family entrepreneurs and friends (often entrepreneurs) are present at the funeral; on the other hand, if the dead person was a poor relative, only a few members of the wealthy branches attend, representing the rest. In the late 1950s the funeral of Pablo Gómez was attended by a crowd of thousands. The president of Mexico, most of his cabinet, and a large number of prominent figures from the political and business world were there.

The cemetery chosen also has a symbolic connection with status. Mamá Inés, Leopoldo Sr., and a few others who died in the 1920s are buried in the old cemetery of the Sanctuary of Guadalupe. It was fashionable during the nineteenth century but is no longer; the Gómez are now buried in the Spanish cemetery. Originally founded by the Spanish community in Mexico, it has become (with the French cemetery) a burial place for the Mexican upper class. Pablo Gómez purchased the most elegant crypt in the cemetery, right next to the entrance, where important traditional families are buried and space is not normally available.

Rosaries are recited and a mass is said at the wake, sometimes at the funeral as well. Speeches are not customary. After the burial people line up to give their condolences to the dead person's next of kin; everyone then leaves separately. Masses or rosaries are said during the following nine days, and later at regular intervals, on behalf of the soul of the deceased. Having masses said during the novena carries a higher status: it requires money as well as connections with the Church, because it involves renting a church and getting a priest to say mass every day for nine days. These masses are normally conducted in the evenings. More commonly the rosary is recited every day of the novena either in a church or at the home. Participation in the *novenario* is optional, and no invitations are required.

The congregation may include people who attended the funeral, as well as others who were unable to go. The next of kin go every evening and note carefully the presence of relatives and friends.

A great funeral mass was formerly conducted on the ninth day after the funeral. It was sung with accompanying choir and was officiated by three priests. This tradition has been practically abandoned; Pablo was perhaps the last of the Gómez who had one. Condolence visits are now much less frequent than they used to be: such visits were formerly mandatory and are still very much in style among the older generation. Dark-colored garments are worn when making such visits, and it is customary to talk about the deceased and to express formal condolences, even among close relatives. The period of mourning for a close relative used to be a full year, during which only black could be worn, even by children. This custom too has become somewhat relaxed, although it is strictly followed by older members of the family.

Funerals are the most widely observed family rituals. They are open to all and are a convenient test of family allegiance. From the presence or absence of kin at funerals it is possible to determine whether or not they still consider themselves relatives.

Secular Rituals

Certain social customs are found among the Gómez kinship network and among similar family networks in Mexico. These may be termed secular rituals, because they complement the religious rituals by giving special form and content to repetitious occasions in the life cycle of an individual (G. Lewis 1977, 39; Moore and Myerhoff 1977). Secular rituals among the Gómez are stylized and prescribed much like religious rituals are. Thus certain social reunions among kin may be described as secular rituals because they are not simply of the normal spontaneous kind but are institutionalized occasions, validated by patterns of symbolic behavior and elevated to the rank of family traditions. They reinforce the sense of belonging of subgroups within the kinship network; they enhance intragroup communication; they create culture and subculture; they mold and transmit ideology; and they shape the selfhood of component individuals in the kinship network through values and norms of behavior that constitute the distinctiveness of a group. Secular rituals also create social arenas in which status differences and internal conflict among members of the group surface and are sometimes resolved.

Secular rituals among the Gómez are considerably more frequent than religious rituals: they are daily occurrences. Prescribed family gatherings occur in the form of celebrations: birthdays, send-offs or welcome-home parties on the occasion of extended trips abroad, weekly gatherings among the grandfamily or cousin groups, entrepreneurial gatherings, and so on. Each of these occasions is associated with a stylized form of behavior: formality or informality of dress, customary dishes or types of cuisine, wines or spirits consumed, whether presents are exchanged and what types, and particularly the length and composition of the list of participants. One finds members of the Gómez family forever discussing their social obligations, how they must call on so and so, buy a present for such and such, be in attendance at some bedside, or go to a formal dinner.

WEEKLY DINNER PARTIES. In urban Mexico one frequently finds the family custom of the weekly dinner, usually on weekends, at the grandparents' home. Weekly gatherings at the grandparents' home include, if possible, all married and unmarried sons and daughters with their spouses and children. Typically three generations are represented. Often other close relatives (e.g., an unmarried or widowed aunt) are also present. Once the custom has been established, attendance is expected on a weekly basis; a visiting relative or friend may occasionally participate on an informal basis. Informal invitations to these weekly gatherings are not easily extended, however, among the Gómez; the grandmother's approval is first secured.

The rationale of the gathering is to enhance and enjoy the solidarity of the grandfamily during the grandparents' lifetime. After their death these gatherings become increasingly difficult to continue, though attempts in this direction are sometimes made by one or another of the daughters. Eventually, each son becomes a paterfamilias and his home becomes the center of similar weekly reunions.

The weekly family dinner is a mechanism for promoting the solidarity of a grandfamily, an occasion where cousins meet and get to know each other from childhood. Each grandfamily has a separate weekly dinner. Conversations are about each member's activities during the week, who ran into whom, what happened in business, who did what on the social and cultural front, and what happened in the kinship network at large. Nearly every week there is a funeral, a wedding, or an important birthday, giving rise to comments about who went and who didn't, how they behaved, what they were wearing, what they said, and so forth. These comments are permeated with family norms and values, transmitted from generation to generation.

The conversation is by no means limited to family affairs: the political and economic situation is also discussed at length. Such comments frequently generate clashes of opposing views between the older and the younger generations; they represent an important arena for the process of adaptation of the family ideology to daily events. Labor problems, the conduct of government, religion, and family and moral issues are topics frequently discussed. It is an opportunity to be outspoken, both in defense of those who have acted correctly and in criticism of those who have been remiss or otherwise inadequate. As the family ideology evolves, so does the range of topics: for example, family planning or birth control, a formerly unmentionable subject, is now openly discussed. The children listen to the arguments and soak up factual information and family ideology together. Some of them may eventually undergo a stage of rebellion, but their socialization in the family system of norms and values usually proves permanent.

Personal problems of individual family members are seldom discussed in the round, even less so when the person concerned is present, unless he or she brings it up. If some family member plans to leave, give up the family business, change lines of work, get divorced, or has a serious illness, this may give rise to comments from person to person (or on the telephone), but not in a weekly gathering. The problem may be known to all those present, possibly because it has been discussed with each family member separately, but it is rarely mentioned. This is not only to avoid embarrassment but also expresses a pervasive etiquette of mutual respect among family members.

Each extended family develops its own style and mode of interaction. Some tend to be more direct and others more oblique in their comments. The patriarch or matriarch may be more or less authoritarian and the relationships between members may be more guarded or more relaxed. On the whole, however, the topics of conversation are largely identical: the kinship network at large, current news, family rituals, and personal gossip including business, social life, and the activities of children. Because of their entrepreneurial orientation, business gossip is of particular interest to the Gómez kinship network.

Seating arrangements also have their rules. Parents sit at the head of the table and uncles and aunts, important guests, and children or grandchildren who have had an important celebration that week (birthday, return from a trip, etc.) may sit nearby. The rest sit according to age: older children and their spouses sit closest to the parents; younger children and grandchildren sit further down the table.

The food served varies a great deal. Usually the extended family looks forward to enjoying grandmother's traditional recipes. If held on a weekday evening the reunion may be over in a matter of one or two hours, but on weekends it may occupy a full day. Among the Gómez it is not the custom to play cards or other games on family occasions. They are communions in the family spirit, and their only purpose is to eat together and converse animatedly on topics of mutual interest.

VISITING THE SICK. When a relative falls ill, particularly in cases of serious illness or hospitalization, the news spreads rapidly through the kinship network. Women are in charge of circulating this information, and all those who can, especially the men, try to provide whatever assistance may be needed. For example, when Herminia Bañuelos (III,63), the poorest member of the Bañuelos branch, fell ill, her sister-in-law, Ana María Jiménez (a centralizing woman) was promptly informed by her nieces, Herminia's daughters. Ana María then informed her brother Pedro as well as her cousins Juana and Leopoldo Jr. Those important family members relayed the news to their spouses, and so on. These branches had had no personal contact for a long time, yet Herminia was visited in the hospital by Leopoldo Jr., Pedro, Modesta, Ana María, and many others, particularly relatives from the third generation. At the hospital they met members of the poor branches, and they had occasion to recall family events and update information on certain members of the family; in short, kinship relations were revived. Information was gathered about the occupations and other vital facts of Herminia's children, and the lives of nearly forgotten relatives from poor branches were discussed once again among the rich. This was the first time that some members of the fifth generation had heard of Aunt Herminia and her children.

Another time, Ana María was operated on and had to be hospitalized for a full month. Because of her daily telephone conversations with Modesta, Juana, Carmelita, her own daughter Lupe, and others, these women were immediately alerted and passed on the information to their respective families and branches. Most of the Gómez family of the third, fourth, and fifth generations, from the poorest to the wealthiest, visited her in the hospital at least once a week. This response to illness is a clear indication of family cohesion and also of family leadership, since the example of the leaders is immediately followed by all. Although such visits do not require an invitation or even a personal notification and are open to all family members, they may be regarded as a ritual; personal response and participation (or nonparticipation) is carefully noted. The closer the kinship tie with the sick person, the greater is the expected frequency of visits: parents and daughters are expected to be at the bedside every day, and sons every evening or as often as they can get away from work. In case of serious illness the nuclear family is expected to be present in full at the bedside, day and night. Uncles, aunts, and cousins, depending on their emotional closeness to the patient, are expected to pay a visit about once a day. More distant relatives are expected to go once a week; such expectations of course depend to some extent on the patient's illness and on his or her status.

Leopoldo Jorge Gómez Chacón (IV,111), a son of Pablo Gómez, suffered a heart attack at 8:00 one morning. By 1:00 that afternoon, representative members of the wealthy branches were gathered at his bedside; throughout the family network everyone was talking about his illness, about the fact that it had struck him at such an early age, and about how his wife must be feeling. Since the patient was a member of a clique of first cousins, the other members of the clique assumed the role of brothers and stood guard at the hospital. Normally a wife is responsible for deciding about doctors and treatments, but in this case the eldest brother took over to such an extent that a conflict between brother and wife on the subject of the patient's care seemed imminent.

When Juan Leopoldo Bañuelos Fábregas (IV,136), a member of a poorer branch, suffered from a long and complicated illness that required a great deal of expensive surgery and care, his wealthy uncles joined forces to pull him through. The initial information had reached them through the female network; but the male kin, once they had the news, visited the patient constantly. In general, visiting the sick among the Gómez kinship network represents one of the crucial arenas for the transmission of information and the consolidation of family unity. Relatives who gather around a hospital bed generate strong sentiments of solidarity and support at critical times in the life of an individual; this response is perceived as the real strength of kinship. It means also that any information about relatives is of the highest interest to family members and must be promptly circulated throughout the kinship network.

Information gathered at the bedside of sick relatives can refer to business matters. An accountant will be consulted on some problem related to income tax; a relative may offer to transport merchandise with his fleet of trucks; others may discuss a possible joint business or renting office space from each other. Many a new business idea was born at the bedside of a sick relative; it happens all the time and at all family rituals.

Status Reinforcement Rituals

Among the Gómez, certain ostentatious customs have become important status symbols in the wealthy branches of the family. They are of three types: family trips, country gatherings, and ritual board meetings.

Family trips may involve anything from weekends in Acapulco to extended trips to Europe. Leopoldo Jr. was particularly addicted to such travel; he instituted annual grand tours to Europe with all the members of his grandfamily. This custom began around 1950 and involved conspicuous consumption: first-class travel, first-class hotels and restaurants, expensive clothes, and costly presents for relatives who stayed home. These tours were entirely planned and paid for by Leopoldo, and the itinerary tended to be the same, year after year. A change of hotel was a major decision.

Similar though perhaps less ostentatious family trips have been customary among family entrepreneurs from time to time; they tend to reinforce the allegiance of sons-in-law and daughters-in-law to the family clan. Nonparticipation on the part of a son or daughter could be interpreted as an act of defiance: at any rate, it represents a distinct show of coolness, however justified by external circumstances.

Normally these ritual trips are not intended as occasions for fraternizing with the local population abroad. On the contrary, they are opportunities for satirizing and criticizing foreign customs (the French are "unpleasant," the Germans "immoral," Americans are rich and well organized but lack family values and so on). Spain is the major exception, because of the common language and respect for Hispanic heritage in the family ideology.

Grand tours are an expression of the patriarchal structure of the grandfamily and particularly of the patron-client relationship between a father and his sons and daughters. It is also a mark of extreme wealth that is much admired and envied by the family at large. Lesser entrepreneurs copy the example of their more powerful kin by organizing family trips to the United States or within Mexico, occasionally sharing expenses with their sons and sons-in-law. Small cliques of brothers or cousins who wish to emphasize their emotional closeness organize weekend trips to Houston, Acapulco, Guanajuato, and so on, sometimes taking their wives and children. The Merino y Pachecos, for example, customarily spend Christmas at a ski resort in the United States, where they own an elegant apartment.

Leopoldo Gómez Benítez (IV,103) and his wife became weary of traveling in large family groups. They had some money invested in the United States and decided to purchase a home in Texas for the exclusive use of their nuclear family. They spent a vacation there together, but as soon as Leopoldo's grandfamily heard of it, they came to visit. Scarcely a month had gone by before Leopoldo's brothers and sister purchased vacation homes in Texas right next door to Leopoldo's, to his wife's dismay. Now they would again have to spend their vacations all together. Leopoldo and his wife finally became resigned to this fact of life; any new attempt to change their vacation spot would merely cause another exodus of the grandfamily, with identical results.

Several extended families of the Gómez network own weekend homes in the country. The Merino y Pacheco brothers, for example, bought a big weekend house in Cuernavaca for their mother, doña Juana. This house includes separate apartments for each of the Merino y Pacheco nuclear families, including the sisters, and it is used practically every weekend. Among the Gómez Chacón, each brother has his own ranch. Javier Gómez Gómez also has a ranch. Members of the poorer branches, the Bañuelos, the Gómez Balbuena, and the Gómez Morenos, have no weekend homes. Vacationing together and spending weekends together represents a positive value in the Gómez ideology because it reinforces relations among members of grandfamilies, particularly among the younger cousins who play together and grow up together. The biggest weekend or holiday gatherings occur at the entrepreneurial ranches; these gatherings are exclusive, but some faithful clients and poor relations are always invited, while other wealthy entrepreneurial relatives, who have their own ranches, might not be invited.

A country gathering is a customary type of gathering that occurs only among the wealthy Gómez. It is a status occasion by definition, not just because of the restricted invitation list but also because it presupposes ownership of country estates, fine horses, and so on. An example is the horseback promenade, one of which took place in 1977. It was organized by four of the wealthier entrepreneurs and their sons. Altogether about fifty people were invited; all but five were relatives. Members of the third, fourth, and fifth generations of the wealthiest and most prestigious branches of the family were included. The promenade began with breakfast at the colonial ranch of one of the patriarchs, who served a typical Mexican menu: fruit, eggs "a la mexicana," beans, *chilaquiles*, coffee, milk, pastry, all in great abundance. The guests arrived in big shiny new cars. The ranch has stable facilities to accommodate up to thirty horses; they had been ferried in the previous evening, by special vans from various other ranches.

After breakfast the cavalcade (about twenty people on horseback) rode out in the direction of the ranch of the second patriarch, about ten miles away. The rest of the party proceeded by car, to await the group on horseback at their destination. Meanwhile, lunch was being prepared at the second ranch, a fine new mansion in the colonial style. The horseback party arrived and drinks were served. The quality of the horses, incidentally, is important: they must be the finest. One of the invited women had declined to go out with the horseback party solely because she felt that her horse was not as highly bred as the others. Some of the horses had been imported from the famous Spanish Riding School in Vienna. Men normally use the traditional Mexican *charro* saddle; until recently they wore the charro costume as well. Women use the English saddle, or Spanish saddles imported from Córdoba.

At leisure, after drinks, a Mexican specialty was served: *chalupas*, made by a "chalupera" who had been brought all the way from Puebla for the occasion. The appetizer was followed by an open-air dinner in the traditional Mexican style. This took most of the afternoon. Toward evening, their chauffeured cars ready, families began to take leave one by one. Stable grooms took charge of the horses and loaded them back into the vans, to be returned to their ranches. Such ritual cavalcades used to be held once a year, at considerable expense.

Country rituals, like trips and vacations, are occasions for families and young cousins to meet. They are also status competitions, involving ranches, fine horses, good service, and displays of art treasures. Membership in the elite of the kinship network is thus given concrete expression and meaning. Conversation is not merely about horses and other status symbols but also very much about family affairs. The symbols connected with housing, food, and dress as well as country customs are meant to stress the "criollismo" of the family tradition, both in its Mexican flavor and in its Spanish accent.

Board meetings are a third kind of status-reinforcing ritual. Gómez enterprises are organized so that the major family entrepreneurs sit on each other's boards of directors. On the average, a board of directors meets once a month; among the Gómez family such meetings are more than mere business affairs. They tend to become business luncheons at elegant downtown restaurants or slightly more formal gatherings at the office or the home of the enterprise's owner. Board meetings are not truly deliberative but resemble boasting sessions held by the entrepreneur for the benefit of his business associates. The idea is to discuss past successful operations and make plans for the future. Whenever a report might be disheartening or contain unhappy news, the president of the enterprise will abstain from calling a board meeting.

In other words, board meetings are ritual occasions for status display among leaders of the family business. The purpose of the meetings appears to be largely one of enhancing the prestige and economic power of an entrepreneur among his peers. Although during years of adversity no board meetings are held, they are reinstated as soon as business picks up again. Membership on a board of directors is seen as a prerogative of major family entrepreneurs, and their sons may also join when they are about thirty years old and working in business. The fact that these individuals meet regularly across the board tables of each other's enterprises is significant as a symbol of their class solidarity over and above the rivalries that may exist between them.

Conclusions

In addition to the described rituals, there are innumerable social occasions, such as birthday parties, wedding anniversaries, and send-offs and welcome-home parties, that have been celebrated among the Gómez since the days of Mamá Inés. These are grandfamily gatherings; sometimes a mass is said. Some occasions are more important than others and may be celebrated among a wider circle of relatives. Originally the entire kinship network residing in Mexico City participated in such events; eventually, however, they came to be celebrated only within a given branch or within a grandfamily of the branch. Members of other grandfamilies or branches, however, are often invited. Among certain Gómez relatives it has become customary to invite the eldest member of each grandfamily in order to perpetuate the tradition of having representatives of the entire kinship network present at such affairs. This primarily occurs on special occasions; ordinary birthday parties, such as children's birthdays, are celebrated among the circle of the child's first cousins or (at most) second cousins if they happen to be friends or go to school together.

Ritual occasions of this type are extremely frequent. As an example, the Gómez Benítez branch currently has about seventy members, if Leopoldo Junior's sons-in-law, daughters-in-law, grandchildren, and their spouses are included. This means one birthday every five days on the average, requiring at least a telephone call from each member. This particular grandfamily includes fifteen couples, whose wedding anniversaries must be commemorated separately year after year. In addition, there is the normal spate of holy communions, weddings, funerals, bridal showers, births and christenings, graduations, and visits to the ill. Personal visits are mandatory in many cases.

Organizing and attending family rituals represents a demanding occupation for Gómez women. A Gómez wife's desire to work for a living is not merely discouraged for traditional reasons: it is impractical, if the woman truly cares for the prestige of her nuclear family among the kinship network at large. In addition, she has to reckon with the social obligations to personal friends and business associates outside the family, as well as her in-laws' grandfamily and kinship network obligations. The more a man values his family connections and personal or business associations, the less he is likely to want his wife to find interests or occupations outside the home. His wife's observance of rituals symbolically expresses the economic worth of the head of the extended family.

Rituals have an economic function not merely because business is transacted at them but because the economic liquidity and stability they express translate into future business opportunities or credit. Ritual behavior in the Gómez family entails a complex system of symbolic actions of great importance to the development of each family member and to the kinship network as a whole. A great many social obligations must be attended to if a member wishes to retain his family status. Each individual discriminates and is discriminated against by invitations made or withheld to certain ritual occasions, and by accepting or failing to accept the same. A wide range of forms of participation is open to each individual, which enables him or her to express status or feelings of conformity (or nonconformity) without actually committing a breach of etiquette.

Gómez family rituals may thus be interpreted as serving a multiplicity of purposes, among which the following may be singled out. First, they define and continually redefine the boundaries of the kinship network versus the rest of society. Family membership and allegiance depend on participation in these rituals. Second, they define the internal stratification and segmentation of the kinship network by branches, grandfamilies, cliques, economic strata, and hierarchies. Each of these subgroups has a distinctive identity that sets it apart from other groups. Family rituals are also power arenas, where status is conferred or confirmed and where allegiance is also visibly enacted, as well as arenas where conflicts between specific individuals and subgroups are acted out and resolved. Third, family rituals are arenas where family ideology and information on individuals and kin groups are circulated and updated. Finally, family rituals are vehicles for the expression of continuity of the family kinship group. This continuity distinguishes a kinship relation from one of simple friendship. Ritualization confers a seal of permanence and sanctity: it consecrates the family as the highest priority among all an individual's obligations.

Ideology

THE IDEOLOGY of the Gómez has been shaped by the social activities of the kinship group. Its creation and re-creation can be traced in time through the changing historical contexts that gave the group its identity.

The dominant ideology of the Gómez family group is the one professed and expressed by the dominant individuals of the group, the entrepreneurs and the centralizing women. Generally speaking, it is an ideology that stresses the role of private initiative in the development of Mexico and exalts the positive values that are attributed to membership in the family group and in the Mexican bourgeoisie. This is reflected in ideas about race, religion, family, property, and authority. Its roots are in the conceptual apparatus of the society at large, but the kinship group has reinterpreted the general conceptual framework of the culture by selecting or emphasizing some elements and ignoring others. This reinterpretation becomes particularly obvious when one analyzes the group's version of its own history, since the selection and interpretation of historical facts and personalities has much to do with the values of the group.

As Cohen has shown in his study of interest groups in complex societies (1974), social groups borrow the elements of their ideology from the general symbolic system of the culture and transform it through reinterpretation in order to create the *distinctiveness* of the group as opposed to other similar groups. Cohen emphasizes the importance of ideology for group identity and stresses the relationship between the ideological system, ritual, kinship, and the political and economic situation of the group.

An ideology is a cultural subsystem dealing with beliefs and values shared by a social group. It includes explanations of who and what we are, why we are, where we come from, what we do or should do, and how we relate to others. In this system the factual is not separated from the desirable: what is and what should be are intermingled. Ideology is a description of how a group sees itself and others and how it wishes to be seen by others (Bock 1974, 306; Cohen 1974, 24; Dumont 1977, 7; Durkheim 1965; Geertz 1973, 144-54; Parsons 1961, 359-67).

Most modern societies are pluralistic, in the sense that they feature a high degree of differentiation into groups and social classes that is based on the division of labor and other factors. The symbolic universe of the society is reinterpreted by each group, and the result of this reinterpretation is the ideology of the group. In general, ideology is not only an attribute of the culture but must be related to a specific group, subgroup, or class within the society. "When a particular definition of reality comes to be attached to a concrete power interest, it may be called an ideology. The distinctiveness of ideology is that the same overall universe is interpreted in different ways, depending upon concrete vested interests within the society in question. . . . Every group engaged in social conflict requires solidarity. Ideology generates solidarity" (Berger and Luckman 1976, 141).

It is important to discuss the methodological problems that confront the anthropologist when studying the ideology of a particular group. Each individual, family, or group shares basic symbols and bodies of knowledge in common with other groups, families, or individuals, while at the same time maintaining specific variants or features that are not shared. Thus, the "Gómez ideology" shares important features with the ideology of Catholicism, of Mexican nationalism, of private enterprise, of the Mexican upper class, and of gender specificities. The same symbolic universe can be reinterpreted in different ways by different individuals or social groups. Such interpretations may vary according to objective changes in reality (e.g., the introduction of new technologies) or the impact of new ideological influences (e.g., modernization). Interpretation is selective, in the sense that the group seeks to survive in a changing social context; ideological change must therefore be understood within the logic of social change.

Ideology is thus circumscribed by a dynamic of continuity and change. Continuity is provided by the history of the group: a common sequence of events with the members of the group as actors, an integrated process in time. Ideology feeds on these events and modifies them through interpretation until they are changed into myth. The history of the Gómez kinship group contains heroes and villains, leaders and dissidents. The historical personage of Mamá Inés, for example, has become a mythological symbol that relates specifically to family values such as unity, the matriarchate, and womanhood in general; these concepts and values are also associated with customs, family dishes, and other symbols. Her national counterpart as a symbol of motherhood is the Virgin of Guadalupe. However, the ideological connotations of the historical figure of Mamá Inés are meaningful only to members of the Gómez kinship group and represent only one specific component of their subculture. The family also claims that they are descendants of the family of San Felipe de Jesús, the Mexican saint who lived in the sixteenth century. This claim symbolizes their old criollo roots and their religious allegiance. The history of the kinship group may be read as a set of symbols that has grown up around historical figures endowed with specific ideological meanings. The distinctive character or "we-ness" of a group is found in its self-transmitted history, beliefs, values, and norms. The survival of a group can be interpreted in terms of its ideological and cultural continuity.

Ideological symbols and forms of knowledge may either be transmitted explicitly, as in the case of religion, or through daily actions, statements, rituals, gestures, comments, value judgments, and life styles. Members of a group are expected to share this ideological system and transmit it to their children. The assimilation of ideology is a major part of the process of socialization.

Ideology is not merely a source of group identity and solidarity; it is also a charter for socialization and individual action. This is because ideology inspires the ideals of individual men or women belonging to the group. Not all members of the group conform to this model at all times, but most of them acknowledge the group ideal in their individual behavior. Conflict occurs when a significant number of members cease to conform to the ideological tenets of the group. In the case of the Gómez, there are ideological expectations attached to all aspects of life: control and power, family solidarity, the role of the male entrepreneur in the economy, child raising, and so forth. As we have seen, socioeconomic reality produces discrepancies between ideal and actual behavior. Ideology has caused Gómez family members to lose power or status within the society, contrary to expectations contained in the ideology itself. Other contradictions appear at the level of the individual: family support is not always as solid as the individual might wish; fathers and sons are not always on good terms; and the rest of the world does not always behave according to the pattern predicted in the Gómez ideology. In a rapidly changing world, individuals are reared on an ideology that is at least one generation out of date by the time they grow up.

Interpretation of Mexican History: Race and Class

The Gómez identify with Mexican attitudes that equate white skin color with high social status. The conquerors were white and the conquered, dark. Indigenous values are despised, not just because they are associated with the losers but also because they stand for a non-Western way of life.

The Gómez credit the Spanish conquerors with having achieved the linguistic, cultural, and political unification of Mexico and with having introduced the Catholic faith. They identify progress with adoption of "white" cultural patterns and equate backwardness with the Indian way of life.

Indians are accepted provided that they behave "like decent people" (*gente decente*). They are despised if they live like "pelados," which means, among other things, eating only tortillas, chile, and beans; having an uncultured form of speech; being lazy; and "leading a promiscuous life." It is recognized that some Indians or lower-class people may be clean-living and respectful of authority: such people are respected and may be warmly patronized. On the other hand, a blond or light-skinned worker will be more readily trusted than a dark one.

These attitudes might be more discriminatory of class than of race: a man with prominent Indian features is not a "pelado" if he adopts a European life style and rises on the social ladder (see also Aguilar 1978; Friedlander 1974). Obvious class connotations are implied in setting white people of Spanish origin and European upper-class life style against dark-skinned people with indigenous life styles. The category of "mestizo" is not used as such. Once individuals adopt a Western life style, they are accepted.

The Gómez family recognizes its mestizo origins yet defines itself as Spanish, white, and typically blue-eyed. Babies at birth are described as "pretty" or "homely" according to this standard, and brides or bridegrooms are described in the same way. The relativity of these concepts is brought home by the fact that "Spanish" in Mexico means being white, blond, and blue-eyed, while in the United States it means being dark-skinned and having black eyes.

The family acknowledges that Mamá Inés was of Indian origin; this is stated as a neutral fact, neither stressed nor glossed over. Her personality is invariably praised: she is said to have been clean, sweet, self-sacrificing, devoted to her children and grandchildren, and family minded. Don Carlos, on the other hand, is always described as tall, blond, white-skinned, blue-eyed, well educated, and very Spanish. If the Indian origins of Mamá Inés are overlooked, the poverty of don Carlos is also not mentioned.

The family mythology has made don Carlos the owner of a hacienda, but in the archives he is described as a *labrador* (farmer) and merchant. Sometimes it is vaguely mentioned that his father owned a hacienda but that don Carlos did not inherit the property or had forfeited it for some gentlemanly reason. Being the owner of a hacienda is important because it means being a "patron" in the old Spanish sense of the term. It means being in a position of authority, being a part of New Spain, and also being a descendant of Spaniards. A "patron" lives in a big house and has servants. He has horses (an important status symbol). He is known in the region; he is a generous and splendid host; he is hospitable to travelers, jealous of his prerogatives, and proud of his station in life. He may do as he pleases with his property, his servants, his wife, and his family. He is a gentleman, righteous, generous, and a "macho." Power and prestige are more highly valued than money. Owning a ranch is an important symbol for a wealthy Gómez business-man. He takes pride in his rural property and everything that goes with it: horses, bulls, servants, old-fashioned hospitality. The intended image is one of an offspring of the landed gentry, with origins as remote as possible in the early days of the Span-ish colony. This image is cultivated despite the fact that the Gómez family is generally recognized as part of the new indus-trial bourgeoisie rather than the old aristocracy. The Gómez are not content with being wealthy; they insist on tradition within the context of the colonial landowner's ideology.

Mexican independence (1810-1821) is hardly mentioned in connection with the family history. It is difficult to understand the lack of interest in this critical period of Mexican history and its heroes. Informants vaguely state that Hidalgo was "good" (he was a criollo) and that Morelos was "bad" (he was a mulatto). There seems to be some vague disapproval of both, perhaps due to the fact that both were defrocked priests who rose up in rebellion against formal authority.

The attitude toward Maximilian's empire (1864-1867) is one of admiration. The French period is seen as glittering and elegant. The display of period furniture and art objects of French origin is favored by the Gómez family to this day, sug-gesting that ostentatiously French taste is a part of the family effort to establish its European upper-class connections.

Benito Juárez is a controversial figure among the Gómez. The older traditionalists often express their distaste for Juárez the anticlerical liberal, who robbed the Church of its posses-sions. On the other hand, progressive entrepreneurs admire Juárez the reformer, who carried out the separation between church and state and inaugurated the ascent to power of the industrial bourgeoisie. The Gómez version of Mexican history claims that Juárez sold out Mexico to the Americans, in order to finance the Liberal war (1857-1867). According to the fam-ily, the loss of Mexican territories to the Americans was not so much the fault of Santa Anna but of Juárez. As in the case of Mamá Inés, the fact that Juárez was an Indian is neither stressed nor glossed over.

The liberal dictatorship of General Porfirio Díaz is seen with approval because of the modernization it introduced and the fact that the family rose to prominence during this period. However, the personality of Porfirio Díaz himself is seen with indifference. The famous *científicos* who administered Mexico during the Porfirio Díaz regime are described as "obnoxious people who made much of themselves because they were technocrats." Older people indulge in nostalgia over the technological marvels of Porfirismo: street lighting, the first motor cars, and the beautiful new suburban areas.

Among the Gómez kin, the Mexican Revolution (1910-1921) is remembered chiefly as a period of personal insecurity. In general there is little political talk in the family, and their ideas about Porfirio Díaz or about the Revolution are influenced by personal considerations rather than by political opinion. There is some difference of opinion about the Revolution itself: the more conservative family members used to criticize land reform because it "promoted laziness" among the peasants. The more progressive members of the family tend to praise it as an instrument that led to social order, yet they criticize it for failing to give full ownership of the land to the peasants and for keeping them as wards of the state.

The revolutionary leaders are not often discussed. Madero is respected but Villa and Zapata are dismissed as bandits, though there is little serious argument on the issue. It is remarkable that this crucial period in the history of Mexico remains almost ignored by family ideology. Their primary interest is family affairs: for example, the marriages of family members into "good families" of the Mexican aristocracy. Thus, Juanita's alliance with the Merino y Pacheco family occupies a great deal more space in family tradition than the whole of the Mexican Revolution. This is consistent with the role of family mythology as a means of social legitimacy. The middle-class branches cooperate in the effort to emphasize the high social status of the family, because it reflects favorably on their own social position.

If the Mexican Revolution is barely a subject of interest to the Gómez clan, there is a great deal of interest in political events during the presidency of Plutarco Elías Calles (1924-1928), particularly the religious persecution. This period is described as one of insecurity, injustice, and secret solidarity between the family and the Church. Calles himself is described as a devil. It is often mentioned that the family helped priests and nuns in this period.

The personality of President Lázaro Cárdenas (1934-1940) is endowed with ambiguity in the family mythology. The main connotation is negative: he was a "communist," because of his unpleasant populist leanings, his left-wing language, his habit of surrounding himself with lower-class people, and his encouragement of subversive ideas. He was always dividing up estates among the peasants and hobnobbing with the unions. As one explores the subject, however, one finds that Cárdenas is much admired for the nationalization of petroleum and for his energetic promotion of economic development in Mexico.

It is true that the methods used by Cárdenas in expropriating the oil are rejected: they infringed on the rights of private property. As a result, an "efficient" private enterprise became a state enterprise, and all state enterprises are considered inefficient by definition. Yet the nationalistic benefits of expropriation are felt to outweigh these drawbacks. The Gómez ideology values private property in a strongly nationalistic context. Foreign investment is good provided that the money stays in Mexico. Here again one finds some ambivalence, because the Gómez, like most business people, have money in foreign banks. But they are astute about the role of foreign corporations in Mexico: their attitude is "let them come in and we'll figure a way to keep the money in the country, without adopting their way of life."

The Gómez see Avila Camacho (1940-1946) as a "great and good" president, an honest man and a good Catholic. His presidency is seen as a time of prosperity. He is much praised for standing up to public opinion and admitting that he was a practicing Catholic, while other presidents and prominent public men hypocritically practiced their faith in secret. (Mexican law bars officeholders from public worship because the separation between church and state must be total. This gives rise to a great deal of mockery about public officials sending their children to religious schools and seeking the spiritual comforts of religion when their end is near.)

President Miguel Alemán (1946-1952) is greatly admired by the Gómez as the best president Mexico ever had. It is conceded that there was much corruption and that the president himself set a bad example, but he is excused on the ground that he only took for himself a small part of what he gave to the country. President Adolfo López Mateos (1958-1964) is also appreciated: he was charismatic, "simpático," and knew how to maintain a balance between the forces in the country. He valued the advice of private business, and industry felt supported even though the president occasionally talked like a leftist.

Gustavo Díaz Ordaz (1964-1970) is seen as a great president. He is credited with having put his foot down during the 1968 student troubles and calling a halt to communism. Students at the National University of Mexico are seen as agitators and intellectual bums; young people should work or study and be respectful of their elders. The university itself is seen as a hotbed of unrest and insubordination and is considered unsuitable for young women: a disorderly place and a breeding ground of perversion. The 1968 Tlatelolco massacre was a bad thing, but in the family's eyes it was justifiable because it saved Mexico's image during the Olympic Games and succeeded in making order prevail. Law and order is seen as a value in itself. The Gómez feel that Mexico's achievement in organizing and successfully hosting the Olympic Games was very important, and they are proud of the more modern image that Mexico attained abroad. They are sensitive to foreign opinion and would like Mexicans to be thought of as civilized, orderly, and progressive.

Alemán, López Mateos, and Días Ordaz were "friendly" presidents, who could be approached personally and who would visit the Gómez homes and consent to be witnesses at their daughters' weddings. Their administrations were a honeymoon period for the relationship between private enterprise and the state. Those who were children at the time recall that they might meet the president or his top officials at some of the entrepreneurs' homes.

President Luis Echeverría (1970-1976) is seen as the "bad guy" of Mexican history. Most deeply resented, at least by the Gómez, was Echeverría's rhetoric that kept harping on class struggle, seeking an opposition between private initiative and the rest of the country. This, they feel, went directly against social peace. He abetted discord between workers and patrons, he printed paper money in quantities that brought about inflation and a huge foreign debt. He is seen as a criminal, because he tore apart the texture and harmony of the social compact. The Gómez were also dismayed at Echeverría's public image, particularly abroad. They recall that he served "jamaica" water to Queen Elizabeth of England and boorishly grabbed her by the elbow. He insisted on foisting his lower-class, "pelado" customs on the rest of Mexico. For all the world to see, the president's wife wore an Indian peasant dress to greet the shah of Iran: this was a mistake and an unforgivable offense. At "Los Pinos," the executive mansion, they threw out all the beautiful French furniture and china and replaced them with coarse Mexican handicrafts. The Gómez are convinced, moreover, that this French furniture is now in Echeverría's private home.

This was the first period in which Gómez business people openly admitted taking money out of the country. Some of them began to express doubts about nationalism and about the future of Mexico. The breach between private enterprise and the state was at its most severe. Entrepreneurs felt that they were being treated as second-class citizens after all they had done for the country and for progress. It was not simply that they felt misunderstood as a group: they were alarmed by what they saw as a fundamental misapprehension of the role of risk taking and entrepreneurial skills in the development of Mexico. The prevailing rhetoric even took hold of the Gómez family, and some of its entrepreneurs began talking about "class struggle."

Until then, the Gómez view of labor relations had essentially been one of cordiality and harmony. The patron was responsible for his workers' well-being: he provided jobs, salaries, social security payments, and guidance. Gómez industrialists saw themselves as benevolent patrons who worked hard and took risks in order to create more and better jobs. In return, workers were expected to join efforts with entrepreneurs on behalf of the enterprise. Patrons feel that they carry their responsibility at all times, day or night, working very hard and risking everything, and that they have therefore earned their position and their standard of living. They do not feel that they exploit labor; on the contrary, they are extremely hurt at such a suggestion. They insist that they comply with all fair demands of labor. It is the union leaders who exploit the workers by extracting dues and union contributions from salaries and by organizing unfair and ruinous strikes for their own political advancement. They are the ones who make unreasonable demands, forcing Mexican industries out of business, reducing the number of jobs and hurting the interests of the workers by making Mexican products less competitive than imports. The Gómez also feel that the workers are easily intimidated and do not have the guts to stand up to union leaders. Such views are permeated with ambivalence because the union leadership is often seen as a necessary evil: they must be placated with tact and money in order to keep industry going. Gómez entrepreneurs feel that the unions exploit patrons as well as workers and that the labor situation is one of corruption, even though they concede that a tiny minority of labor leaders may be devoted to the interests of the workers. (Still, they feel such honest leaders would find it difficult to get promoted within the union hierarchy and would certainly never get to the top.) Fidel Velázquez, the boss of the Mexican Labor Federation (CTM), is admired as a great man who has done much for the development of Mexico and who has always been an approachable sort of person.

For the Gómez, the present internal structure of the country is beyond comprehension: there are masses of pelados in the streets (the result of the population boom), yet no one wants to work, and everyone has claims and grievances. People would rather not eat than get an honest job. Beaches and other public places are overrun by pelados who act as if they owned the country. The Gómez are frightened at the idea of having to live with such people: those without manners, who do not respect lines at supermarkets, dump their garbage on the beaches, shout at each other, have children without being properly married, use foul language, and do not respect people of position.

The Gómez think that since the beginning of the Echeverría regime, there is no longer any real good will between private business and the state. The family feels that it is the proper role of the state to create and maintain the infrastructure that private business requires to run Mexican industrial and commercial enterprises. The state should not operate industries or produce things: it doesn't know how. All state enterprises operate in the red; none of them is productive; why does the state insist on controlling the economy if it cannot manage it? Rather, the proper role of government is to keep order in the country and build a solid infrastructure (up to and including oil). The Gómez accept the principle of a mixed economy to the extent that it is required to solve specific Mexican problems, such as the petroleum industry, that private enterprise could not manage by itself. They recognize and appreciate the state's role as a protector of the poor, but they also claim that the state, like a foolish parent, is spoiling the poor by lavishing benefits without exacting duties in return.

This ideological framework must be kept in mind if one is to understand the peculiar fury of the Gómez family over Echeverría. Why did they see him as a madman who was tearing down everything that had been achieved in Mexico during earlier decades? They were used to political rhetoric about the poor and about redistributing wealth: this did not disturb them or affect their negotiating power vis-à-vis the state. But Echeverría used insulting language, calling them "riquillos" (roughly, "the insignificant or poor rich") and thus making wealth itself ridiculous and derogatory.

The López Portillo administration began auspiciously for the entrepreneurs, who regained some measure of confidence in the Mexican system. The president reestablished formal diplomatic relations with Spain and acknowledged the contribution of Spanish culture to Mexico's national roots: this was well received by the family. Moreover, the López Portillo administration was for the most part a time of economic growth and prosperity. Still, however, the business community remained mistrustful and much capital left the country. The middle class became more cosmopolitan and less nationalistic, partly as a result of increased travel opportunities abroad. Imitation of everything foreign became fashionable once again.

It seems that the family had no inkling that an economic crisis was approaching. When it came in 1982, with drastic currency devaluations and the nationalization of the banking system, the Gómez suffered a deep shock. They had no vested interests in the private banking system: on the contrary, they had been paying outrageous interest rates that could hardly get any worse with nationalization (and in fact the rates came down considerably right after nationalization). Yet their reaction was one of class solidarity with the bankers, who the Gómez thought had served the country well. The family felt that the entire business community was threatened.

Religious Ideology

It may be said that religion and family are the primary ideological leitmotifs of the Gómez kin. Other aspects of their ideology, including economics and politics, are imbedded in the concepts of religion and family and derive their validity and cohesion from these principal concepts. Such issues as family morality, the position of individuals within the family, authority, economy, and political ideology can only be properly understood and explained in terms of Catholicism. Catholicism is considered the only true religion and there is no conceivable alternative for a Gómez family member.

The Catholicism favored by the Gómez has a conservative and traditional flavor. Some branches are more devout than others, but all are strict Catholics with social ties to the Church hierarchy. Many have personal friends among bishops, priests, and nuns. Yet they are not inclined toward the contemplative life and are strangely unwilling for their own sons or daughters to enter religious orders. Family positions on ritual, economics, social ideology, and politics are similar to those of the Church, but do not actually identify with it.

Historically speaking, the social doctrine of the Church has always had considerable influence on the Gómez ideology, as far as it can be reconstructed from the positions of the older generation of Gómez entrepreneurs. There are correspondences between their views and those of the Church during the early years of the present century, as derived particularly from the encyclical *De Rerum Novarum*. An example of this position, which continues to influence economic and political attitudes within the Gómez family, is this statement by a leader of the Mexican Acción Católica (a Catholic organization) during the period of the Christero wars (1923): "Catholic teachings . . . admonish the employer to consider the laborer as his powerless brother and to treat him with charity. They teach the worker to respect his boss as his superior, for all authority comes from God; the rich must love the poor; the poor must love the rich, and they must mutually respect each other's legitimate rights; the industrial worker must respect the property of the capitalist, who must in turn respect the personal dignity of the worker; the artisan must work with honor; the capitalist must pay a just salary" (Quirk 1973, 27).

The phrase "a good Catholic entrepreneur," as used currently by the Gómez, should be understood in the context of this statement. The religious order that is in particular favor with the Gómez is known to subscribe to this doctrine. However, during the 1960s the Second Vatican Council introduced substantial doctrinal changes that greatly influenced the ideology and internal organization of the Church. These alterations have made inroads in the social ideology of all classes, particularly in Latin America (Levine 1980a, 21). Generational differences have appeared among the Gómez, and many younger members of the family feel that the traditional social doctrine held by Gómez entrepreneurs is old-fashioned and should be modified according to the teachings of the Second Vatican Council, which defines the obligations of a patron toward his workers as going far beyond those of charity. This is particularly true of young men who have been educated by the Jesuits or who have studied at universities beyond the influence of the religious order that the family sponsors. Discussions arise on this point in many Gómez homes, and the current position of the Church in Latin America is hotly debated. Conservatives in the family feel that the Church is forsaking its traditional mission and is participating in politics, which is not its rightful field of action. Some of the younger people cite recent post-Council doctrine in support of a more active Church policy in the pursuit of social justice. One thing is certain: religious doctrine has been and continues to be of decisive importance in the activity of the Gómez entrepreneurs.

Political ideology too is influenced by religious thought. The Gómez hold that the poor have a right to be fed, clothed, lodged, and given suitable jobs. They may even become entrepreneurs, as long as they respect capital and capitalists, and then they are respected as such. The issue of church and state is no longer controversial, in the sense that though the Gómez voice reprobation toward the nineteenth-century liberals who deprived the Church of its privileges, they have long come to accept that the Church should not be involved in politics (Levine 1980b; Quirk 1973, 17).

The Gómez view all authority as sacred. In this, they follow the pre-Council view of the Church. All authority comes from God: a father's authority is sacred at home, and so that of a boss in business. Yet the Gómez are anything but meek in submitting to the authority of politicians, bosses, or even the Church. Conflicts of authority are often resolved by appealing to the fact that a father has the last word as God's representative in all walks of life.

The impact of the Second Vatican Council amounts to "a major attempt to rethink the nature of the Church, the world, and the proper relation between the two" (Levine 1980a, 21). The world can and should be changed through the intervention of human will, a view that scorns passivity and resignation. This model "helps move emphasis within the Church away from a predominant concern with the roles, rank and juridically defined hierarchy, and towards testimonial witness as source of authority and model for action. . . . The link of authority to action . . . had a major impact on the scope and meaning of obedience within the Church" (Levine 1980a, 21-22). The new position of the Church not only undermines the image of the father as the ultimate authority; it also opens a gateway to social analysis. The position of the Church with respect to sin has also shifted. Sin is increasingly seen as the result of a structural situation derived from social dominance, oppression, and injustice, rather than a matter of personal attitudes and individual morality. Charity and correct behavior are not enough; a good Catholic should actively contribute to uproot sin from the social system. Some among the younger generation are faithful followers of this new Church doctrine (just as their elders follow the doctrine that was preached to them), in order to better understand society and to promote those changes felt to be desirable by the Church. This certainly does not mean that any Gómez family member has enrolled in extremist radical groups or even in leftist political organizations. Rather, they follow the teachings of the bishops, which amounts to a "central" position in the spectrum of Catholic opinion.

These trends in religious life have had interesting results. Some of the more old-fashioned aspects of religious practice, such as masses in the home or religious schools on the ranches, have disappeared. Other traditions continue to be observed, including almsgiving, moral counseling of servants by patrons, and all relevant aspects of Catholic ritual. The attitudes of the young differ according to whether they belong to the upper classes or to the middle class. Some of the younger upper-class members of the Gómez family continue to emphasize the importance of religious teaching to children.

Religious ideology has been strongly influenced by the Jesuits, who teach (among other things) that workers have formal rights whose observance is as important as almsgiving. They tend to be informal about Church rituals and reject the orientation toward the Church hierarchy. They have also strongly opposed the accumulation of wealth by the Church. Gómez family members who have been raised in a modern religious spirit of this kind are still deeply Catholic and participate actively in rituals, though favoring the modern liturgy. Middle-class members of the family are, on the whole, less active in the Church, and their Catholic observance remains more or less one of following formal ritual. The level of religious performance is thus another distinguishing hallmark of the elite.

As far as relations with other faiths are concerned, the ideological behavior is perhaps best illustrated by the following anecdote. A family patriarch was holding a conversation with a relatively open-minded member of the family, and the latter asked: "Did you know, uncle, that Jesus and the Virgin Mary were Jews?" The old man was shocked: "Never say a thing like that. Don't you know it's a sin?" Similar attitudes are found with respect to Protestants. One young Gómez woman had a housemaid who was a Protestant; her mother became exceedingly concerned about the possibility that she might be trying to convert the other servants of the house.

Among the younger generations Protestantism is no longer regarded as a threat, and some Gómez children are educated in German or American secular private schools. Gómez businessmen have become more widely traveled and have had some contacts with foreign businessmen of other faiths. But the marriage of a daughter to someone who was not Catholic would be another matter. Gómez parents continue to be actively concerned about the performance of their children's religious duties, their going to mass regularly, and their taking Communion, long after they are married. The reading of books on religious subjects is also encouraged.

In recent years the Catholic Church has welcomed lay discussion on matters such as birth control, social justice, and the political position of the Church. Members of the Gómez family, old and young, have followed this lead and have talked about religious matters more than in the past. On the whole, the older members let themselves be ruled by the Church hierarchy and the younger people follow the dictates of their own conscience. For example, they use birth control if they feel it is right. Formerly only priests were felt to be sufficiently well informed on questions of religion; now, however, the young people read and study matters related to the conduct of their own lives and feel supported by the Church in so doing.

It should be noted, on the other hand, that the Gómez ideology contains an element of anticlericalism. This appears to derive from the liberal ideology of the nineteenth century, although liberals themselves are despised. Older people often make disparaging comments about the Church as a power group and about priests who do not live up to Church standards and who may be hypocrites. Priests at all levels of the hierarchy are invited as guests and are consulted as indispensable technicians in ceremonial matters; yet they are often criticized as bureaucrats and even dismissed as a necessary evil. Gómez family members never fail to make a clear distinction between the Eternal Religion on the one hand and the Church as a temporal institution on the other. This could explain their reluctance for family members to enter the Church as priests or nuns. Such attitudes are not uncommon among other Catholic groups. Ianni and Reuss-Ianni (1973, 222) point out, for example, that "Italians, even those of the south who are deeply religious, do not really trust their Church as an institution. They have always seen the Church as an independent temporal power as well as a religious institution, and distrust it just as much as any form of government."

Family Values

The grandfamily is regarded as the basis and the center of social life among the Gómez. The couple must remain united. Parents regard their entire life, including business and social prestige, as existing solely for the sake of their children. From the ideal point of view, children take precedence over financial prestige and commercial success. Brothers and sisters always must remain close to each other.

The most prized value is family unity. The importance of fulfilling family duties and remaining loyal to the family is greatly stressed, particularly toward children. In this sense, as in many others, Ianni's description of the Sicilian family ideal closely corresponds to that of the Gómez: "The pattern of family roles mirrors the divine family or Catholicism. The stern, authoritarian father is a patriarch who commands immediate obedience: the true pater familias, who represents the family's power and status within the community. The mother is subservient to the father: her humility, fidelity and willingness to bear all burdens, enshrine the honor of the family and win the respect of her children. Daughters, like mothers, are humble and their chastity is a matter of great moment" (Ianni and Reuss-Ianni 1973, 20-21).

The Gómez family is patrifocal. Status and power are the rewards of masculinity. A man must be in charge, particularly in his home: his wife and children should respect him and even fear him. Within the extended family, status is acquired through the dispensation of patronage, for example, by providing jobs for relatives and by being in a position to grant favors. Man is the protector and the provider; he is an intermediary between the family and the outside world. He has no other domestic duties and none should be required of him. He expects to be waited on and even pampered: it is his due as head of the household. His participation in raising children is indirect; he may occasionally play with his small children or, when they grow up, gradually introduce his sons to certain aspects of a man's world. Child rearing is the direct and formal responsibility of the mother. She must answer to her husband for any details of dress, manners, or scholastic record that may displease him. The children's health too is the mother's responsibility: it is her fault if they are frequently ill, and she will have to correct the situation by herself. Women frequently use the father's authority to discipline children: "watch out, here comes daddy." She is not supposed to have independent authority.

The male ideal is expressed by the three F's: "feo, fuerte, y formal" (ugly, strong, and formal).[1] To be homely (*feo*) means that a male should leave prettification to women and not be

---

[1] See also de la Peña 1984, 211.

concerned with physical appearance. To be strong (*fuerte*) means exercising power over wife and children, being sexually active, and being capable of protecting himself and the members of his family; and being *formal* means being a good Christian, a respectable man, and an unfailing provider. Male children begin learning the masculine role in their relationships with their sisters and female cousins. Later in life, it will be a brother's obligation to watch out for his sisters and protect them, even after they marry; this responsibility also extends to a sister's children. After a father dies the son has the obligation to look after his mother as well.

Male ideology among the Gómez is closely entwined with economic ideology. In many ways there is a correspondence between economic and political beliefs and the ideal masculine role. The heroes of the Gómez embody the ideal values expected of a male. Thus, the gallery of family heroes whose example is held up to the younger generations includes Leopoldo, Leopoldo Jr., Pablo, Saúl, Pedro, and Maximiliano Merino y Pacheco. They have in common the qualities of being "hard working," "good fathers," "good uncles," "loyal to the family," "protective of women," "generous," and "good Catholics," as well as being good providers of income and family status. Some Gómez personalities are held to embody specific aspects of the male ideal: Saúl, Roberto, and Javier embody the physical ideal because they were tall, blond, white-skinned, blue-eyed, and distinguished. There are other blond and fair-skinned members of the Gómez family, but the issue of don Carlos Gómez' first marriage are singled out as representative. Praised for their business skills are Pablo, Pedro, and Ramiro; Saúl and his children Alvaro and Enrique are held up as examples of honesty and rectitude. Pablo and particularly Roberto are cited as having been very fond of women, an ambivalent trait that is nevertheless admired.

Negative traits that detract from the masculine ideal are the opposite of the above. Saúl's sons Alvaro and Enrique, the "poor darlings," were lifelong employees of their uncles and never managed to own a business of their own. Modesto, second son of Mamá Inés, was a "grey" man, without any qualities of distinction. Being under one's wife's authority is a particularly negative trait that is only acknowledged of certain affine relatives. A few Gómez family members, of course, have been cited as opposed in every way to the male ideal: for example, the flamenco dancer and Modesto Jr., who left his wife and served a jail sentence. Extramarital affairs are forgiven as long as family duties are not neglected, but homosexuality or occupations thought to be dishonorable or nonproductive are not tolerated.

Affine males are particularly praised for being good husbands and for showing appreciation of their Gómez wives. This can be overdone, and an affine husband who allowed his wife to take a job would be criticized.

If the masculine ideal among the Gómez is to be in control, the traditional feminine ideal is to be controlled, to be loyal, and to be pure. Female chastity is closely connected with the ideal of virginity at marriage, faithfulness in marriage, and motherhood. Another important feminine ideal is religious devotion.

But the central value of femininity is certainly motherhood. Until recently this meant having a large number of children; a smaller number (three or four) is now acceptable, provided that they are "very well brought up." The mother is held responsible for her children's care and is expected to devote her best efforts to this task; except for the menial tasks of child rearing, such as washing and ironing, she is expected to do everything herself. She will breast-feed her babies, change their diapers, get up at night if they cry, and (later on) select their school, pick them up after school every day, assist them with their homework, and teach them the basics of religion. In recent years, many Gómez girls have taken courses on child care and child psychology as a preparation for marriage and motherhood.

Women who marry a Gómez are expected to be wealthy and it is hoped that they will give their loyalty to their husband, surrendering their private assets so that these can be transferred to their husband's business. The ideal in-law should be submissive and close to the Gómez. Gómez girls, on the other hand, are expected to remain loyal to the Gómez; outstanding Gómez women have been "strong" and this strength implies pulling their husbands and children toward the Gómez side. As a result, there is a double standard for females: an affine is expected to yield allegiance to her husband, but this is contradictory to what is expected from his sisters. The latter are expected to marry for love within a socially acceptable group, which means middle-class professionals of good Catholic stock who are not connected with the world of politics or the government.

A Gómez woman is valued in terms of her capacity to absorb affinal groups in order to raise a nuclear family that identifies with the Gómez tradition. This does not imply that the Gómez sons-in-law should be less than manly: on the contrary, they are expected to conduct themselves in exactly the same patriarchal style as a true Gómez. But the wife remains responsible for ritual and for the conduct of social life in general. Without ceasing to be submissive to their husbands, Gómez daughters are expected to transmit the Gómez ideology to their offspring.

The female ideal thus consists in embodying, reflecting, and amplifying, if possible, the prestige of the male and at the same time being loyal to the group of the Gómez, both as consanguineous and as affinal relatives. The most respected women in the genealogy are the "centralizing women" (Yanagisako 1977, 208-219). These women derive prestige from their self-assumed role of gathering and transmitting family information and from being consulted as authorities on family lore and family tradition. This implies a total commitment to the group, not only in circulating information but in the participation, promotion, and organization of social events. So high is the value attached to these family meetings that their promotion has become a central tenet of female ideology. A woman must be warm and friendly toward relatives and interested in family matters. Her female friends should preferably be relatives, so that most of her daily activities (including shopping or socializing with each other's children) take place within the Gómez family circle. Women frequently initiate informal social contacts between related nuclear families, including small dinner parties, dining out, or going to the movies. Women are expected to be housewives in exchange for the economic protection afforded by their husband: they are not openly allowed to manage their own capital.[2] Female business abilities can only be exercised indirectly, through a husband, a brother, or a son. This ideology is reflected in the process of socialization: girls are expected to listen and learn but not to speak or act; eventually they may have a voice in economic matters but no participation in the decision-making process. Their area of activity outside the home is supposed to be strictly social, not economic (de la Peña 1984, 211-12).

Being a good wife is as important as being a good mother. In fact, being a good mother is also being a good wife and vice versa. A good wife must accept the intellectual and economic superiority of her husband and subordinate her own interests and tastes to those of her husband, often extending to personal matters such as her style of dress. She must be ready to accept and enforce the family ideology in every aspect, including the socialization of her daughters in the feminine ideal. She must maintain good relations with relatives on her own as well as her husband's side. She must be well informed on current family matters, in order not to miss important engagements or ritual activities. In addition she should take the initiative in promoting social reunions within the family, remember the birthdays of relatives, and go to see them if they are ill; she must choose suitable presents for all occasions and provide adequate help for needy relatives. She is also expected to be always ready to welcome her husband's friends and business associates in the home and entertain them as befits the family status, postponing her own social engagements in order to participate in any social gatherings her husband, brothers, or sons may independently have decided to attend. Finally, within these social activities it is expected that a good Gómez wife will

---

[2] Wainerman found the same ideals expressed in the messages of the Catholic Church during the 1950s in Argentina (1980, 16, 29-30).

encourage and further whatever personal connections may be advantageous for the family business.

A statement from an address by Justo Sierra, Porfirian secretary of education in 1901, typifies the feminine ideal in Mexican society: "The educated woman will be truly dedicated to the home; she will be a companion and collaborator of man in the formation of the family. That is what we want. . . . Your calling is to form souls, and to sustain the soul of your husband; for this reason we educate you. Dear child, do not become the feminist in your midst. . . . No, you and we are mutually complementary; we are a single person called upon to continue the perpetuation of the Fatherland . . . while men earn the bread, you are responsible for order, tranquility and the well-being of the home, and above all, you contribute . . . to the formation of souls; this a supreme task. . . . Let men struggle with political questions and write laws; you fight the good fight of the sentiments . . . shaping souls is better than writing laws" (in Vaughan 1979, 66-67).

A woman's desirable qualities will be found embodied in the heroines of Gómez family history. The most frequently cited examples of female perfection are Mamá Inés, prototype of the centralizing mother; Anita, a strong woman who, though childless, was devoted all her life to her nephews and nieces and to the family in general; Cecilia, who endured great suffering because of the early death of two of her sons; Ana María, Cecilia's daughter, a charming, strong, centralizing woman who also endured suffering as a mother. Anita, who was blonde and blue-eyed, is praised as the paramount of physical beauty, though most Gómez women are brunettes. Quite a few Gómez women are held to be excellent wives, good-looking, devoted mothers, or talented cooks.

Juana was admired for her determination and strength of character in standing up to her husband, but the same qualities would not necessarily be admired in an affine woman. Women who are devout are also much admired. Some affine women are admired for their success in boosting the prestige of their husbands, or for their patience in bearing their husband's faults.

As in the case of men, negative qualities are the opposite of the ideal traits. Infidelity is singled out in the case of Elisa, who ran away from home with a servant; Modesta, who married the widower of her own wealthy cousin; the three sisters who successively married their cousin Bernabé; and Dolores, who married a minor politician. Widows who remarry are automatically criticized, because widowhood is held to be sacred. Some women are reputed to be ugly; for example, Roberto's wife is remembered as a good woman who was too dark-skinned, "like a monkey." Some in-laws, including Leopoldo's wife and the wife of Juan Gómez Chacón, are criticized for their aloofness or for putting on airs. On the other hand, kindness in a woman is much admired. María Elvira, Leopoldo's youngest daughter, is much remembered because she adopted her sister's baby daughter after her sister died.

In summary, the ideal woman is a submissive wife and an effective full-time mother. She is kind-hearted and devout; but if strong-willed and powerful she will be especially admired, provided that she is a Gómez and completely loyal to the clan.

Education

Gómez attitudes on education are closely related to those on economics and family values. From early childhood, members are made to feel that belonging to the family is not only an honor but a material advantage. Gómez children have rich uncles who give nice presents; they go to parties and are the object of more attention and care than other children. They may meet a cabinet minister or a famous bullfighter over Sunday breakfast. Their relatives seem to be practically everywhere. The educational value of such experiences is fully realized by the Gómez.

There have been generational changes in the educational ideology of the family, in addition to individual variations depending on the attitude of the affinal parent. On the whole, children are the acknowledged center of attention in the nuclear family. Everything is done for their sake, in the expectation that they will follow in their parents' footsteps and become "the glory and crown of their old age." The informal education of a Gómez child, particularly among the wealthier branches, includes a taste for the good life: good schools, fine cars, swimming pools, travel, and friendships with the sons and daughters of important people. Children give orders to servants with their parents' approval; they are taught values pertaining to their social class. On family occasions children are permitted to listen to favorable or critical comments concerning other people, including family members. These case histories are effective in promoting the internalization of family values.

The formal education of Gómez children is entrusted to private schools. The choice of school depends on the period and family branch. Up to the fourth generation, children were sent to two schools (one for boys and one for girls) belonging to a French religious order. These were the most prestigious upperclass schools in Mexico City at the time, and even the less wealthy among the Gómez sent their children there. They met children from the same social background; the school friends they brought home would be suitable marriage prospects. A wider selection of private schools became available after 1940, and new considerations came into play. Thus, the Merino y Pacheco family began sending their children to the American School, primarily because they felt that English had become a more important language than French. During the 1950s several schools for "Christian businessmen" were opened under the direction of a new religious order sponsored by Pablo Gómez, among other wealthy businessmen, with the active participation of Leopoldo Jr. and Pedro Jiménez. Most members of the wealthy branch now send their children to these schools and eventually to the University of Anahuac, created by the same group during the 1960s. The less wealthy families send their children to middle-class religious schools.

Economics and Power

The prevailing economic ideology among the Gómez stresses private property as a fundamental, self-evident value. They share the nineteenth-century view of private enterprise as "a system characterized by the predominance of rather small, competing firms, each under the guidance of an enterprising and resourceful businessman, who at his own risk continually experiments with various combinations of the productive factor" (Parsons 1961, 150). In this view, the role of government should be limited to maintaining public services and providing the general conditions under which independent business can prosper. These conditions include the maintenance of social order and the basic infrastructure for industrial development. Participation of the state in the production of goods and services is rejected.

The Gómez feel that government lacks the capability for generating profit due to bureaucracy, corruption, and politics in general. This a country like Mexico cannot afford. Rather, the state should support private enterprise because it is productive, efficient, progressive, and patriotic. The entrepreneurs were the builders of modern Mexico, and they alone can serve the nation. State-owned enterprises lose money and hamper the development of the country.

A business enterprise is seen as a device for making money quickly. Long-term investments are uninteresting, and planning is not a major component of business activity. The current heads of the family business still operate under the traditional assumption that a business enterprise is a vehicle for the prestige and the personal power of the owner. By extension, the family itself derives prestige from business ownership. The entrepreneur is not interested in the accumulation of capital for its own sake, but rather as a means for gaining power and prestige.[3]

---

[3] A highly placed government official told us of the following illustrative incident. He had succeeded in interesting a French corporation in marketing a kind of Mexican sweets in France. He then contacted the largest manufacturer of these sweets. This man, a wealthy Mexican entrepreneur, was invited to France and eventually signed an export agreement with the French corporation. However, after a time the Mexican industrialist unilaterally broke the agreement and cancelled the deal. He explained his decision as follows: "You see, the French are sending young men to stick their noses into my factories. They demand quality control and new kinds of packaging, and they conduct themselves as if I were their employee. I'm somebody around here: I play golf with important government people everyday, and I have breakfast with the governor whenever I feel like it. I'm the boss in my industry. I don't need to

Absolute personal control is indispensable; otherwise the entrepreneur would not be in a position to provide jobs for family members at will or to withdraw funds when his prestige requires it. Money is for spending: high living is generosity, because everything is shared with family and friends. Mansions are for lavish entertaining; even travel is done in family groups. Thus, prestige is gotten from money to the extent that it is shared with others.[4]

Hard work as such is not a source of prestige. Family obligations take precedence over business: if an aunt is taken ill, the entrepreneur is expected to drop everything and hurry to her bedside.

Some relevant differences with the ideology of the classical North European entrepreneur can be noted. According to Weber (1965, 155-56), entrepreneurs believe in the value of thrift. So do the Gómez, to the extent that they have a keen sense of the value of money and are sagacious in their purchases, but these are subordinate values that are overruled by generosity. The noble *caballeros* of colonial days were notoriously careless with their money, and thriftiness was regarded as a sign of meanness and low birth. Regard for work is another ideological value found among Weber's entrepreneurs. The Gómez stress the value of hard work; but they do not equate time with money. Thus, important family rituals are held during working hours and family members are expected to attend, regardless of their business commitments. Illness in the family has already been cited as another reason for interrupting the normal work schedule; but even ordinary socializing with relatives or friends may take precedence over work commitments. In fact, social contacts are regarded as an important part of the job, because credit and contracts depend to a large extent on social

---

export even if I do make more money; I have all the money I can use for my prestige and my way of life." Our informant claims that at least three hundred similar cases could be found in recent records. The meaningful element in business for these industrialists is status and personal power: capital is not valued in itself but rather as a means to gain status.

[4] Ladd (1976, 52, 164) found among the Mexican nobility at the time of Independence (around 1910) that lavish expenditure in homes and social entertainment was seen as part of an economic investment.

relations and entertainment. The frugality and work ethic described by Weber is not necessarily conducive to better business in such an environment.

Time spent with relatives or friends is time well spent, in both social and economic terms. On the other hand, cultural activities such as reading, going to a concert, or visiting a museum, which are highly appreciated among other bourgeois cultures, are viewed by the Gómez as a complete waste of time.

Other aspects of Western bourgeois culture, for example, technological development and rational business organization, are admired by the Gómez. However, they tend to view technology as something to be bought ready-made rather than developed for the enterprise. Technology is an expensive import: they will spend on it as much as is strictly necessary and no more. Modernization of an enterprise will not be carried to the extent that it begins to interfere with the authority and the life style of the entrepreneur. Thus, for example, modern accounting procedures are applied reluctantly in compliance with government regulations of which the family disapproves, another difference with Weber's entrepreneurs, who tended to value bureaucratic rationalization.

In their attitudes toward investment, the Gómez place industrial productivity at the top of the scale. However, they tend to feel that long-term investments in real estate or in foreign currency are safer. They do not buy stocks or bonds, nor are they interested in selling shares of their own enterprises to the general public. They prefer to retain total control. Investment in agricultural properties is socially prestigious. Commerce as such is seen as necessary and important but not particularly interesting.

Employment in a firm is seen as a normal stepping stone toward entrepreneurship, but lifelong employees are despised as conformists. Independent professions are esteemed insofar as they carry their own prestige (physicians) or may be useful in building up a business enterprise (architects, engineers, chemists). Political jobs or employment in state corporations or in the civil services are rejected as unsuitable for a Gómez.

Corruption is regarded as inseparable from public office. If an honest, hard-working young man in private business decides to accept a job in public administration, the invariable comment is: "You watch! He'll get rich quickly." Practically all contacts with the civil service are expected to be based on deals of one kind or another, and all bureaucrats are assumed to expect a material reward for their services. Though taking a bribe is considered immoral, offering one is normal business practice and carries no moral stigma. This double standard may be changing; members of the younger generations are beginning to accept positions in civil service. The growing technocratic nature of government has made a career in public administration seem attractive to some individuals with social standing comparable to the Gómez. The government has become increasingly powerful and there are more well-paid officials who no longer depend on small handouts from business people for a living, even if their chiefs still accept large bribes.

Attitudes toward Political Activity

The Gómez tend to reject all political activity as basically demeaning. The only Gómez known to have been a full-time government official was Saúl, during the Porfirio Díaz regime, before the Revolution. Politics is left to the politicians, a peculiar breed not to be antagonized, but who, on the whole, are people with no idea of what business is about.

No Gómez has been known to take any interest in party politics to the extent of becoming a member of the official party or of any other party. Yet the Gómez are definitely politically aware. They have clear concepts about the role of the state and the ideal organization of society. Furthermore, they have been quite effective in promoting and furthering their political ideas through the business associations and the related groups that exist in Mexico as negotiating partners of the state.

One important political activity is informal contact with politicians. Political friendships and acquaintances may be based on an exchange of political services, business, or personal favors. Gómez industrialists are usually personal friends of the mayor in the city or town in which they operate. They are always willing to cooperate with public welfare projects.

They contribute toward building funds for new schools, highways, sanitation works, and so on. They organize testimonial dinners for visiting governors or congressmen and can be counted upon to foot the bill. Whenever they sponsor a community improvement, they carefully leave the final responsibility to the local authorities. And if local officials are in trouble, they will be well received in a Gómez home, where they are certain to find moral and financial support. This policy has earned the Gómez family a vast network of political friendships that can be put in motion as business demands it. Their political prestige extends beyond the authorities, furthermore, to the local population in general.

In general it may be said that the Gómez are not primarily politically minded individuals and do not wish to participate in party politics. Their politicking in the business world is not viewed as a form of partisanship but rather as an aspect of their business activities and as a defense of their special interests as a group. They have no desire to appoint representatives or to found political parties. Neither the PRI nor any other political party is felt to represent them or their interests. Their spokesmen in the trade associations or chambers will use every opportunity to expound through the media the private enterprise ideology with which the family identifies, but this is not seen as politics.

To the extent that the Gómez share the views of the private sector on political economy, any statement that questions the legitimacy of private property is viewed with alarm. Any leftist tendency is automatically labeled communism. This is particularly noticeable among the older family members. The main threat from the Left is perceived as loss of status: it is the one thing the Gómez resent most directly. They feel acutely that communism would deprive them of their social standing; only as an afterthought do they fear that communism would set up a strong state that would meddle with their business. Communism is to be feared primarily because it goes against family values. It will "take the children away," in the sense that the state will take over education and turn the children against the values of tradition and family loyalty. The Gómez are worried about the secularization of society for the same reason. Most family members feel that education as currently imparted at Mexican state universities is communistic. Some of the younger generation, however, reject the Soviet system but agree with a number of left-wing claims, including the need for more social equality and increased state participation in accordance with the new teachings of the Church. This annoys some of the older generation, who are disconcerted about the change in Church politics in Latin America. There are considerable differences in political views even among the younger generation: women, for example, are more frightened by communism, as they are by anything that seems to threaten their family life.

Nationalism

The Gómez pride themselves on being nationalists. They feel that they have built up business enterprises and thereby helped to develop and modernize Mexico. They affirm their love of their country and feel that it should occupy a position among the most civilized nations. The Mexico they have in mind is definitely the part of the country that springs from Spanish roots. The Indian heritage, they feel, is a heavy burden that has to be thrown off in order to enable the country to rise in the modern world. This attitude is not without ambivalence: for example, affines of Spanish origin are welcomed into the family but are also made to feel that they are foreigners and not true Mexicans.

Nationalism among the Gómez is frequently expressed by the adoption of country-life patterns, "charro" traditions, Mexican food, and particularly veneration for the Virgin of Guadalupe.

The Gómez have ambivalent attitudes toward Americans. They are admired and frequently visited: some Gómez businessmen own real estate in the United States and travel there regularly on shopping trips. They admire American progress, highways, orderly traffic, and advanced medical technology. They dislike and sharply disagree with its family life: Americans allow their marriages to break up and their children to leave home at an early age. The children are spoiled brats who talk back to their parents; aged persons cannot rely on their sons to take care of them; brothers and sisters don't get along; young girls lead immoral lives. Thus, admiration for the United States as a place to visit and as a bulwark against communism does not encourage them to send their young children to be educated there. They are apprehensive about their sons becoming bad-mannered and eventually marrying an American.

A somewhat similar ambivalence may be observed in respect to multinational corporations operating in Mexico. Foreign investments are welcomed because they bring money into the country: how else could Mexico get the necessary capital for development? If they closed down the multinationals, thousands would become jobless. The multinationals are private corporations and must be respected as such; if they want to take their profits out of the country, they have a right to do so. Competition between Mexican industry and foreign multinationals is not particularly emphasized. The more traditional Gómez entrepreneurs dislike multinationals as partners because they refuse to relinquish control of their businesses to the corporations. Yet they find it logical that a more powerful partner will attempt to take them over and they do not see multinationals as intrinsically evil. This interesting attitude about foreign business may be partly due to the idea that a Latin businessman, and particularly a Gómez, is supposed to be brighter and less naive than a "gringo."

The Gómez world traveler allows his nationalistic ideology to be expressed in all sorts of comments about foreign peoples and customs. In general, foreigners are stereotyped and compared unfavorably with people and customs back home. Thus, Germans are held to be stiff though unquestionably hardworking and meticulous. Frenchmen are unpleasant, though something can be said for their culture, their elegance, and their cooking. The English are insufferable, and the Italians are absolutely chaotic, which makes their excellent art, industry, and cooking all the more mysterious. The Gómez do not see the Orient: it is far too frightening. As for the rest of Latin

America, it has almost nothing to show or teach the Gómez. Visiting such places is held to be a waste of time.

The Spanish are the only foreigners who seem to be exempt from such criticism. Spain after the Second World War and before the death of Franco represented the ideal country to many Gómez, who admired progress and a strong centralized state, respect for the Catholic religion, solid family values, and the nobility of men and women who prided themselves on their origins. "Even the lowliest fisherman has a decent home," they would say. After the Second World War, members of the family traveled frequently to Spain and became increasingly identified with that country and adopted Spanish customs. For example, on the Gómez ranches the Mexican saddle was replaced by the Cordoban saddle and the traditional Mexican charro costume fell into disuse.

It can be said that the Gómez nationalism is of a special kind. The Mexican upper classes were once of purely European extraction; but the mestizo industrialists who rose to power on the wave of the Revolution proclaimed themselves Mexicans. Mexican traditions became upper-class values. Thus, the Gómez are proud of their devotion to the Virgin of Guadalupe, of their fine Mexican cooking, and of their traditional Mexican hospitality. They feel deeply that they stand for everything that is best in Mexican values; and in this sense they do not behave as representatives of a relatively small interest group but of Mexico itself. If challenged, they will defend their values and their world view as true and valid for all Mexicans irrespective of class or party allegiance.

The Gómez view of Mexican society and Mexican politics may be summarized as follows: entrepreneurs are at the top of Mexican society and deservedly so, because the nation owes its development to the efforts of business and industry. It is deplorable that the state is continuously encroaching upon the area of competence of private business. The recent increase in public investments and the gradual takeover of major industries by the state are seen as tragic developments in which private business is forced to play a secondary role in industrial development. Yet an organized political response to these statist tendencies is seen as inappropriate and perhaps futile. The political elite already owns the country: "They live like lords, if ever there were lords who enjoyed that kind of high living. . . . They have everything and risk nothing." Politics is equated with corruption, nepotism, and demagogy: the politicians have taught the lower classes to expect everything without working harder in return. They do not teach them their obligations because they rely on the support of the masses for remaining in power.

Discussion

There are interesting and revealing inconsistencies and ambivalences in the family ideology. An ideology is not a static system: on the contrary, it reflects social change and conflict. On the one hand, conduct becomes institutionalized through repetition; on the other, some members of the group, especially the young, begin to perceive inconsistencies between the ideology and reality or absorb ideological features from other social groups. Such new elements may eventually become incorporated into the family ideology without necessarily displacing older and possible contradictory features. The coexistence of contradictory elements within the same ideology enables individuals or subgroups in the kinship network to identify with different positions and still remain in the fold as recognized members, with a valid claim to participating in the family tradition. New ideological elements may eventually become modified to fit the general orientation of the family ideology, which corresponds to a well-defined class position. But certain key motifs in the family ideology have not varied over time: the importance of power and status, the central role of private property, male supremacy, Catholicism, and loyalty to family values.

Ambivalences in the Gómez family ideology have occurred when traditional or even feudal values, corresponding to the criollo ideal, clash with bourgeois industrial values or, more recently, with modern technocratic values. The social roles corresponding to each of these ideals may require entirely different attitudes and skills. The criollo is lordly and extrava-

gant, the bourgeois is hard-working and thrifty, and the technocrat is clever and pragmatic. All three may have authority,
dominance, and status. What matters in the end is prestige,
family pride, skill in the exercise of power, and loyalty toward
relatives and dependents, particularly women.

Another source of contradiction is found in the racial attitude of the family. Admiration for the white race and Spanish
lineage is accompanied by deprecation of everything dark-
skinned and Indian. Yet the family is mestizo and its Indian
heritage cannot be denied. This contradiction is usually solved
by making Indian-ness a matter of behavior and life style
rather than one of blood. Being dark-skinned does not matter
if one lives like a white man (Aguilar 1978).

There is considerable ambivalence also in the Gómez attitude toward foreigners. This refers particularly to the United
States, though Spain was formerly regarded with the same
mixture of admiration and mistrust. Americans are admired
and imitated on the one hand and ridiculed or dismissed on the
other. Individualism, practicality, and rationality of conduct in
business and public affairs are traits that are widely admired,
though they are also perceived as threatening to cherished personal and family values. This ambiguity is seen most sharply in
the areas of child care and education. Most Gómez children
are sent to private schools where foreign language instruction
is included as part of a conscious philosophy of modernity that
is derived directly from America or Europe, but schools that
succeed too well in this are avoided. Parents have a very real
fear of losing control over their offspring because of the negative influence of schooling.

As for religion, being wealthy and a good Christian was not
thought of as an inconsistency in the past, when the orientation of the Catholic church was still overwhelmingly conservative. Almsgiving and caring for the poor, going to mass, and
building churches were the essence of being a good Christian.
More recently there has been a great deal of pastoral emphasis
on social injustices that the Church sees as its mission to correct. Among the younger family members some have strongly

identified with this position, thus generating a certain amount of conflict in the family.

Attitudes toward the state represent another source of ideological contradiction. The political establishment is openly criticized and rejected; individual politicians are not socially accepted. The central power of government is constantly disparaged due to its corruption and its inefficiency or lack of economic ability. On the other hand, it is accepted as self-evident that the state must be there to protect private industry; in fact, the Gómez entrepreneurs are strongly dependent on the state. They work for and with state organizations and are frequently in personal contact with representatives of official agencies. They also criticize the official party but would be seriously concerned were the party to be truly threatened. They entertain high government officials like lords and then criticize them because of their lordly pretentions. The growth of the state apparatus is viewed with alarm, yet simultaneously there is a desire for national greatness, as expressed, among other things, by a powerful state apparatus.

Contradictions can also be detected in the social self-image of the Gómez. Although they are at the top of Mexican society, they feel utterly dependent on others. Both feelings may be real in a sense, but the importance of the Gómez social position is probably more a thing of the past than of the present. In this respect the Gómez ideology may well prove a hindrance in the process of successful adaptation to changing social and economic conditions.

An important ideological contradiction arises over the tension and conflict between consanguinity and affinity. There is a double standard in the sense that the behavior expected of a sister is the opposite of that expected of a wife. However, there is no real inconsistency in that both are expected to behave in the best interest of the Gómez family. The same is true of male relatives and male affines: in-laws are expected to cleave to the Gómez, but a Gómez man is sharply criticized when he identifies with his own in-laws. Open conflict is avoided through following social formalities. Thus, affines are respected for maintaining their formal obligations toward their consanguinity group. Close relatives of an affine are respectfully treated and children are acknowledged to belong to both family groups. The conflict is always there even if latent, however, and is never fully solved. An affine woman once complained that "the ideal of a Gómez man is to marry a test-tube baby." And a Gómez woman replied that her ideal husband would be an "orphan."

There is some contradiction in the ideal of womanhood. Two opposite types of women are admired: the heroic woman who is authoritarian, strong, domineering, and powerful and the meek, submissive, and utterly devoted housewife. Both types have been valuable assets in the history of the Gómez kin; in their own way, both have contributed to maintaining the social dominance of the family.

In general, it may be said that the contradictions and inconsistencies in the family ideology are more apparent than real. They can usually be resolved by deferring to the first priority, family interest.

There might be another contradiction between the values of the male (which include being a conqueror of women) and the values of a good husband and a good Christian. This is dealt with at the individual level rather than in general. What is a grievous offense in a man of low prestige may be regarded as a minor fault or even an endearing quality in a highly regarded family member. Infringing a norm is one matter; breaking them all is another. An excess of machismo is easily forgiven in an aggressive and successful businessman, since it seems somehow connected with his qualities of leadership. Straying from the straight and narrow path may be excusable in a man, but is definitely forbidden to a woman.

The ideology of an upper-class Mexican family can be traced to heterogeneous beliefs and values taken from the dominant ideology in areas such as religion, class, nationalism, and modernization. These ideas are reinterpreted by the group according to its historical experience, which is a result of its occupying a well-defined place in the economic and social structure of Mexico. There are individual shadings of opinion, discrepancies, and even internal contradictions among the

Gómez on any or all of these ideological points. However, when such apparent inconsistencies are analyzed more closely, they can usually be resolved on grounds of family interest. No ideology is monolithic; it develops according to the contradictions and conflicts within the group and in society at large. Some conflicts (as between consanguineous and affinal kin) are perennial, however, and cannot be resolved.

It is here that the value of ideology as an instrument of group solidarity becomes most clearly apparent. Ideology does not have to be consistent: it is enough for it to provide answers that will enable the group interests to prevail on every issue. The Gómez ideology should not be analyzed critically as a single doctrine or dismissed as fantasy or wishful thinking; it is an organized body of values and beliefs that provides specific responses to all conceivable situations members of the group may encounter.

Conclusions

THE GÓMEZ family is representative of what might be called the "family bourgeoisie" of Mexico. Its history is typical of the rise of new urban classes in Mexico, including the bourgeoisie and some middle-class sectors. The bourgeoisie did not originate from within the class of landowners but sprang from traders and small manufacturers who became industrialists. This transition took place in Mexico after the mid-nineteenth century in a specific cultural context and as part of the historical stage of modernization.

The ethnographic description of the Gómez has provided examples of economic behavior that seem at variance with classical forms of capitalism. As a mode of production, capitalism implies a set of relationships between actors in production. When introduced into a different sociocultural setting from the one in which it originated, it tends to adapt to the new local conditions, including the historical context, socio-economic conditions, and local culture. Thus the relations of production are modified both ways: through changes that affect the recipient society and through a cultural redefinition of the capitalistic mode of production in terms of the prevailing cultural system. Individuals turned actors of capitalism behave according to their values and their traditional system of social relations.

A society is shaped by its culture. It incorporates and transforms innovation within its own terms of reference; eventually, innovation also becomes a part of the culture and transforms it. British capitalism was an integral part of a specific sociocultural system, though some of its peculiarities may have been heralded as "laws" of the mode of production, in the belief that their logic was part of the supracultural logic of economics.

In Mexico, capitalism was introduced under different conditions. It arose during a period of structural change and initially it was not self-supporting. The state was weak and capital accumulation did not suffice to introduce a new system of production. Therefore the early bourgeoisie had to resort to existing family strategies in order to create its own conditions of survival and development. These family strategies had always been a part of the Mexican social system. The family was and remains a privileged symbol of exchange throughout history. It is the pivot of the culture and the core of social networks. Thus the family defines the strategies for gaining access to resources (economic and social) by members of the society. For example, in the early days of faltering state power, weak institutions, and frequent political changes, the system increasingly relied on personal connections. Social networks became the main vehicles for mobilizing available resources: they became social capital.

It is because social capital is convertible to economic capital that a broad range of activity was (and continues) to be deployed in order to maintain and extend social networks. This effort costs money. Conspicuous consumption and an expensive life style are the symbolic trappings of social position and group affiliation: not only are they a symbolic language, they also represent an investment.

If the local conditions were inhospitable to capital accumulation, the fledgling entrepreneurs had to manage their transition from traders to industrialists by leaning on groups or institutions with independent means. Outside the state, these were primarily the Church and foreign capital. The efforts of the early Mexican capitalists were aimed at extending their social networks in the direction of these capital resources. When one source dried out or was replaced by new sources, the capitalists modified their social strategies. Thus, after the Revolution some members of the Gómez family sought to gain access to the circle of state politicians: in some cases such connections were even ritualized by compadrazgo. Leadership in the family has always gone to the innovators who found appropriate social strategies for gaining access to new resources.

The pattern of social relations based on the cultural meaning of the family and the importance of personal networks has not always served the process of capitalization. At times it has been a hindrance. The fragmentation of property at death works against the continuity of capital accumulation. Even in the entrepreneur's lifetime, there is a trend toward scattering of resources due to the cultural power ideal, in which each grown son must head a subsidiary firm. Patterns of centralized authority and patronage have sometimes restricted the scope of development of enterprise. These features of family business may be attributed to cultural factors, such as the position of the father as patron of his sons and protector of his sisters and their children. The restrictive aspects of family enterprise may have made it less competitive with modern corporate intruders on the Mexican economic scene.

On the other hand, and in the light of recent historical trends such as the nationalization of the banks and Mexico's financial troubles of the 1980s, the family enterprise remains a viable form of confronting economic crisis. An economic system in which the grandfamily is still a central entrepreneurial organization can be expected to work tolerably well. It provides a basis for confidence and loyalty that is often lacking in the more individualistic corporate life in the United States, and it also has a certain flexibility that helps it adjust to a chronically unstable economic and political environment.

Internal Organization of the Family Enterprise Complex

Understanding the "family bourgeoisie" requires an unconventional approach to the study of business enterprise. The relevant economic unit is not the enterprise or even the group of enterprises headed by a given owner. It is a cluster of businesses of different sizes and in different fields of the economy, an informal conglomerate that is controlled by the family as a whole. This point of view is essential; it affords a new insight into decision making that is hardly possible when one looks at the component firms one by one.

The family bourgeoisie is based on an articulated network of minor or complementary firms tied to the main group of enterprises by kinship and patronage. They can be derived from the structure of the grandfamily, and they parallel the process of kin segmentation. A young man may start his business career working directly under his father or uncle. His capital of social connections will increase until the time comes for him to establish himself as an independent entrepreneur. Depending on his kinship rank he will be assigned a parallel or subordinate role in the general structure of family businesses: jobbing, manufacturing parts, contracting, trucking, or managing wholesale or retail outlets. The patron will make it his business and his responsibility as a father or kinsman to vouch for the new entrepreneur and to guide him through the financial arrangements. Once established, the patron will be his principal business partner or client.

The entrepreneur's sons will inherit separate business firms upon his death, yet these firms will in general be interdependent because the entrepreneur will have set them up with an eye for complementarity or cooperation. Thus there is a continuing solidarity involving exchange of information, sharing of contacts, temporary deals, and joint ventures between brothers. The Mexican family bourgeoisie cannot be studied from the vantage point of a firm-by-firm approach. Rapid informal communication between widely separated branches of the business network affords a tremendous flexibility and ease of adaptation to changing situations. This flexibility extends to coping with the problem of changing technological conditions; a technologically well-trained relative may be more reliable in a firm than an unrelated one because of his expected loyalty. Thus the kinship group is able to survive in a high-risk environment with a low level of investment.

It is essential to keep in mind, however, that an informal network of kin enterprises is not the same thing as a corporation or a financial group. There is no central management, no joint policy, no common financial backing. This difference between family and corporate business helps explain the peculiarities of large Mexican groups, such as the Monterrey group, which are "corporate" in name only. Such groups tend to favor protectionist policies because they are more interested in their survival as a high-status kinship network than in challenging the supremacy of new, anonymous, capital-intensive capitalist corporations.

Cultural Features of the Family

The kinship system in Mexico is based on the three-generation grandfamily. This is the building block of the society, its fundamental unit of economic, ritual, and social solidarity. Its cohesion is consanguinity by bilateral descent.

The larger unit that is recognized in the kinship system is the kindred, a network that radiates outward from the grandfamily and includes alliances with other grandfamilies through affinity. The kindred thus includes a large group of people bound by mutual acknowledgment of kinship: it is a social ego-centered network with rules of inclusion and exclusion. The significant interaction among members of the society generally creates areas of intersection between different kindreds or within a given kindred. Whenever these areas of intersection generate a community of interest between segments of kinship networks, the resulting alliances or efforts toward assimilation tend to evolve a shared symbolic language that includes a life style, a political ideology, an educational background, and so on.

These features of the kinship system can be found throughout history and across social classes: they are an outstanding feature of Mexican culture. The specific outward expressions of kin solidarity, as well as the strategies of alliances, vary according to social classes and according to the economic and political conditions of the social system. However, the basic elements of the kinship system appear to have been essentially invariant since colonial times in its expression in the economy (e.g., occupational and survival solidarity), social life (rituals, social networks, and life styles), and politics. These manifestations include residential patterns, kinds of goods and services exchanged, the extension of the kindred utilized in exchange patterns, and the choice of marriage partners. The formal communalities of the Mexican kinship system allow a flexible range of uses of the relationships that it engenders.

The Gómez family affords an example of the ways in which

the Mexican family bourgeoisie fuses its family ideals with its economic strategies: the family enterprise complex. Other classes and social groups, however, display different forms of articulation between kinship and economic subsistance. The peasant economic system relies on kinship relations not only for its internal organization but for its relations with other levels of integration. For the urban "informal sector," previous migration constitutes a key economic strategy, limiting the capacity to gather the entire grandfamily together. On the other hand, extreme employment insecurity promotes intense economic and social interaction with kin and residential proximity to them. The salaried middle class has an even lesser ability to control the residential proximity of kin than the urban informal sector; nevertheless, the greater continuity of the middle class in an urban environment allows occasional interaction with the larger circle of the kindred. Interactions in urban middle-class kinship networks are more diversified than among the urban poor and somewhat less formal than in the hierarchical family bourgeoisie. The relatively diversified kinship network in the urban middle class is crucial for job placement as well as for acquiring the bonuses that are crucial for maintaining a comfortable life style in a highly bureaucratized environment.

A key problem for the analysis of any cross-class kindreds is that some of them have developmental sequences that imply class diversification. The urban poor have or can acquire peasant and proletarian working-class relatives; middle-class professionals may have upper or lower middle-class or bourgeois relatives. It is known, however, that the ideology of family unity ("family consciousness") prevails over that of class distinction.

In the case presented here, economic differences inside the grandfamily have not resulted in recognition of class differentiation. Wealth and status differences within the grandfamily are recognized only as differences in "life style."

As the family branches out and stratification continues, class differences in the kindred do become recognized, though grandfamilies within it are seen as belonging to a single class.

At some point the kindred recognizes itself to be an entity within which there is a communality of status that prevails over the tensions emerging from class oppositions.

Members of the Gómez kindred are conscious of the class affiliations of the different grandfamilies. Nevertheless, the kindred is a stronger source of group loyalty than class membership. At the same time, the existence of class tension within the kindred is a fundamental explanation for the importance of ritual life. The patron-client ties and the set of mutual loyalties and obligations that are reinforced and expressed within these rituals and in the economic environment are the reason for the predominance of family over class.

Political Participation

In the corporative structure of Mexican politics, the Gómez belong to the sector known as "private initiative." The other two formal sectors are: the public sector (i.e., the federal and state administrations and the related network of agencies, systems, public corporations, and services) and the labor sector.

From the time of their inception, the Gómez were active participants in the organizations of the private initiative sector, the chambers and the associations. These formal entrepreneurial organizations are recognized by the Mexican state as representatives of business. Hence the government deals with chambers and associations and not with individual business concerns. Membership in these organizations is compulsory for any established business, but the Gómez have always occupied prominent positions in the sectoral leadership.

Historically, the Mexican state sees itself as a protector and patron of the private initiative sector; in exchange, private initiative has had a function—namely, to industrialize the country. The Mexican state is not a classical bourgeois state in the sense that other capitalistic societies are described as such. Instead, the symbiotic relationship between the public sector and the private initiative sector may be seen as a complex interaction, part cooperation and part competition, between two social classes: the "new class" of politicians and administrators, and the bourgeoisie. The power elite of Mexico is not identical with the class of owners of the means of production: one deals in capital, the other deals in power. Their class interests are different. The relations between the two dominant sectors involve ongoing negotiations for an increasing share of the national resources.

Each sector has its loyalties and preferences that amount to a life style. However, there is enough complementarity between their respective class interests to allow for a variety of personal contacts. Thus the top politicians place their investments in the private initiative sector and the sons and daughters of entrepreneurs may occupy administrative or technical positions in the bureaucracy.

The verticality of structural relations based on patron-client loyalties poses a problem for social class theory. A sector is not a horizontally stratified social formation with a common relationship to the means of production. It is a vertical bloc cemented by loyalty networks: the cohesion afforded by loyalty, including family loyalty, can overcome some of the effects of income differentials between different levels within the sector.

Among the Gómez, for example, the lower-income branches have often depended on the patronage of their more affluent relatives; therefore, their system of loyalties is organized vertically along patron-client relationships, in which the patron's economic and social position represents prestige and security for the clients. These patron-client bonds tend to weaken and disappear as genealogical, social, and economic distances widen, and when that occurs, one may begin to talk about the appearance of social class differences and the disappearance of kinship bond recognition.

Personal loyalty has been remarkably neglected in theories of class struggle. Had cultural factors been taken into account, these theories would have done more exploration of the loyalty and *confianza* and their role in the class structure. On the basis of our ethnographic findings, we believe that both the economic system (and its relations of production) and the political system are shaped by the kinship system.

The Gómez family is a part of Mexico, solidly incorporated in the private initiative sector, a label that locates them in terms of the Mexican economic and political system. Examining Gómez kinship, however—their relationship among themselves and with the world at large—is a means of apprehending the basic family metaphor on which the system patterns its relationships, both of domination and subordination and of cooperation and solidarity. Understanding kinship is thus a way of attaining insight into the inner workings of the society itself.

Five Generations of the Gómez Family

A s in the text, Roman numerals in the appendix indicate generation. Arabic numbers indicate the family member's individual code. A first spouse is coded e′, the second e″. Nuclear families of one generation may appear with no direct descendants listed in the next generation if most of our Gómez have lost touch with them. When spouses or children are known to exist but their first names are unknown, a code number is assigned but no name given. (S) after a name indicates an adult who never married; no symbol is given if the individual has not yet reached adulthood or if information is lacking. (≠) is placed after a spouse's name if the marriage ended in separation or divorce. (†) indicates an individual who died young, usually before reaching marriageable age.

GENERATION I

I 1	Pedro Luis Gómez
I e′1	María de Jesús Mora y Mota
I e″1	Carmen Ponce de León
I 2	Antonio Gómez
I e′2	name unknown
I 3	Carlos Gómez
I e′3	Ana Balbuena Barrientos
I e″3	Inés Aburto (Mamá Inés)
I 4	Catalina Gómez
I 5	nun; name unknown (S)
I 6	nun; name unknown (S)
I 7	nun; name unknown (S)
I 8	female; name unknown
I e′8	name unknown

GENERATION II

nuclear family of 1,1 and 1,e′1

II 9	Amable Gómez

II e'9	Josefina Salinas
II 10	Luis Gómez
II e'10	María de Jesús Fernández Amieva
II 11	María Guadalupe Gómez
II e'11	Juan Miranda

nuclear family of 1,2 and 1,e'2

II 12	Manuel Gómez
II e'12	name unknown

nuclear family of 1,3 and 1,e'3

II 13	Carlos Gómez Balbuena
II e'13	name unknown
II 14	Roberto Gómez Balbuena
II e'14	Albina Mora
II 15	Saúl Gómez Balbuena
II e'15	María Campos

nuclear family of 1,3 and 1,e"3

II 16	Leopoldo Gómez Aburto (Leopoldo Sr.)
II e'16	Juana Casés
II 17	Modesto Gómez Aburto (Modesto Sr.)
II e'17	Amada Moreno
II 18	Magdalena Gómez Aburto (S)
II 19	Augusto M. Onofre Gómez Aburto†
II 20	Rosalía Gómez Aburto
II e'20	Ramiro Bañuelos
II 21	Cecilia Gómez Aburto
II e'21	Blas Jiménez
II 22	Anita Gómez Aburto
II e'22	David Camarena

GENERATION III

III 23	Bernabé Gómez Salinas
III e'23	same as III,55
III e"23	same as III,56
III e‴23	same as III,60

nuclear family of II,10 and II,e'10
(spouses unknown)

III 24	Luis Gómez Fernández
III 25	Leopoldo Gómez Fernández
III 26	Amalia Gómez Fernández

nuclear family of II, II and II,e'II
(most spouses unknown)

III 27	Juan Miranda Gómez
III e'27	name unknown
III 28	Amado Miranda Gómez
III 29	María Miranda Gómez
III 30	Amalia Miranda Gómez
III 31	Luis Miranda Gómez
III 32	Conchita Miranda Gómez
III 33	Soledad Miranda Gómez
III 34	Juanita Miranda Gómez
III e'34	Javier Ordóñez

nuclear family of II,13 and II,e'13

III 35	Carlos Gómez (second family name unknown)

nuclear family of II,14 and II,e'14

III 36	José Gómez Mora
III e'36	Micaela Gutiérrez de Gómez
III 37	Lourdes Gómez Mora (S)
III 38	Felipe Gómez Mora (S)
III 39	Javier Gómez Mora
III e'39	same as III,42 ($\neq$)

nuclear family of II,14 (adopted by II,22)

III 40	Carmelita Gómez (S)

nuclear family of II,15 and II,e'15

III 41	Rosalía Gómez Campos (S)
III 42	Josefina Gómez Campos
III e'42	same as III,39 ($\neq$)
III 43	Alvaro Gómez Campos
III e'43	Cecilia Villa
III 44	Lucrecia Gómez Campos (S)
III 45	Amalia Gómez Campos (S)
III 46	Enrique Gómez Campos
III e'46	María del Carmen González
III 47	Luz María Gómez Campos
III e'47	José Ortíz

nuclear family of II,16 and II,e'16

III 48	Juana Gómez Casés
III e'48	Agustín Merino y Pacheco
III 49	María de Lourdes Gómez Casés†

III e′ 49	Adolfo Aguirre (later III,e′ 57)
III 50	Leopoldo Gómez Casés (Leopoldo Jr.)
III e′ 50	Magdalena Benítez
III 51	Pablo Gómez Casés (Pablo Sr.)
III e′ 51	Juana Chacón
III 52	María Leticia Gómez Casés
III e′ 52	Genaro Montalvo
III 53	Elvira Gómez Casés
III e′ 53	Fausto Corona (≠)
III 54	María Elisa Gómez Casés
III e′ 54	Patrocinio Aguilar

nuclear family of II,17 and II,e′17

III 55	Inés Gómez Moreno
III e′ 55	same as III,23
III 56	Amalia Gómez Moreno
III e′ 56	same as III,23
III 57	Modesta Gómez Moreno
III e′ 57	same as III,e′ 49
III 58	Susana Gómez Moreno
III e′ 58	Lucio Ramos
III 59	Modesto Gómez Moreno (Modesto Jr.)
III e′ 59	Elvira Núñez
III 60	Celina Gómez Moreno
III e′ 60	same as III,23
III e″ 60	Manuel Dávila

nuclear family of II,20 and II,e′20

III 61	Rosalía Bañuelos Gómez
III e′ 61	Ruperto Mújica
III 62	Alfredo Bañuelos Gómez
III e′ 62	Amalia Fábregas
III 63	Herminia Bañuelos Gómez
III e′ 63	Teófilo Gutiérrez
III 64	Roberto Bañuelos Gómez (S)
III 65	Consuelo Bañuelos Gómez (S)
III 66	Ramiro Bañuelos Gómez
III e′ 66	same as III,69
III 67	Juan Leopoldo Bañuelos Gómez
III e′ 67	(first name unknown) Roca
III 68	Soledad Bañuelos Gómez(S)

nuclear family of II,21 and II,e′21
III 69   Ana María Jiménez Gómez
III e′69   same as III,66
III 70   Blas Jiménez Gómez†
III 71   Blas Jiménez Gómez†
III 72   Pedro (Joaquín) Jiménez Gómez
III e′72   María Mercedes Larrázuri

GENERATION IV

nuclear family of III,55 and III,e′55 (III,23)
(spouses unknown)
IV 73   Bernabé Gómez Gómez (Bernabé Jr.)
IV 74   Alfredo Gómez Gómez
IV 75   Carlos Gómez Gómez
IV 76   Amalia Gómez Gómez
IV 77   Rodrigo Gómez Gómez

nuclear family of III,60 and III,e′60 (III,23)
IV 78   María Guadalupe Gómez Gómez(S)

nuclear family of III,39 and III,e′39 (III,42) (≠)
IV 79   María Gómez Gómez
IV e′79   Oscar Garza Ruíz
IV 80   Javier Gómez Gómez
IV e′80   Maritte Coure

nuclear family of III,43 and III,e′43
IV 81   Enrique Gómez Villa
IV e′81   María del Consuelo Alvarez
IV 82   Consuelo Gómez Villa
IV e′82   Panfilo Suárez
IV 83   Alvaro Gómez Villa
IV e′83   Diana Ortíz
IV 84   Alma Gómez Villa
IV e′84   Ernesto Ascencio
IV 85   Amelia Gómez Villa (S)
IV 86   Arcelia Gómez Villa
IV e′86   Alfonso Mijares

nuclear family of III,46 and III,e′46
IV 87   María del Carmen Gómez González (S)
IV 88   Enrique Gómez González
IV e′88   Cecilia Ruíz

IV 89	Susana Gómez González
IV e'89	(first name unknown) Vertíz
IV 90	Luz María Gómez González
IV e'90	Ernesto (surname unknown)
IV 91	Lupe Gómez González
IV e'91	Miguel Kemper
IV 92	Lucila Gómez González
IV e'92	Martín Núñez
IV 93	Carolina Gómez González (S)
IV 94	Guillermo Gómez González

nuclear family of III,47 and III,e'47
(In addition to IV,95, there were five more sons and one daughter; names unknown; spouses and further descendants unknown.)

IV 95	Javier Ortíz Gómez
IV e'95	Paloma Casas

nuclear family of III,48 and III,e'48

IV 96	Juana Merino y Pacheco Gómez
IV e'96	Celso Iturriaga
IV 97	Agustín Merino y Pacheco Gómez
IV e'97	Emilia Toriello
IV 98	Alicia Merino y Pacheco Gómez
IV e'98	Pedro Benítez
IV 99	Maximiliano Merino y Pacheco Gómez
IV e'99	Berta Ascencio
IV 100	Josefina Merino y Pacheco Gómez
IV e'100	Enrique Heinze

nuclear family of III,49 and III,e'49

IV 101	Lourdes (Luli) Aguirre Gómez
IV e'101	Miguel Romero(≠)

nuclear family of III,50 and III,e'50

IV 102	Lupe Gómez Benítez
IV e'102	Jorge Toriello
IV 103	Leopoldo Gómez Benítez (Leopoldo III)
IV e'103	Magdalena Durán
IV 104	Juana Gómez Benítez
IV e'104	Jorge Garza
IV 105	Magdalena Gómez Benítez
IV e'105	Federico Piña Solórzano
IV 106	Ramiro Gómez Benítez
IV e'106	Berta Gómez (no relation)

IV 107	Lourdes Gómez Benítez
IV e'107	Adolfo Gutiérrez
IV 108	Lucila Gómez Benítez
IV e'108	Samuel Urbina

nuclear family of III,51 and III,e'51

IV 109	Pablo Gómez Chacón (Pablo Jr.)
IV e'109	Covadonga Gómez (no relation)
IV 110	Juan Gómez Chacón
IV e'110	Montserrat Mingot
IV 111	Leopoldo Jorge Gómez Chacón
IV e'111	María Elvira Romero
IV 112	María Guadalupe Gómez Chacón
IV e'112	Alberto Alcocer
IV 113	Juana Gómez Chacón
IV e'113	César Calvo

nuclear family of III,52 and III,e'52

IV 114	Genaro Montalvo Gómez
IV e'114	Soledad Lippert
IV 115	María Leticia Montalvo Gómez
IV e'115	Pablo Palacios Galván (≠)

nuclear family of III,53 and III,e'53 (≠)

IV 116	Alberto Corona Gómez
IV e'116	name unknown
IV 117	Carmen Corona Gómez (S)
IV 118	María Corona Gómez (S)
IV 119	Fausto Corona Gómez
IV e'119	name unknown

nuclear family of III,54 and III,e'54

IV 120	Pilar Aguilar Gómez
IV e'120	Enrique W.
IV 121	Patrocinio Aguilar Gómez (S)
IV 122	Ernesto Aguilar Gómez†

nuclear family of III,57 and III,e'57 (III,e'49)

IV 123	Adolfo Aguirre Gómez
IV e'123	Betty (surname unknown)
IV 124	Felipe Aguirre Gómez
IV e'124	Carolina Ramos

nuclear family of III,59 and III,e'59

IV 125	Modesto Gómez Núñez
IV e'125	same as IV,130 (≠)

nuclear family of III,61 and III,e'61

IV 126	Alvaro Mújica Bañuelos
IV e'126	name unknown
IV 127	Soledad Mújica Bañuelos (S)
IV 128	Berta Mújica Bañuelos
IV e'128	Alfredo Galán (later IV,e'131)
IV 129	Alfredo Mújica Bañuelos (S)
IV 130	Inés Mújica Bañuelos
IV e'130	same as IV,e'125 (≠)
IV 131	Magdalena Mújica Bañuelos
IV e'131	same as IV,e'128

nuclear family of III,60 and III,e'60
five children; names unknown

nuclear family of III,62 and III,e'62

IV 132	Amalia Bañuelos Fábregas (S)
IV 133	Ramiro Bañuelos Fábregas
IV e'133	Sofía (surname unknown)
IV 134	Roberto Bañuelos Fábregas
IV e'134	name unknown
IV 135	Alfredo Bañuelos Fábregas
IV e'135	name unknown
IV 136	Juan Leopoldo Bañuelos Fábregas (S)
IV 137	Inés Bañuelos Fábregas
IV e'137	name unknown
IV 138	Carmen Bañuelos Fábregas
IV e'138	name unknown
IV 139	Hector Bañuelos Fábregas
IV e'139	name unknown
IV 140	Pilar Bañuelos Fábregas
IV e'140	name unknown

nuclear family of III,63 and III,e'63

IV 141	Alberto Gutiérrez Bañuelos
IV e'141	(woman of Spanish parentage)
IV 142	Juan Gutiérrez Bañuelos (S)
IV 143	Rosalía Gutiérrez Bañuelos
IV e'143	name unknown
IV 144	Magdalena Gutiérrez Bañuelos (S)
IV 145	Patricia Gutiérrez Bañuelos (S)

nuclear family of III,66 and III,e'66(III,69)

IV 146	María Auxiliadora Bañuelos Jiménez†

IV 147	Cecilio Bañuelos Jiménez
IV e'147	Juanita Monroy
IV 148	Lupita Bañuelos Jiménez
IV e'148	Gustavo Arredondo
IV 149	Pedro Bañuelos Jiménez
IV e'149	Covadonga Núñez
IV 150	Ricardo Bañuelos Jiménez
IV e'150	Rosalía Villa
IV 151	Ramiro Bañuelos Jiménez
IV e'151	Graciela Gimeno
IV 152	Juan José Bañuelos Jiménez
IV e'152	Mercedes Riverol
IV 153	Ana María Bañuelos Jiménez
IV e'153	Ricardo Romo (≠)

nuclear family of III,67 and III,e'67

IV 154	Juan Leopoldo Bañuelos Roca
IV e'154	name unknown

nuclear family of III,69, see above, IV,146–153

nuclear family of III,72 and III,e'72

IV 155	María Mercedes Jiménez Larrázuri
IV e'155	Joseph Bazin
IV 156	Paloma Jiménez Larrázuri
IV e'156	Miguel Barrios
IV 157	Pedro Jiménez Larrázuri (Pedro Jr.)
IV e'157	Verónica Moritz
IV 158	Cecilia Jiménez Larrázuri
IV e'158	Jean Jacquard
IV 159	Alvaro Jiménez Larrázuri
IV e'159	Carolina Durán
IV 160	Higinio Jiménez Larrázuri
IV e'160	Amalia Font
IV 161	Alejandra Jiménez Larrázuri
IV e'161	Rodrigo López
IV 162	Blas Jiménez Larrázuri
IV e'162	Berta Mendoza
IV 163	María Jiménez Larrázuri (S)

GENERATION V

nuclear family of IV,79 and IV,e'79

V 164	Oscar Garza Gómez

V 165	Pilar Garza Gómez
V 166	Javier Garza Gómez
V 167	Pía Garza Gómez
V 168	Laura Garza Gómez
V 169	Raúl Garza Gómez

nuclear family of IV,80 and IV,e'80

V 170	Mariette Gómez Coure
V e'170	Manuel Becerra
V 171	Ivonne Gómez Coure
V e'171	A. Batiz
V 172	Diana Gómez Coure
V e'172	(son of entrepreneur)
V 173	Louise Gómez Coure
V e'173	(man of French nationality)
V 174	Javier Gómez Coure
V 175	Roberto Gómez Coure
V e'175	name unknown
V 176	Mirelle Gómez Coure
V 177	Guillermo Gómez Coure

nuclear family of IV,81 and IV,e'81

V 178	Pilar Gómez Alvarez
V 179	Ernesto Gómez Alvarez
V 180	Gisela Gómez Alvarez
V 181	Marcos Gómez Alvarez
V 182	Francisco Gómez Alvarez

nuclear family of IV,82 and IV,e'82

V 183	Paola Suárez Gómez
V 184	Ramón Suárez Gómez
V 185	Enrique Suárez Gómez
V 186	Alvaro Suárez Gómez
V 187	Celso Suárez Gómez

nuclear family of IV,83 and IV,e'83

V 188	Alvaro Gómez Ortíz
V 189	Felipe Gómez Ortíz
V 190	Federico Gómez Ortíz
V 191	Diana Gómez Ortíz
V 192	José Miguel Gómez Ortíz

nuclear family of IV,84 and IV,e'84

V 193	Mirtala Ascencio Gómez
V 194	María Ascencio Gómez

nuclear family of IV,86 and IV,e'86

V 195	Alfonso Mijares Gómez
V 196	Arcelia Mijares Gómez
V 197	Ramiro Mijares Gómez
V 198	María Elisa Mijares Gómez
V 199	Azucena Mijares Gómez
V 200	Paulina Mijares Gómez

nuclear family of IV,88 and IV,e'88

V 201	Cecilia Gómez Ruíz
V 202	Consuelo Gómez Ruíz
V 203	Enrique Gómez Ruíz

nuclear family of IV,96 and IV,e'96

V 204	Juana Iturriaga Merino y Pacheco
V e'204	Hector Palacios Roel
V 205	Celso Iturriaga Merino y Pacheco
V 206	Manuela Iturriaga Merino y Pacheco
V e'206	name unknown
V 207	Carmelita Iturriaga Merino y Pacheco
V e'207	name unknown
V 208	Alfredo Iturriaga
V 209	male; name unknown
V e'209	(Costa Rican woman)

nuclear family of IV,97 and IV,e'97

V 210	Agustín Merino y Pacheco Toriello
V e'210	Mercedes Sirvent
V 211	Emilia Merino y Pacheco Toriello
V e'211	Alvaro Gutiérrez ($\neq$)
V 212	Diego Merino y Pacheco Toriello
V e'212	Montserrat Sirvent
V 213	Lupe Merino y Pacheco Toriello
V e'213	Ignacio Villegas
V 214	Marianela Merino y Pacheco Toriello
V e'214	Miguel Covarrubias
V 215	María Elisa Merino y Pacheco Toriello

nuclear family of IV,98 and IV,e'98

V 216	Prudencio Benítez Merino y Pacheco
V e'216	Angélica Martínez
V 217	Alicia Benítez Merino y Pacheco
V e'217	Celso Navarro y Nájera
V 218	Ramiro Benítez Merino y Pacheco†

APPENDIX

v 219	Felipe Benítez Merino y Pacheco
v e′219	Cecilia Kruger
v 220	Leopoldo Benítez Merino y Pacheco
v e′220	Teresita (surname unknown)
v 221	Benito Benítez Merino y Pacheco
v e′221	Mónica Kruger

nuclear family of IV,99 and IV,e′99

v 222	Berta Merino y Pacheco Ascencio
v e′222	name unknown
v 223	Malú Merino y Pacheco Ascencio
v 224	Maximiliano Merino y Pacheco Ascencio

nuclear family of IV,100 and IV,e′100

v 225	Enrique Heinze Merino y Pacheco
v 226	Juan Heinze Merino y Pacheco
v 227	Verónica Heinze Merino y Pacheco
v 228	female; name unknown
v 229	male; name unknown
v 230	male; name unknown
v 231	twin; name unknown
v 232	twin; name unknown

nuclear family of IV,101 and IV,e′101 (≠)

v 233	Lulú Romero Aguirre
v e′233	name unknown
v 234	"La Nena" Romero Aguirre
v e′234	name unknown
v 235	Miguel Romero Aguirre

nuclear family of IV,102 and IV,e′102

v 236	Jorge Toriello Gómez
v e′236	Elvira Solana
v 237	Leopoldo Toriello Gómez
v e′237	(woman from San Luis)
v 238	Lupe Toriello Gómez
v e′238	Miguel Yedid
v 239	Rosa Toriello Gómez
v e′239	Javier Urquijo
v 240	Jaime Toriello Gómez

nuclear family of IV,103 and IV,e′103

v 241	Leopoldo Gómez Durán
v 242	Felipe Gómez Durán
v 243	Pedro Gómez Durán

v 244   Magdalena Gómez Durán
v 245   José Pablo Gómez Durán
v 246   Manuel Gómez Durán

nuclear family of IV,104 and IV,e'104
v 247   Juana Garza Gómez
v 248   Jorge Garza Gómez
v 249   José Garza Gómez
v 250   Carolina Garza Gómez

nuclear family of IV,105 and IV,e'105
v 251   Federico Piña Solórzano Gómez
v e'251   (first name unknown) Romo
v 252   Magdalena Piña Solórzano Gómez
v 253   Leopoldo Piña Solórzano Gómez
v 254   Pedro Piña Solórzano Gómez
v 255   Lupita Piña Solórzano Gómez
v 256   Marilí Piña Solórzano Gómez
v 257   Juan Carlos Piña Solórzano Gómez
v 258   Mari Nieves Piña Solórzano Gómez

nuclear family of IV,106 and IV,e'106
v 259   Berta Gómez Gómez
v 260   Lucila Gómez Gómez
v,261–v,266 (name, sex unknown) Gómez Gómez

nuclear family of IV,107 and IV,e'107
v 267   Adolfo Gutiérrez Gómez
v 268   Lourdes Gutiérrez Gómez

nuclear family of IV,108 and IV,e'108
v 269   Samuel Urbina Gómez
v,270–v,275 (name, sex unknown) Urbina Gómez
v 276   (female, name unknown) Urbina Gómez

nuclear family of IV,109 and IV,e'109
v 277   Pablo Gómez Gómez
v 278   Juan Gómez Gómez
v 279   Pedro Gómez Gómez

nuclear family of IV,110 and IV,e'110
v 280   Juan Gómez Mingot
v 281   Pablo Gómez Mingot
v 282   Montserrat Gómez Mingot
v 283   María de Lourdes Gómez Mingot

nuclear family of IV,111 and IV,e'111

V 284	Leopoldo Jorge Gómez Romero
V 285	Alicia Gómez Romero
V 286	Mónica Gómez Romero
V 287	Ricardo Gómez Romero

nuclear family of IV,112 and IV,e'112

V 288	María Guadalupe Alcocer Gómez
V 289	Ana Alcocer Gómez
V,290–V,293	(name, sex unknown) Alcocer Gómez
V 294	Pedro Alcocer Gómez
V 295	Juan Alcocer Gómez
V 296	Milagros Alcocer Gómez

nuclear family of IV,113 and IV,e'113

V 297	César Calvo Gómez
V 298	Pablo Calvo Gómez
V 299	Juana Calvo Gómez
V 300	Lupe Calvo Gómez

nuclear family of IV,114 and IV,e'114

V 301	Genaro Montalvo Lippert
V 302	Sofía Montalvo Lippert
V 303	Andrés Montalvo Lippert
V 304	Lourdes Montalvo Lippert

nuclear family of IV,120 and IV,e'120

V 305	Pilar W. Aguilar
V 306	Elisa W. Aguilar
V 307	Enrique W. Aguilar
V 308	Patrocinio W. Aguilar
V 309	Ernesto W. Aguilar

nuclear family of IV,128 and IV,e'128

V,310–V,314	(name, sex unknown) Galán Mújica

nuclear family of IV,147 and IV,e'147

V 315	Juana María Bañuelos Monroy
V 316	Cecilio Bañuelos Monroy
V 317	Ramiro Bañuelos Monroy

nuclear family of IV,149 and IV,e'149

V 318	Pedro Bañuelos Núñez
V 319	Covadonga Bañuelos Núñez
V 320	Javier Bañuelos Núñez
V 321	Verónica Bañuelos Núñez

nuclear family of IV,150 and IV,e'150
V 322   Diana Bañuelos Villa
V 323   Débora Bañuelos Villa
V 324   Rosalía Bañuelos Villa

nuclear family of IV,151 and IV,e'151
V 325   María Graciela Bañuelos Gimeno
V 326   Lorenza Bañuelos Gimeno
V 327   Ramiro Bañuelos Gimeno

nuclear family of IV,152 and IV,e'152
V 328   Mercedes Bañuelos Riverol
V 329   Nuria Bañuelos Riverol
V 330   Alina Bañuelos Riverol

nuclear family of IV,153 and IV,e'153 ($\neq$)
V 331   Maricela Romo Bañuelos
V 332   Ana María Romo Bañuelos
V 333   Ricarda Romo Bañuelos

nuclear family of IV,155 and IV,e'155
V 334   María Mercedes Bazin Jiménez
V 335   Amalia Bazin Jiménez
V 336   José Bazin Jiménez

nuclear family of IV,156 and IV,e'156
V 337   Paloma Barrios Jiménez
V 338   Santiago Barrios Jiménez

nuclear family of IV,157 and IV,e'157
V 339   Pedro Jiménez Moritz
V 340   Mónica Jiménez Moritz

nuclear family of IV,158 and IV,e'158
V 341   Juan Jacquard Jiménez
V 342   Carolina Jacquard Jiménez
V 343   Higinio Jacquard Jiménez

nuclear family of IV,159 and IV,e'159
V 344   Carolina Jiménez Durán
V 345   Alvaro Jiménez Durán

GENERATION VI

The sixth generation had sixteen members known as of December 1978.

Adams, Richard N. 1978. "Brokers and Career Mobility Systems in the Structure of Complex Societies." *Southwestern Journal of Anthropology* 26 (4):315-27.

Aguilar, A., and F. Carmona. 1977. *México: Riqueza y miseria*. Mexico City: Nuestro Tiempo.

Aguilar, John L. 1978. "Class Ethnicity as Ideology: Stratification in a Town." *Ethnic Groups* 2 (2):109-131.

Aguilar Camín, Héctor. 1977. *La frontera nómada: Sonora y la Revolución Mexicana*. Mexico City: Siglo XXI.

Aguilar Zinzer, Adolfo. 1978. "Historia de una industrialización fallida (1940-1946)." *Sábado: Suplemento de Uno Mas Uno* 42 (Sept. 2):2-7.

Alcaraz, Marco Antonio. 1977. *Las agrupaciones patronales en México*, 2d ed. Mexico City: El Colegio de México, Jornadas (66). 1st ed. 1970.

Alejo, Francisco Javier. 1969. "La estrategia del desarrollo económico de México en 1920-1970." Thesis, Facultad de Economía, Universidad Nacional Autónoma de México.

Alonso, Jorge, ed. 1980. *Lucha urbana y acumulación de capital*. Mexico City: CISINAH. Ediciones de la Casa Chata.

Anderson, Charles W. 1968. "Bankers as Revolutionaries: Politics and Development Banking in Mexico." In *The Political Economy of Mexico*, ed. W. P. Glade, pp. 104-196. Milwaukee: University of Wisconsin Press.

Archivo General de Notarías del Distrito Federal. Mexico City, Mexico.

Arizpe, Lourdes, 1973. *Parentesco y economía en una sociedad Náhua*. Mexico City: Instituto Nacional Indigenista/Secretaría de Educación Pública.

———. 1978. *Migración, etnicismo y cambio económico*. Mexico City: El Colegio de México.

Aronoff, Myron J. 1978. "A Framework for a Political Anthropological Approach to the Study of Ideology." Paper presented at the panel "Boundaries and Limits of Analysis in Political Anthropology." Tenth meeting of the International Congress of Anthropological and Ethnological Sciences, New Delhi, Dec. 10-11.

REFERENCE LIST

Arriola, Carlos. 1981. *Los empresarios y el estado*. Col. SEP 80. Mexico City: Secretaría de Educación Pública.

Aubey, Robert T. 1979. "Capital Mobilization and Patterns of Business Ownership and Control in Cultural Context." In *Entrepreneurs in Cultural Context*, ed. S. Greenfield, A. Strickon, and R. Aubey, pp. 225-42. Albuquerque: University of New Mexico Press.

Azevedo, Thales de. 1965. "Family, Marriage and Divorce in Brazil." In *Contemporary Cultures and Societies of Latin America*, ed. Dwight B. Heath and Richard N. Adams, pp. 257-87. New York: Random House.

Bailey, David. 1974. *Viva Cristo Rey! The Cristero Rebellion and the Church-State Conflict in Mexico*. Austin: University of Texas Press.

Banca Cremi. 1980. *Análisis-79: La economía mexicana*. Mexico City.

Banck, Geert A. N.d. "Survival Strategies of Low-Income Urban Households in Brazil: A Case Study." Mimeo.

Banfield, E. 1958. *The Moral Basis of a Backward Society*. New York: Free Press.

Banks, Joseph Ambrose. 1964. "The Structure of Industrial Enterprise in Industrial Society." In *The Development of Industrial Society*, ed. Paul Richard Halmos. *Sociological Review* Monograph 8. Staffordshire: University of Keele.

Barkin, David. 1972. *Los beneficiarios del desarrollo regional*. Col. SEP 70's. Mexico City: Secretaría de Educación Pública.

Barnes, J. A. 1973. *Three Styles in the Study of Kinship*. Berkeley: University of California Press.

Barnett, Steve. 1977. "Identity Choice and Caste Ideology in Contemporary South India." In *Symbolic Anthropology*, ed. Janet L. Dolgin, David S. Kemnitzer, and David Schneider, pp. 270-309. New York: Columbia University Press.

Barret, Richard A. 1978. "Desarrollo económico y las clases altas en una ciudad española." *Ethnicas* (Barcelona) 14:9-19.

Barth, Fredrick. 1963. *The Role of the Entrepreneur in Social Change in Northern Norway*. Oslo: Scandinavian University Books.

———. 1970. *Models of Social Organization*. Occasional Paper no. 23. London: Royal Anthropological Institute of Great Britain and Ireland. 1st ed. 1969.

Bazant, Jan. 1971. *Los bienes de la Iglesia en México (1856-1875)*. Mexico City: Centro de Estudios Históricos, El Colegio de México.

Bazdrech, P. Carlos. 1974. "El dilema de la política económica." In

La vida política en México 1970-73. Centro de Estudios Internacionales, El Colegio de México.

Beato, Guillermo. 1979. "Los profesionales intermediarios, el estado y las empresas extranjeras. Un caso durante el porfiriato." In *Simposio sobre empresarios en México.* Vol. 2, *Intermediación: Fracciones étnicas de clase,* ed. G. Beato, G. de la Peña, and R. Salazar. Cuadernos de la Casa Chata (22). Mexico City: CISINAH.

Beato, Guillermo, and Doménico Síndico. 1980. "Los comienzos de la industria regiomontana: Un análisis estructural." Paper presented at the ninth meeting of the Latin American Studies Association, Bloomington, Ind., Oct. 17-19.

Befu, Harumi. 1963. "Patrilineal Descent and Personal Kindred in Japan." *American Anthropologist* 65:1328-41.

Belote, Jim, and Linda Belote. 1977. "The Limitation of Obligation in Saraguro Kinship." In *Andean Kinship and Marriage,* ed. Enrique Mayer and Ralph Bolton, pp. 106-116. Special Publication no. 7. Washington, D.C.: American Anthropological Association.

Belshaw, C. 1955. "The Cultural Milieu of the Entrepreneur: A Critical Essay." In *Exploration in Entrepreneurial History,* vol. 7, no. 3. Cambridge: Harvard University.

Benedict, Burton. 1968. "Family Firms and Economic Development." *Southwestern Journal of Anthropology* 24 (1):1-11.

Bennett, Douglas, and Kenneth Sharpe. 1977. "Controlling the Multinationals: The Illogic of Mexicanization." Mimeo.

———. 1979. "Formación de la industria automotriz mexicana (1958-1964)." In *Dinámica de la empresa mexicana,* ed. V. Márquez, pp. 151-85. Mexico City: El Colegio de México.

———. 1980. "El estado como banquero y empresario: El carácter de la última instancia de la intervención económica del estado mexicano, 1917-1970." *Foro Internacional XX* 79:29-72.

Berger, Brigitte, and Peter Berger. 1983. *The War over the Family.* New York: Anchor Press, Doubleday.

Berger, Peter, and Thomas Luckman. 1976. *The Social Construction of Reality: A Treatise in the Sociology of Knowledge.* New York: John Wiley and Sons.

Bernal, John D. 1965. *Science in History.* Cambridge: M.I.T. Press.

Blau, Peter. 1964. *Exchange and Power in Social Life.* New York: John Wiley and Sons.

Blehr, Otto. 1963. "Action Groups in a Society with Bilateral Kinship: A Case Study from the Faroe Islands." *Ethnology* 2:269-75.

Bloch, Maurice. 1973. "The Long Term and the Short Term: The

Economic and Political Significance of the Morality of Kinship." In *The Character of Kinship*, ed. Jack Goody, pp. 75-88. Cambridge: Cambridge University Press.

Blok, Anton. 1974. *The Mafia of a Sicilian Village, 1860-1960*. Oxford: Basil Blackwell.

Bock, Phillip K. 1974. *Modern Cultural Anthropology*. 2d ed. New York: Knopf.

Bordieu, Pierre. 1980. "Le capital social." *Actes de la recherche en sciences sociales* 31:2-4.

Brading, D. A. 1975. *Mineros y comerciantes en el México Borbónico (1763-1810)*. Mexico City: Fondo de Cultura Económica.

————. 1978. *Haciendas and Ranchos in the Mexican Bajío: León 1700-1860*. London: Cambridge University Press.

Brandenburg, Frank. 1962. "A Contribution to the Theory of Entrepreneurship and Economic Development: The Case of Mexico." *Inter-American and Economic Affairs* 16 (Winter):3-23.

————. 1972. "The Development of Latin American Private Enterprise." In *Workers and Managers in Latin America*, ed. Stanley M. Davis and L. W. Goodman, pp. 179-84. Lexington, Mass.: D. C. Heath and Co.

Brito, Enrique M. 1969. *La población en México: Datos fundamentales*. Mexico City: Centro de Investigación y Acción Social (CIAS).

Brooke, Nigel, John Oxenham, and Angela Little. 1977. "Qualifications and Employment in Mexico." Report of the Institute of Development Studies (IDS). Sussex. Mimeo.

Brun Martínez, Gabriel. 1974. "Problemas metodológicos en el estudio de las estructuras familiares, ciudad de México, 1811." Paper presented at the seminar on methodological problems of urban history. Departamento de Investigaciones Históricas, Instituto de Antropología e Historia. Mimeo.

————. 1978a. "La organización del trabajo y la estructura de la unidad doméstica de los zapateros y cigarreros de la Ciudad de México 1811." Paper presented at the symposium "Organization of the Production and Work Relations in the Nineteenth Century in Mexico." Seminar in Urban History, Departamento de Investigaciones Históricas, Instituto de Antropología e Historia, Feb. 14-19. Mimeo.

————. 1978b. "Breve bibliografía sobre la historia de la familia en México." Seminar on Urban History, Instituto de Antropología e Historia. Mimeo.

Bruner, Edward M. 1973. "Kin and Non-Kin." In *Urban Anthropol-*

ogy, ed. Aidan Southall, pp. 373-92. New York: Oxford University Press.

Bryce-Laporte, Roy Semor. 1970. "Urban Relocation and Family Adaptation in Urban Ethnography." In *Peasants in Cities: Readings in the Anthropology of Urbanization*, ed. W. Manguin. Boston: Houghton Mifflin Co.

Butterworth, Douglas. 1962. "Study of the Urbanization Process of Mixtec Migrants of Tilaltongo in Mexico City." *América Indígena* 22 (3):257-74.

Calderón, Francisco R. 1965. "La república restaurada, vida económica." In *Historia moderna de México. La república restaurada: Vida económica*, ed. Daniel Cosío Villegas. Mexico City: Hermes.

———. 1973. "Los ferrocarriles en México." In *Historia moderna de México. El Porfiriato: Vida económica*, ed. Daniel Cosío Villegas, pp. 608-661. Mexico City: Hermes.

Calderón de la Barca, Frances Erskine. 1970. *La vida en México*. Mexico City: Porrúa.

Calneck, Edward. 1978. "The Internal Structure of Cities in America: Pre-Columbian Cities; The Case of Tenochtitlan." In *Urbanization in the Americas from Its Beginnings to Its Present*, ed. R. Schaedel, J. Hardoy, and N. Knitzer, pp. 315-26. The Hague: Mouton.

Camacho, Manuel. 1974. "El poder: Estado o feudos políticos." In *La vida política en México: 1970-73*, pp. 77-100. Centro de Estudios Internacionales, El Colegio de México.

———. 1981. *La clase obrera en la historia de México*. No. 15, *El futuro inmediato*. Mexico City: Universidad Nacional Autónoma de México/Siglo XXI.

Camp, Roderic Ai. N.d. "The University and Political Leadership in Mexico." Mimeo.

———. 1980. "Family Relationships in Mexican Politics." Mimeo.

Campbell, J. K. 1976. *Honor, Family and Patronage*. Oxford: Oxford University Press.

Cancian, Frank. 1976. *Economía y prestigio en una comunidad Maya*. Mexico City: Instituto Nacional Indigenista.

Cardoso, Fernando Henrique. 1970. "The Industrial Elite." In *Elites in Latin America*, ed. S. M. Lipset and A. Solari, pp. 94-116. 2d ed. London: Oxford University Press.

———. 1972. "The Industrial Elite in Latin America." In *Workers and Managers in Latin America*, ed. Stanley M. Davis and L. W. Goodman, pp. 53-56. Lexington, Mass.: D. C. Heath and Co.

Cardoso, Fernando Henrique. 1976. *Ideologías de la burguesía industrial en sociedades dependientes.* 5th ed. Mexico City: Siglo XXI.

Cardoso Fernando Henrique, and E. Faletti. 1967. *Dependencia y desarrollo en América Latina.* Serie Documentos Técnicos 1. Lima: Instituto de Estudios Peruanos.

Carlos, Manuel L., and Lois Sellers. 1972. "Family, Kinship Structure, and Modernization in Latin America." *Latin American Research Review* 7, no. 2 (Summer):95-124.

Carrasco, Pedro. 1976. "The Joint Family in Ancient Mexico: The Case of Molotla." In *Essays on Mexican Kinship*, ed. Hugo G. Nutini, Pedro Carrasco, and James Mounsey Taggart, pp. 45-64. Pittsburgh: University of Pittsburgh Press.

————. 1967. "Relaciones sobre la organización social indígena en el siglo XVI." *Estudios de Cultura Náhuatl* (7):119-54.

Carrol, John. 1965. *The Filipino Manufacturing Entrepreneur.* Philadelphia: University of Pennsylvania Press.

Cerutti, Mario. 1980. "Producción capitalista y articulación del empresario en Monterrey (1880-1910)." Facultad de Filosofía y Letras, Universidad Autónoma de Nuevo León. Mimeo.

Chance, John. 1978. *Race and Class in Colonial Oaxaca.* Stanford: Stanford University Press.

Cinta, Ricardo. 1971. "Burguesía nacional y desarrollo." In *Perfil de México* (3). Mexico City: Siglo XXI.

Cohen, Abner. 1969. *Custom and Politics in Urban Africa.* London: Routledge and Kegan Paul.

————. 1974. *Two-Dimensional Man.* London: Routledge and Kegan Paul.

————. 1977. "Symbolic Action and the Structure of the Self." In *Symbols and Sentiments*, vol. 1, ed. Joan Lewis, pp. 117-29. London: Academic Press.

Comas, Juan. 1964. *La antropología social aplicada en México.* Mexico City: Instituto Indigenista Interamericano (Serie Antropología Social).

CONAPO. 1975. *México demográfico.* Mexico City: Consejo Nacional de Población.

CONCAMIN. 1969. Series of conferences presented by associations and chambers of the National Federation of Industrialists. Mimeo.

Cordero, Salvador. 1977. *Concentración industrial y poder económico en México.* Mexico City: Cuadernos del Centro de Estudios Sociológicos (23), El Colegio de México.

Cordero, Salvador, and G. Santín. 1977. *Los grupos industriales:*

Una nueva organización económica en México. Mexico City: Cuadernos del Centro de Estudios Sociológicos (23), El Colegio de México.

Cosío Villegas, Daniel. 1976. *Memorias.* Mexico City: Joaquín Mortiz.

Cosío Villegas, Daniel, ed. 1965. *Historia moderna de México. La república restaurada: Vida económica.* Mexico City: Hermes.

————. 1973. *Historia moderna de México. El Porfiriato: Vida económica.* Mexico City: Hermes.

————. 1974a. *Historia moderna de México. La república restaurada: Vida social.* Mexico City: Hermes.

————. 1974b. *Historia moderna de México. El Porfiriato: Vida social.* Mexico City: Hermes.

Cotler, Julio. 1970. "The Mechanics of Internal Domination and Social Change in Peru." In *Masses in Latin America,* ed. Irving L. Horowitz, pp. 407-444. New York: Oxford University Press.

Craig, Daniel. 1979. "Immortality through Kinship: The Vertical Transmission of Substance and Symbolic Estate." *American Anthropologist* 81 (1):94-95.

Cumberland, Charles S. 1968. *Mexico: The Struggle for Modernity.* New York: Oxford University Press.

Dahl, Robert. 1963. *Modern Political Analysis.* Englewood Cliffs, N.J.: Prentice Hall.

Davenport, William. 1959. "Nonunilinear Descent and Descent Groups." *American Anthropologist* 61 (4):557-72.

Davis, Peter, and Douglas Stern. 1979. "Adaptation, Survival and Growth of the Family Business: A Family Systems Perspective." Working paper, International Meeting of the Institute of Management Sciences, Hawaii, June. Mimeo.

Davis, Stanley M. 1972a. "United States versus Latin America: Business and Culture." In *Workers and Managers in Latin America,* ed. Stanley M. Davis and L. W. Goodman, pp. 57-62. Lexington, Mass.: D. C. Heath and Co.

————. 1972b. "Authority and Control in Mexican Enterprise." In *Workers and Managers in Latin America,* ed. Stanley M. Davis and L. W. Goodman, pp. 259-305. Lexington, Mass.: D. C. Heath and Co.

de la Peña, Guillermo. 1979. "Empresarios en el sur de Jalisco: Un estudio de caso en Zapotlán el Grande." In *Simposio sobre empresarios en México.* Vol. 2, *Intermediación: Fracciones étnicas de clase*, ed. G. Beato, G. de la Peña, and R. Salazar, pp. 47-84. Cuadernos de la Casa Chata (22). Mexico City: CISINAH.

―――. 1980. *Herederos de promesas: Agricultura, política y ritual en los altos de Morelos*. Mexico City: CISINAH.

―――. 1984. "Ideology and Practice in Southern Jalisco: Peasants, Rancheros and Urban Entrepreneurs." In *Kinship, Ideology and Practice in Latin America*, ed. Raymond T. Smith, pp. 204-236. Chapel Hill: University of North Carolina Press.

de Mendizábal, Miguel Othón et al. 1975. *Ensayo sobre las clases sociales en México*. 5th ed. Mexico City: Nuestro Tiempo.

Derossi, Flavia. 1972a. "Familism in Industry." In *Workers and Managers in Latin America*, ed. Stanley M. Davis and L. W. Goodman, pp. 75-82. Lexington, Mass.: D. C. Heath and Co.

―――. 1972b. *El empresario mexicano*. Mexico City: Universidad Nacional Autónoma de México.

Dolgin, Janet L., David S. Kemnitzer, and David Schneider. 1977. *Symbolic Anthropology*. New York: Columbia University Press.

Domhoff, G. William. N.d. "Social Clubs, Policy Planning Groups, and Corporations: A Network Study of Ruling-Class Cohesiveness." Dept. of Sociology, University of California, Santa Cruz. Mimeo.

Donner, Patricia. 1974. "Algunos aspectos para la discusión del concepto de movimientos sociales." In *Hacia una conceptualización del fenómeno de los movimientos universitarios en América Latina*, pp. 51-75. Santiago: Corporación de Promoción Universitaria 31.

Dumont, Louis. 1977. *From Mandeville to Marx*. Chicago: University of Chicago Press.

Duncan, Hugh D. 1968. *Symbols in Society*. Oxford: Oxford University Press.

Durkheim, Emile. 1965. *The Elementary Forms of Religious Life*. New York: Free Press. 1st ed. 1915.

Echeverría, Luis. 1974. "Declarations about Entrepreneurs." *El Día* 1A, Sept. 2.

Elmendorf, Mary. 1977. "Mexico: The Many Worlds of Women." In *Women: Roles and Status in Eight Countries*, ed. J. Z. Grete and A. Chapman, pp. 127-72. New York: John Wiley and Sons.

Escobar, Gabriel. 1980. "Análisis preliminar del parentesco y la familia de clase media de la ciudad del Cuzco." In *Parentesco y matrimonio en los Andes*, ed. Ralph Bolton and Enrique Mayer, pp. 681-720. Lima: Pontificia Universidad del Perú.

Evans, Peter. 1972. "The Latin American Entrepreneur: Style, Scale and Rationality." In *Workers and Managers in Latin America*, ed. Stanley M. Davis and L. W. Goodman, pp. 195-202. Lexington, Mass.: D. C. Heath and Co.

Evens, Terence M. S. 1975. "Stigma, Ostracism and Expulsion in an Israeli Kibbutz." In *Symbols and Politics in Communal Ideology*, ed. Sally Falk Moore, pp. 166-209. Ithaca: Cornell University Press.

Fajnzylber, F., and Trinidad Martínez. 1975. *Las empresas transnacionales: Expansión a nivel mundial y proyección en la industria*. Mexico City: CONACYT/Centro de Investigación y Docencia Económica (CIDE).

Faron, L. 1964. *Hawks of the Sun*. Pittsburgh: University of Pittsburgh Press.

Firth, Raymond. 1964. "Family and Kinship in Industrial Society." In *The Development of Industrial Society*, ed. Paul Richard Halmo, pp. 65-87. *Sociological Review* Monograph no. 8. Staffordshire: University of Keele.

———. 1971. "The Nature of English Kinship." In *Readings in Kinship and Social Structure*, ed. N. Graburn, pp. 385-89. New York: Harper and Row.

———. 1973. *Symbols: Public and Private*. Ithaca: Cornell University Press.

Firth, Raymond, Jane Hubert, and Anthony Forge. 1970. *Families and Their Relatives: Kinship in a Middle-Class Sector of London*. London: Routledge and Kegan Paul.

Flanders, Jean Louis. 1979. *Orígenes de la familia moderna*. Barcelona: Grijalbo.

Forbes, Jean T. 1971. "El sistema de compadrazgo en Santa María Belén Atzitzinitillán, Tlaxcala." M.A. thesis, Universidad Iberoamericana, Mexico City.

Forde, Daryll. 1962. "Death and Succession." In *Essays on the Ritual of Social Relations*, ed. Max Gluckman, pp. 89-123. Manchester: Manchester University Press.

Forman, Shepard. 1975. *The Brazilian Peasantry*. New York: Columbia University Press.

———. 1976. "The Significance of Participation: Peasants in the Politics of Brazil." Paper presented at the conference "Faces of Citizen Participation in Latin America," at San Antonio, Texas, Nov. 12-14. Mimeo.

Fortes, Meyer. 1966. "Ritual and Office in Tribal Society." In *Essays on the Ritual of Social Relations*, ed. Max Gluckman, pp. 53-87. Manchester: Manchester University Press.

———. 1969. *Kinship and the Social Order*. London: Routledge and Kegan Paul.

Foster, George M. 1972. *Tzintzuntzán*. Mexico City: Fondo de Cultura Económica.

Freeman, J. Derek. 1961. "On the Concept of the Kindred." *Journal of the Royal Anthropological Institute* 91, part 2:199-220.

Friedel, F. 1970. "The Family in a Greek Village: Dowry and Inheritance, Formal Structure." In *Readings in Kinship in Urban Society*, ed. C. C. Harris, pp. 121-61. Oxford: Pergamon Press.

Friedlander, Judith. 1974. *Being an Indian in Hueyapan*. New York: St. Martin's Press.

Friedman, John. 1980. "The Politics of Space: Five Centuries of Regional Development in Mexico." *International Journal of Urban and Regional Research* 46, no. 3 (Sept.):319-49.

Fuentes, Carlos. 1972. *La región más transparente del aire*. Mexico City: Fondo de Cultura Económica.

———. 1975. *Tiempo mexicano*. Mexico City: Joaquín Mortiz.

Furtado, Celso. 1973. *La economía desde la conquista ibérica: Historia económica hasta la revolución urbana*. Mexico City: Siglo XXI.

Gamio, Manuel. 1960. *Forjando partria*. Mexico City: Porrúa. 1st ed. 1916.

Gamst, Frederick C. 1977. "An Integrating View of the Underlying Premises of an Industrial Ethnology in the United States and Canada." *Anthropological Quarterly* 50, no. 1 (Jan.):1-8.

———. 1979. "An Application of the Model, the Image of Limited Good in Industrial Urban Society." In *From Tzintzuntzan to the Image of Limited Good*, ed. Mark Wayne Clark, Robert Kemper, and Cynthia Nelson, pp. 131-52. Berkeley: Kroeber Anthropological Society.

García Acosta, Virginia. 1979. "La integración económica de los españoles en la ciudad de Puebla y los asturianos en el Distrito Federal." In *Inmigrantes y refugiados españoles en México*, ed. M. Kenny et al. Mexico City: Ediciones de la Casa Chata (8), CIS INAH.

Geertz, Clifford. 1973. *The Interpretation of Cultures*. New York: Basic Books.

Geertz, Hildred, and Clifford Geertz. 1975. *Kinship in Bali*. Chicago: University of Chicago Press.

Gilbert, Dennis. 1977. "The Oligarchy and the Old Regime in Peru." Dissertation Series 69, Cornell University (Jan.).

Gillin, John. 1969. "Ethos Components in Modern Latin American Culture." In *Contemporary Cultures and Societies of Latin America*, ed. A. D. Heath and R. Adams, pp. 503-517. New York: Random House.

Glade, William P., Jr., and Charles W. Anderson. 1963. *The Political Economy of Mexico*. Madison: University of Wisconsin Press. 2d ed. 1983.

————. 1979. "Entrepreneurship in the State Sector: CONASUPO of Mexico." In *Entrepreneurs in Cultural Context*, ed. S. Greenfield, A. Strickon, and R. Aubey, pp. 191-222. Albuquerque: University of New Mexico Press.

Gluckman, Max. 1961. "Ethnographic Data in British Social Anthropology." *Sociological Review* 9:5-17.

————. 1962. *Essays on the Ritual of Social Relations*. Manchester: Manchester University Press.

Godau, Rainer, and Viviane B. de Márquez. 1981. "Burocracia pública y empresa privada: El caso de la industrialización mexicana." El Colegio de México. Mimeo.

Gold, Gerald. 1975. *St. Pascal*. Toronto: Holt, Rinehart and Winston of Canada.

González, Luis. 1979. *Los artífices del Cardenismo*. Mexico City: El Colegio de México.

González Casanova, Pablo. 1965. *La democracia en México*. Mexico City: Era.

González y Gonzalez, Luis, Ema Cosío Villegas, and Guadalupe Monroy. 1974. "La república restaurada, la vida social." In *Historia moderna de México. La república restaurada: Vida social*, ed. Daniel Cosío Villegas. Mexico City: Hermes.

González Navarro, Moisés. 1974. "El Porfiriato, la vida social." In *Historia moderna de México. El Porfiriato: Vida social*, ed. Daniel Cosío Villegas. Mexico City: Hermes.

Goode, William J. 1968. "The Theoretical Importance of Love." In *Selected Studies in Marriage and the Family*, ed. Robert Winch and Louis W. Goodman, pp. 469-80. New York: Holt, Rinehart and Winston.

————. 1970. *World Revolution and Family Patterns*. New York: Macmillan, Free Press.

Goodenough, W. H. 1951. *Property, Kin and Community on Truk*. New Haven: Yale University Press.

Goodenough, W. H. 1955. "A Problem of Malayo-Polynesian Social Organization." *American Anthropologist* 57 (1):71-83.

———. 1975. "Cultura, lenguaje y sociedad." In *El concepto de cultura: Textos fundamentales*, ed. José R. Llobera, pp. 157-248. Barcelona: Anagrama.

Goody, Jack, ed. 1973. *The Character of Kinship*. Cambridge: Cambridge University Press.

———. 1976. *Production and Reproduction*. Cambridge: Cambridge University Press.

Graburn, Nelson, ed. 1971. *Readings in Kinship and Social Structure*. New York: Harper and Row.

Gramsci, Antonio. 1971. *Selections from the Prison Notebooks*. London: Laurence and Wishart.

Greenfield, Sidney M. 1969. "Differentiation, Stratification and Mobility in Traditional Brazilian Society." *Luso-Brazilian Review* 66, no. 2 (Winter):3-21.

Greenfield, Sidney M., and Arnold Strickon. 1979. "Entrepreneurship and Social Change: Toward a Populational, Decision-Making Approach." In *Entrepreneurs in Cultural Context*, ed. S. Greenfield, A. Strickon, and R. Aubey, pp. 329-50. Albuquerque: University of New Mexico Press.

Grindle, Merilee Serrill. 1977. *Bureaucrats, Politicians and Peasants in Mexico*. Berkeley: University of California Press.

Guadarrama, S. Graciela. 1977. *Origen y formación de la burguesía industrial en México*. Thesis, Facultad de Sociología, Universidad Iberoamericana.

Guiteras Holmes, C. 1965. *Los peligros del alma*. Mexico City: Fondo de Cultura Económica.

Gulliver, P. H. 1971. *Neighbors and Networks*. Berkeley: University of California Press.

Gutiérrez de Pineda, Virginia. 1976. *Estructura, función y cambio de la familia en Colombia*. Vols. 1 and 2. Bogota: Asoc. Colombiana de Facultades de Medicina.

Hamilton, Nora. 1982. "The State and the National Bourgeoisie in Postrevolutionary Mexico: 1920-1940." *Latin American Perspectives* 9 (4):31-54.

Hansen, Roger D. 1974. *The Politics of Mexican Development*. Baltimore: Johns Hopkins University Press.

Hareven, Tamara K. 1977. "Family Time and Historical Time." *Daedalus* (Spring):57-70.

Harms, Hans, and Ronaldo Ramírez. 1979. "The Role of the Informal Sector in the Third World Countries." Paper presented at a symposium organized by the Graduate School of the Architect Association, School of Architect and Development Planning Unit, University College, London, March. Mimeo.

Harris, C. C., ed. 1970. *Readings in Kinship in Urban Society*. Oxford: Pergamon Press.

Harris, Charles H. 1975. *A Mexican Family Empire*. Austin: University of Texas Press.

Hartman, Heinz. 1958. "Managers and Entrepreneurs: A Useful Distinction?" *Administrative Science Quarterly*.

Heath, A. D., and R. Adams, eds. 1965. *Contemporary Cultures and Societies of Latin America*. New York: Random House.

Holzberg, Carol S. 1977. "Notes and Queries on Industrial Development: Illustrations from Jamaica." Paper presented at the meeting of the American Anthropological Association in Houston, Texas. Mimeo.

————. In press. "The Social Organization of Jamaican Political Economics: Ethnicity and the Jewish Segment." *Ethnic Groups*.

Hosono, Akio. 1971. "Industrial Development and Employment: A Mexican Village." In *Kinship and Culture*, ed. F.L.K. Hsu, pp. 106-143. Chicago: Aldine.

Hunt, Robert. 1969. "The Development Cycle of the Family Business in Rural Mexico." In *Essays in Economic Anthropology*, ed. June Helm, Paul Bohannan, and Marshall D. Sahlins. Proceedings of the 1965 annual Spring meeting. Seattle: American Ethnological Society.

Ianni, Francis A. J., and Elizabeth R. Reuss-Ianni. 1973. *A Family Business*. New York: Mouton Publishers.

Isbell, Billie Jean. 1977. "Those Who Love Me." In *Andean Kinship and Marriage*, ed. Enrique Mayer and Ralph Bolton, pp. 81-105. Special Publication no. 7. Washington, D.C.: American Anthropological Association.

Iturriaga, José. 1951. *La estructura social y cultural de México*. Mexico City: Fondo de Cultura Económica.

Jones, Delmos J. 1977. "Social Complexity and the Institutionalization of Cultural Diversity." *Review in Anthropology* 4 (5):451-62.

Jurgensen, Edgardo. 1972. "Risk, Diversification and Profits." In *Workers and Managers in Latin America*, ed. Stanley M. Davis and L. W. Goodman, pp. 185-90. Lexington, Mass.: D. C. Heath and Co.

Kaufman, Robert. 1977. "Mexico and Latin American Authoritarianism." In *Authoritarianism in Mexico*, ed. José Luis Reyna and Richard Weinart, pp. 193-232. Philadelphia: Institute for the Study of Human Issues.

Keefe, Susan E., Amado M. Padilla, and Manuel L. Carlos. 1979. "Family as an Emotional Support System." *Human Organization* 38, no. 2 (Summer):144-52.

Keesing, Roger. 1975. *Kin Groups and Social Structure*. New York: Holt, Rinehart and Winston.

Kemper, Robert V. 1976. *Campesinos en la ciudad: Gente de Tzintzuntzán*. Mexico City: SepSetentas, no. 170.

Kempner, Thomas, K. Macmillan, and K. Haukins. 1976. *Business and Society: Tradition and Change*. Harmondsworth: Penguin Books.

Kenny, Michael, Virginia García Acosta, Carmen Icazurriaga, Clara Elena Suárez, and Gloria Artis E. 1979. *Inmigrantes y refugiados españoles en México: Siglo XX*. Mexico City: Ediciones de la Casa Chata (8), CISINAH.

Keremitsis, Dawn. 1973. *La industria textil mexicana en el siglo XIX*. Col. Sep70. Mexico City: Secretaría de Educación Pública.

Kicza, John E. 1983. *Colonial Entrepreneurs*. Albuquerque: University of New Mexico Press.

Knowlton, Robert. 1976. *Church Property and the Mexican Reform 1810-1910*. De Kalb: Northern Illinois University Press.

Krauze, Enrique, with the collaboration of Jean Meyer and Cayetano Reyes. 1977. *La reconstrucción económica. Período 1924-1928. Historia de la Revolución Mexicana*, no. 10. Mexico City: El Colegio de México.

Ladd, Davis M. 1976. *The Mexican Nobility at Independence, 1780-1826*. Austin: Institute of Latin American Studies, University of Texas.

Lafaye, Jacques. 1976. *Quetzalcóatl and Guadalupe: The Formation of Mexican Consciousness 1531-1813*. Chicago: University of Chicago Press.

———. 1977. "The Spanish Diaspora: The Enduring Unity of Hispanic Culture." Working Paper 2. The Wilson Center, Latin American Program. Washington, D.C.

Lambert, Bernard. 1977. "Bilaterality in the Andes." In *Andean Kinship and Marriage*, ed. Enrique Mayer and Ralph Bolton, pp. 1-27. Special Publication no. 7. Washington, D.C.: American Anthropological Association.

Lauterbach, Albert. 1972. "Management, Entrepreneurship, and Development Needs." In *Workers and Managers in Latin America*, ed. Stanley M. Davis and L. W. Goodman, pp. 173-77. Lexington, Mass.: D. C. Heath and Co.

Leach, Edmund. 1954. *Political Systems of Highland Burma*. London: Bell.

————. 1973. "Complementary and Bilateral Kinship." In *The Character of Kinship*, ed. Jack Goody, pp. 53-88. Cambridge: Cambridge University Press.

————. 1976. *Culture and Communication*. Cambridge: Cambridge University Press.

Leeds, Anthony. 1969. "Brazilian Careers and Social Structure: A Case History and Model." In *Contemporary Cultures and Societies of Latin America*, ed. A. Dwight Heath and R. Adams, pp. 379-404. New York: Random House.

Lefebvre, Henri. 1977. "Ideology and the Sociology of Knowledge." In *Symbolic Anthropology*, ed. Janet L. Dolgin, David S. Kemnitzer, and David Schneider, pp. 254-69. New York: Columbia University Press.

Leff, Nathaniel. 1978. "Industrial Organization and Entrepreneurship in the Developing Countries: The Economic Groups." *Economic Development and Cultural Change* 26 (4):661-75.

Levine, Daniel H. 1980a. "Religion and Politics, Politics and Religion." In *Churches and Politics in Latin America*, ed. Daniel H. Levine, pp. 16-40. Beverly Hills: Sage Publications.

————, ed. 1980b. *Churches and Politics in Latin America*. Beverly Hills: Sage Publications.

Lewin, Linda. 1979a. "Kinship in Brazil." *Hispanic American Historical Review*:269-92.

————. 1979b. "Some Historical Implications of Kinship Organization for Family Basical Politics in the Brazilian Northeast." *Comparative Studies in Society and History* 21 (2):262-92.

Lewis, Gilbert. 1977. "A Mother's Brother to a Sister's Son." In *Symbols and Sentiments*, ed. Joan Lewis, pp. 39-60. London: Academic Press.

Lewis, Joan. 1977. "Introduction." In *Symbols and Sentiments*, ed. Joan Lewis, pp. 1-24. London: Academic Press.

Lewis, Oscar. 1959. "The Culture of the Vecindad in Mexico City: Two Case Studies." *Actas del XXIII Congreso Internacional de Americanistas* 1, San José, Costa Rica.

————. 1969. *Antropología de la pobreza: 5 Familias*. Mexico City: Fondo de Cultura Económica.

Lewis, Oscar. 1970. *Una muerte en la familia Sánchez*. Mexico City: Mortiz.

———. 1976. *Tepoztlán: Un pueblo en México*. Mexico City: Mortiz.

Lipman, Aaron. 1972. "The Colombian Entrepreneur: Rationalism and Deviance." In *Workers and Managers in Latin America*, ed. Stanley M. Davis and L. W. Goodman, pp. 63-68. Lexington, Mass.: D. C. Heath.

Lipset, Seymour Martin, and Aldo Solari, eds. 1970. *Elites in Latin America*. London: Oxford University Press. 1st ed. 1967.

Lisón-Tolosana, C. 1970. "The Family in a Spanish Town." In *Readings in Kinship in Urban Society*, ed. C. C. Harris, pp. 163-78. Oxford: Pergamon Press.

Littlefield, Alice. 1976. *La industria de las hamacas en Yucatán, México*. Mexico City: Instituto Nacional Indigenista.

Llano Cifuentes, Carlos. N.d.a. "Ventajas y límites de la empresa familiar." *Istmo: Revista del Pensamiento Actual* 85:23-45.

———. N.d.b. "La sucesión en las empresas familiares." *Istmo: Revista del Pensamiento Actual* 86:25-44.

Lobo, Susan Blum. 1977. "Journey Home: The Process of Urbanization in the Squatter Settlements of Lima." Thesis, Dept. of Anthropology, University of Arizona.

Lomnitz, Larissa. 1971. "Reciprocity of Favors in the Urban Middle Class of Chile." In *Studies in Economic Anthropology*, ed. G. Dalton, pp. 93-106. Washington, D.C.: American Anthropological Association.

———. 1977. *Networks and Marginality: Life in a Mexican Shantytown*. New York: Academic Press.

———. 1982. "Horizontal and Vertical Relations and the Social Structure of Urban Mexico." *Latin American Research Review* 17, no. 2 (Summer):51-74.

Lomnitz, Larissa, and Alicia Morán. 1978. "Estudio de un grupo de egresados mexicanos de una universidad extranjera." *Pensamiento Universitario*, no. 12. Universidad Nacional Autónoma de México.

Lomnitz, Larissa, and Marisol Pérez-Lizaur. 1979. "Kinship Structure and the Role of Woman in the Urban Upper Class of Mexico." *Signs: Journal of Women in Culture and Society* 5, no. 1 (Autumn):164-68.

———. 1981. "Significados culturales y expresión física de la familia en México." *Actas de la 2a. Reunión nacional de demografía* (Mexico City), Nov.

―――. 1982. "Culture and Ideology among Mexican Entrepreneurs." In *Culture and Ideology: Anthropological Perspectives*, ed. Jean R. Barstow, pp. 23-43. Latin American Series, no. 1. Minneapolis: University of Minnesota Press.

Lomnitz-Adler, Claudio. 1982. *La evolución de una sociedad rural: Historia del poder en Tepoztlán*. Mexico City: Secretaría de Educación Pública/Fondo de Cultura Económica.

Long, Norman. 1972. "Kinship and Associational Networks among Transporters in Rural Peru: The Problem of the 'Local' and the 'Cosmopolitan' Entrepreneur." Paper presented at the "Kinship and Social Networks in Latin America Seminar," Institute of Latin America Studies, London University. Mimeo.

―――. 1977. "Commerce and Kinship in the Peruvian Highlands." In *Andean Kinship and Marriage*, ed. Enrique Mayer and Ralph Bolton, pp. 153-76. Special Publication no. 7. Washington, D.C.: American Anthropological Association.

―――. 1979. "Multiple Enterprise in the Central Highlands of Peru." In *Entrepreneurs in Cultural Context*, ed. S. Greenfield, A. Strickon, and R. Aubey, pp. 123-58. Albuquerque: University of New Mexico Press.

Maccoby, Michael. 1978. *The Games Man*. New York: Bantam.

Macfarlane, Alan. 1979. *The Origins of English Individualism*. Cambridge: Cambridge University Press.

Malinowsky, Bronislav. 1948. *Magic, Science, and Religion*. Boston: Free Press.

Malloy, James M. 1977. "Authoritarianism and Corporatism in Latin America: The Model Pattern." In *Authoritarianism and Corporatism in Latin America*, ed. James M. Malloy, pp. 3-19. Pittsburgh: University of Pittsburgh Press.

Mancilla, Esteban L., and Olga Pellicer de Brody. 1978. *El entendimiento con los Estados Unidos y la situación del desarrollo estabilizador. Historia de la Revolución Mexicana*, no. 23. Mexico City: El Colegio de México.

Mangin, William. 1970. *Peasants in Cities: Readings in the Anthropology of Urbanization*. Boston: Houghton Mifflin.

Mark, Lindy Li. 1972. "Taiwanese Lineage Enterprises: A Study of Familiar Entrepreneurship." Ph.D. thesis, Department of Anthropology, University of California, Berkeley. Mimeo.

Márquez, Viviane B. de, ed. 1979. *Dinámica de la empresa mexicana*. Mexico City: El Colegio de México.

Márquez, Viviane, and R. Godau. 1980. "Burocracia y sociedad: Una perspectiva desde América Latina." Mexico City: El Colegio de México. Mimeo.

Martín, Abelardo. 1978a. "La pequeña y mediana industria, los más aptos para dar empleo." *Uno Mas Uno* (July 1).

———. 1978b. "La excesiva concentración de industrias desnacionalizadas." *Uno mas Uno* (July 1).

Mayer, Adrian. 1968. "The Significance of Quasi-Groups in the Study of Complex Societies." In *The Social Anthropology of Complex Societies*, ed. M. Banton. Association of Social Anthropologists (ASA) monograph #4. London: Tavistock.

Mayer, Enrique. 1977. "Beyond the Nuclear Family." In *Andean Kinship and Marriage*, ed. Enrique Mayer and Ralph Bolton, pp. 60-80. Special Publication no. 7. Washington, D.C.: American Anthropological Association.

Mayer, Enrique, and Ralph Bolton, eds. 1977. *Andean Kinship and Marriage*. Special Publication no. 7. Washington, D.C.: American Anthropological Association.

Mead, George M. 1972. *Espíritu, persona y sociedad*. Buenos Aires: Paidos.

Medina, Luis. 1974. "Origen y circunstancia de la idea de unidad nacional." In *Vida Política de México 1970-1973*, pp. 7-22. Mexico City: Centro de Estudios Internacionales, El Colegio de México.

———. 1978. *Del Cardenismo al Avilacamachismo. Historia de la Revolución Mexicana*, no. 18. Mexico City: El Colegio de México.

Meyer, Jean A. 1977. "La ciudad de México, ex de los palacios." In E. Krauze, ed., *La reconstrucción económica. Historia de la Revolución Mexicana*, no. 10. Mexico City: El Colegio de México.

———. 1980. "Los franceses en México durante el siglo XIX." *Relaciones: Estudios de Historia y Sociedad* (El Colegio de Michoacán) 1, no. 2 (Spring): 5-54.

Meyer, Jean A., with the collaboration of Enrique Krauze and Cayetano Reyes. 1977. *Estado y sociedad con Calles. Período 1924-1928. Historia de la Revolución Mexicana*, no. 11. Mexico City: El Colegio de México.

Meyer, Lorenzo. 1978a. *Los inicios de la institucionalización: La política del maximato. Período 1928-1934. Historia de la Revolución Mexicana*, no. 12. Mexico City: El Colegio de México.

———. 1978b. *El conflicto social y los gobiernos del Maximato. Período 1928-1934. Historia de la Revolución Mexicana*, no. 13. Mexico City: El Colegio de México.

Michaelson, Karen L. 1976. "Patronage, Mediators, and the Historical Context of Social Organization in Bombay." *American Anthropologist* 78, no. 2 (May):281-92.

Michel, A. 1970. "Mate Selection in Various Ethnic Groups in France." In *Readings in Kinship in Urban Society*, ed. C. C. Harris, pp. 227-44. Oxford: Pergamon Press.

Millon, René. 1975. "Teotihuacán como centro de transformación." In *Las ciudades de América Latina y sus áreas de influencia a través de la historia*, ed. Jorge E. Hardoy, pp. 19-26. Buenos Aires: Siap.

Mills, C. Wright. 1975. *La élite del poder*. Mexico City: Fondo de Cultura Económica.

Mintzberg, Henry. 1980. "Configurations of Organizational Power." Burg Wartenstein Symposium 84, "The Exercise of Power in Complex Organizations," July 19-28. Mimeo.

Mitchell, William E. 1976. "Comments on *Working-Class Kinship: Studies in Social and Economical Process*, ed. George S. Rosenberg and Donald F. Auspach, [Lexington, Mass.: D. C. Heath, 1973]." *American Anthropologist* 78, no. 2:400-401.

―――. 1978. *Mishpokhe*. New York: Mouton Publishers.

Molina Enríquez, Andrés. 1979. *Los grandes problemas nacionales*. Colección Problemas de México. Mexico City: Era. 1st ed. 1909.

Moore, Sally Falk. 1975. "Uncertainties in Situations, Indeterminancies in Culture." In *Symbol and Politics in Communal Ideology*, pp. 211-39. Ithaca: Cornell University Press.

Moore, Sally Falk, and B. G. Myerhoff. 1977. *Secular Ritual*. Assen/ Amsterdam: Van Gorcum.

Murdock, George P. 1949. *Social Structure*. New York: Macmillan.

―――. 1964. "The Kindred." *American Anthropologist* 66:129-32.

―――. 1965. "Cognatic Forms of Social Organization." In *Culture and Society Essays*, ed. G. P. Murdock. Pittsburgh: University of Pittsburgh Press. 1st ed. 1960.

NAFINSA, Comisión Económica para América Latina. 1971. *La política industrial en el desarrollo económico de México*. Mexico City: Nacional Financiera.

―――. 1982. "Pequeña y mediana industria." *Nacional Financiera* 2, no. 18.

Nofziger, E. 1969. "The Effect of the Nigerian Extended Family on Entrepreneurial Activity." *Economic Development and Cultural Change* 18:25-33.

Nutini, Hugo G. N.d. "A Formal Comparison of Kinship and Compadrazgo in Belen." Typescript.

Nutini, Hugo G. 1968. *San Bernardino Contla*. Pittsburgh: University of Pittsburgh Press.

———. 1971. "Science and Ideology." *Bijdragen tot. de taal-, land-, en volkenkkunde* 127 (1):1-14.

———. 1984. *Ritual Kinship: Ideological and Structural Integration of the Compadrazgo System in Rural Tlaxcala*. Vol. 2. Princeton: Princeton University Press.

Nutini, Hugo G., and Betty Bell. 1980. *Ritual Kinship: The Structure and Historical Development of the Compadrazgo System in Rural Tlaxcala*. Vol. 1. Princeton: Princeton University Press.

Nutini, Hugo G., Pedro Carrasco, and James Mounsey Taggart, eds. 1976. *Essays in Mexican Kinship*. Pittsburgh: University of Pittsburgh Press.

Nutini, Hugo G., and Douglas R. White. 1977. "Community Variations and Network Structure in the Social Function in Rural Tlaxcala, Mexico." *Ethnology* 16, no. 4 (Oct.).

O'Donnell, Guillermo. 1977. "Corporatism and the Question of the State." In *Authoritarianism and Corporatism in Latin America*, ed. James M. Malloy, pp. 47-87. Pittsburgh: University of Pittsburgh Press.

———. 1978. "Notas para el estudio de la burguesía local." *CEDES*, no. 12. Buenos Aires: Centro de Estudios de Estado y Sociedad.

Oliven, Ruben George. N.d. "Culture Roles O.K.: Class and Culture in Brazilian Cities." Mimeo.

Olivera, Mercedes. 1976. "The Barrios of San Andres Cholula." In *Essays on Mexican Kinship*, ed. Hugo G. Nutini, Pedro Carrasco, and James Mounsey Taggart, pp. 65-96. Pittsburgh: University of Pittsburgh Press.

Ortega y Gasset, José. 1948. "España invertebrada." *Revista de Occidente* (Madrid).

Otero, Mariano. 1967. *Obras*. Ed. J. Reyes Heroles. Mexico City: Purrúa.

Oyarzábal, Shanty. 1979. "Antonio Alonso Terán: Participante en el comercio con Asia (1790-1834)." In *Simposio sobre empresarios en México*, ed. Gloria Artis et al., pp. 53-98. Mexico City: Cuadernos de la Casa Chata, CISINAH.

Palerm, Angel. 1980. *Antropología y Marxismo*. Mexico City: Nueva Imagen.

Pareto, Vilfredo. 1965. *Selections from His Treatise with an Introductory Say by Joseph Lopreato*. New York: Thomas G. Crowell Co.

Parkin, David. 1972. *Palms, Wine and Witnesses*. London: Intertext Books.

Parsons, Talcott. 1961. *The Structure of Social Action*. New York: Free Press. 1st ed. 1943.

Paz, Octavio. 1976. "The Flight of Quetzalcóatl and the Question of Legitimacy." Foreword in *Quetzalcóatl and Guadalupe*, ed. J. Lafaye, pp. ix-xxii. Chicago: University of Chicago Press.

———. 1959. *El laberinto de la soledad*. Mexico City: Fondo de Cultura Económica.

———. 1978. "1978: Entre las convulsiones y la inmovilidad." *Proceso*, nos. 92-95 (Aug.).

Pellicer de Brody, Olga, and José Luis Reyna. 1978. *El afianzamiento de la estabilidad política. Periodo 1952-1958. Historia de la Revolución Mexicana*, no. 22. Mexico City: El Colegio de México.

Peranio, Roger D. 1961. "Descent, Descent Line and Descent Group in Cognatic Social Systems." Proceedings of the American Ethnological Society meeting.

Pereyra, Carlos. 1979. "Ideología y ciencia." In *Ideología y ciencias sociales*, pp. 53-73. Mexico City: Universidad Nacional Autónoma de México.

Pérez-Lizaur, Marisol. 1970. "Asentamiento e historia demográfica: Cuatro comunidades del Acolhuacán." M.A. thesis, Dept. of Social Anthropology, Universidad Iberoamericana, Mexico City.

Pherson, R. 1971. "Bilateral Kin Groupings as a Structural Type: A Preliminary Statement." In *Readings in Kinship and Social Structure*, ed. Nelson Graburn, pp. 192-94. New York: Harper and Row.

Piddington, Ralph. 1973. "The Kinship Network among French Canadians." In *Community and Culture in French Canada*, ed. G. Gold and M. A. Tremblay, pp. 123-41. Toronto: Holt, Rinehart and Winston of Canada.

———. 1970. "A Study of French Canadian Kinship." In *Readings in Kinship in Urban Society*, ed. C. C. Harris, pp. 71-98. Oxford: Pergamon Press.

Pitt-Rivers, Julian A. 1973. "The Kith and the Kin." In *The Character of Kinship*, ed. Jack Goody, pp. 99-106. Cambridge: Cambridge University Press.

———. 1974. *The People of the Sierra*, 3d ed. Chicago: University of Chicago Press.

Polanyi, Karl, C. Arensberg, and H. W. Pearson, eds. 1957. *Trade and Market in the Early Empires*. New York: Free Press.

Portes, Alejandro. 1977. "On the Sociology of National Development: Theories and Issues." In *Third World Urbanization*, ed. J. A. Linghod and R. Hay, pp. 108-127. Chicago: Maarufa Press.

———. 1978. "The Informal Sector and the World Economy: Note on the Structure of Subsidised Labour." *IDS Bulletin* 9, no. 4 (June):35-39.

———. 1983. "The Informal Sector: Definition Controversy and Relation to National Development." *Review* 7, no. 1 (Summer):151-74.

Purcell, John F. H., and Susan Kaufman Purcell. 1977. "Mexican Business and Public Policy." In *Authoritarianism and Corporatism in Latin America*, ed. James M. Malloy, pp. 191-227. Pittsburgh: University of Pittsburgh Press.

Quirk, Robert E. 1973. *The Mexican Revolution and the Catholic Church, 1910-1929*. Bloomington: Indiana University Press.

Radcliffe-Brown, A. R. 1933. *The Andaman Islanders*. Cambridge: Cambridge University Press.

Ramos, Donald. 1978. "City and Country: The Family in Minas Jerais, 1804-1836." *Journal of Family History* 3 (4):365-75.

Ratcliff, Richard E. 1974. "Kinship and Class: Wealth and Family Ties in the Chilean Upper Class." Paper presented at the American Anthropological Association annual meeting, Mexico. Mimeo.

Reyna, José Luis. 1977. "Redefining the Authoritarian Regimen." In *Authoritarianism in Mexico*, ed. José Luis Reyna and Richard Weinart, pp. 155-71. Philadelphia: Institute for the Study of Human Issues.

Reyna, José Luis, and Richard Weinart, eds. 1977. *Authoritarianism in Mexico*. Philadelphia: Institute for the Study of Human Issues.

Ribeiro, Darcy. 1969. *Propuestas acerca del subdesarrollo: Brasil como problema*. Montevideo: Libros de la Pupila.

Richards, Aubey. 1956. *Chisungu*. London: Faber and Faber.

Robert, Bryan. 1980. "State and Region in Latin America." Paper presented at the Urbanization in Latin America Symposium, Social Science Research Council, Carmel, Calif., March. Mimeo.

Roeder, Ralph. 1968. *Juárez and His Mexico*. New York: Greenwood Press.

———. 1973. *Hacia el México moderno: Porfirio Díaz*. 2 vols. Mexico City: Fondo de Cultura Económica.

Rojina Villegas, Rafael. 1976. *Compendio de derecho civil*, vol. 1. "Introducción. Personas y familia." Mexico City: Purrúa.

Romney, Kimball, and Romaine Romney. 1966. *The Mixtecas of*

Juxtlahuaca, Mexico. Six Cultures Series, 4. New York: John Wiley and Sons.

Roxborough, Ian. N.d. "The Mexican Working Class and the Mexican Labour Movement: 1930-1975." London School of Economics. Mimeo.

Safa, Helen I. 1974. *The Urban Poor of Puerto Rico.* New York: Holt, Rinehart and Winston.

Sahlins, Marshall D. 1976a. *Culture versus Practical Reasons.* Chicago: University of Chicago Press.

―――. 1976b. "Economía tribal." In *Antropología económica,* ed. M. Godelier, pp. 233-59. Barcelona: Anagrama.

Salaff, Janet W. 1980. "Marriage Relationships as a Resource: Poor and Affluent Singapore Chinese Families, 1974-76." Paper prepared for the Conference on Face-to-Face Interaction in Chinese Society, Rutgers, New Jersey, Apr. 19. Mimeo.

Salas-Lizaur, Jesús, N.d. "Herederos legítimos." Mimeo.

Salazar, Roberto G. 1971. "El empresario industrial: Patrones tradicionales de constitución y sucesión empresarial." M.A. thesis, Centro de Estudios Económicos y Demográficos, El Colegio de México.

Schefler, Harold W. 1973. "Kinship, Descent and Alliance." In *Handbook of Social and Cultural Anthropology,* ed. J. J. Honigmann, pp. 747-95. Chicago: Rand McNally.

Schmidt, Henry C. 1978. *The Roots of "lo Mexicano": Self and Society in Mexican Thought, 1900-1934.* College Station: Texas A&M University Press.

Schneider, David M. 1968. *American Kinship: A Cultural Account.* Englewood Cliffs, N.J.: Prentice Hall.

Schneider, David M., and B. Calvert-Cottrell. 1975. *The American Kin Universe: A Genealogical Study.* Studies in Anthropology. Series in Social, Cultural and Linguistic Anthropology 3. Chicago: University of Chicago Press.

Schneider, David M., and R. T. Smith. 1973. *Class Differences and Sex Roles in American Kinship and Family Structure.* Englewood Cliffs, N.J.: Prentice Hall.

Schumpeter, Joseph. 1961. *The Theory of Economic Development.* New York: Oxford University Press.

Schusky, Ernest L. 1965. *Manual for Kinship Analysis.* New York: Holt, Rinehart and Winston.

Schwartzman, Simon. 1977. "Back to Weber: Corporatism and Patrimonialism in the Seventies." In *Authoritarianism and Corpora-*

tism in Latin America, ed. James M. Malloy, pp. 89-106. Pittsburgh: University of Pittsburgh Press.

Selby, Henry A., Wayne Kappel, and Clyde M. Woods. 1982. "Male Rules But Females Decide: A Formal Analysis of Marriage and Residence in Traditional Mesoamerica." Mimeo.

Selby, Henry A., and A. Murphy. 1982. "The Mexican Household and the Decision to Migrate to the United States." Occasional Papers on Social Change, no. 4. Philadelphia: Institute for the Study of Human Issues.

Selman, Jean Michel. 1979. "La familia en Italia del siglo XV al siglo XIX." Paper for a conference at the Department of History, Instituto Nacional de Antropología e Historia. Mimeo.

Shafer, Robert. 1973. *Mexican Business Organization*. Syracuse: Syracuse University Press.

Silva Herzog, Jesús. 1970. *Breve historia de la Revolución Mexicana*. 6th ed. Mexico City: Fondo de Cultura Económica, Colección Popular.

Simmel, George. 1964. *The Sociology of George Simmel*, ed. K. H. Wolff. New York: Free Press.

Simmons, Ozzie G. 1965. "The Criollo Outlook in the Mestizo Culture of Coastal Peru." In *Contemporary Cultures and Societies of Latin America*, ed. A. D. Heath and R. Adams, pp. 518-79. New York: Random House.

Smith, Peter. 1977. "Does Mexico Have a Power Elite?" In *Authoritarianism in Mexico*, ed. José Luis Reyna and Richard Weinart, pp. 129-51. Philadelphia: Institute for the Study of Human Issues.

———. 1979. *Labyrinths of Power: Political Recruitment in Twentieth-Century Mexico*. Princeton: Princeton University Press.

Smith, Raymond T. 1973. "The Matrifocal Family." In *The Character of Kinship*, ed. Jack Goody, pp. 121-44. Cambridge: Cambridge University Press.

———. 1978. "The Family and the Modern World System: Some Observations from the Caribbean." *Journal of Family History* 3 (4):337-60.

———. 1982. "Family, Social Change and Social Policy in the West Indies." *New West Indian Guide* 56 (3/4):111-42.

Soustelle, Jacques. 1974. *La vida cotidiana de los Aztecas*. Mexico City: Fondo de Cultura Económica. 1st ed. 1955.

Stavenhagen, R., and F. Zapata. 1976. "Sistemas de relación obrero-patronales en América Latina." *Cuadernos del Centro de Estudios Sociológicos*, no. 1. El Colegio de México.

Stehonwer, J. 1970. "Relations between Generations and the Three-Generation Household in Denmark." In *Readings in Kinship in Urban Society*, ed. C. C. Harris, pp. 337-66. Oxford: Pergamon Press.

Stevens, Evelyn. 1977. "Mexico's PRI: The Institutionalization of Corporatism." In *Authoritarianism and Corporatism in Latin America*, ed. James M. Malloy, pp. 227-58. Pittsburgh: University of Pittsburgh Press.

Steward, Julian. 1963. *Theory of Culture Change*. Urbana: University of Illinois Press.

Stock, Carol. 1974. *All Our Kin*. New York: Harper and Row.

Stolcke, Verena. 1974. *Marriage, Class and Colour in Nineteenth-Century Cuba*. Cambridge: Cambridge University Press.

———. 1980. "Woman's Labours." Mimeo.

Stone, Samuel, 1975. *La dinastía de los conquistadores*. San José, Costa Rica: Edit. Universidad Latinoamericana (EDUCA).

Strathern, Andrew. 1975. "Kinship, Descent and Locality." In *The Character of Kinship*, ed. Jack Goody, pp. 3-21. Cambridge: Cambridge University Press.

Strickon, Arnold. 1965. "Class and Kinship in Argentina." In *Contemporary Cultures and Societies of Latin America*, ed. A. D. Heath and R. Adams, pp. 324-41. New York: Random House.

Suárez, Clara Elena. 1979. "Organización social y socialización de los españoles en las ciudades de México y Tehuacán." In *Inmigrantes y refugiados españoles en México: Siglo XX*, M. Kenny et al. Mexico City: Ediciones de la Casa Chata (8), CISINAH.

Sunkel, Osvaldo, and Edmundo Fuenzalida. 1976. "An Interdisciplinary Research Programme on the Transnationalization of Capitalism and National Development." Sussex: International Development Studies Inform.

Taggart, James Mounsey. 1975. *Estructura de los grupos domésticos de una comunidad Náhuatl de Puebla*. Mexico City: Instituto Nacional Indigenista/Secretaría de Educación Pública.

Taietz, P. "The Extended Family in Transition: A Study of the Family Life of Old People in the Netherlands." In *Readings in Kinship in Urban Societies*, ed. C. C. Harris, pp. 321-36. Oxford: Pergamon Press.

Tokman, Victor. 1977. "An Exploration into the Nature of Informal-Formal Sector Interrelationships." Organización Internacional del Trabajo (OIT), Programa Regional del Empleo para América Latina y el Caribe (PREALC). April. Inform.

Torres, Blanca. 1979. *México en la II Guerra Mundial. Historia de la Revolución Mexicana*, no. 21. Mexico City: El Colegio de México.

Trejo Reyes, Saúl. 1973. *Industrialización y empleo en México*. Mexico City: Fondo de Cultura Económica.

Turner, Víctor. 1974. *Dramas, Fields and Metaphors: Symbolic Action in Human Societies*. Ithaca: Cornell University Press.

———. 1977. "Symbols in African Ritual." In *Symbolic Anthropology*, ed. J. Dolgin, D. Kemnitzer, and D. Schneider, pp. 183-94. New York: Columbia University Press.

Unikel, L., C. Ruiz Chiapetto, and G. Garza Villareal. 1978. *El desarrollo urbano de México*. Mexico City: El Colegio de México. 1st ed. 1976.

Useem, Michael. 1980. "The British Corporate Elite and the Formulation of State Policy." Paper presented at the Burg Wartenstein Symposium 84, July. Mimeo.

Uzzell, Douglas J. 1980. "Mixed Strategies and the Informal Sector: Three Faces of Reserve Labour." *Human Organization* 39 (1):40-49.

Van Gennep, Arnold. 1977. *The Rites of Passage*. London: Routledge and Kegan Paul. 1st ed. 1908.

Van Velson, J. 1967. "The Extended Case Method and Situational Analysis." In *The Craft of Social Anthropology*, ed. A. L. Epstein, pp. 129-52. London: Tavistock.

Vaughan, Mary K. 1979. "Women, Class and Education in Mexico." In *Women in Latin America*, pp. 63-80. Special publication of *Latin American Perspectives*, Riverside, Calif.

Vázquez de Knauth, Josefina. 1975. *Nacionalismo y educación en México*. Mexico City: El Colegio de México.

Verdon, Michel. 1980. "Descent: An Operational View." *Man: The Journal of the Royal Anthropological Institute* 15, no. 1. (March):129-50.

Vernon, Raymond. 1977. *El dilema del desarrollo económico de México*. Mexico City: Diana.

Versiani, Flavio Rabelo. 1971. "Technical Change, Equipment, Replacement and Labor Absorption: The Case of the Brazilian Textile Industry." Ph.D. thesis, Dept. of Economics, Vanderbilt University.

Villarreal, René. 1977. "The Policy of Import-Substituting Industrialization, 1929-1975." In *Authoritarianism in Mexico*, ed. José Luis Reyna and Richard Weinart, pp. 67-107. Philadelphia: Institute for the Study of Human Issues.

Villaseñor, Víctor Manuel. 1976. *Memorias de un hombre de Izquierda*. Mexico City: Grijalbo.

Villoro, Luis. 1979. "El concepto de ideología en Marx y Engels." In *Ideología y ciencias sociales*, ed. Mario H. Otero, pp. 11-39. Mexico City: Universidad Nacional Autónoma de México.

Vogt, E. Zartman. 1964. *Ensayo sobre Zinacantán*. Mexico City: Instituto Nacional Indigenista.

Von Bertrab, Herman. 1979. "Adaptación de la tecnología: El caso de las empresas europeas en México." In *Dinámica de la empresa mexicana*, compil. Viviane B. de Márquez, pp. 15-54. Mexico City: El Colegio de México.

Wagley, Charles. 1959. "Formas de parentesco Luso-Brasileño." Comunicaç IV Coloquio Intern. de Estudos Luso-Brasileiros, Bahia. Mimeo.

———. 1965. "On the Concept of Social Race in the Americas." In *Contemporary Cultures and Societies of Latin America*, ed. A. D. Heath and R. Adams, p. 531-44. New York: Random House.

Wainerman, Catalina H. 1980. "La mujer y el trabajo en la Argentina desde la perspectiva de la iglesia católica." *Cuaderno del CENEP* 16. Buenos Aires: Centro de Estudios de Población.

Walker, David. 1979. "Las ubérrimas ubres del Estado." *Nexos* 15 (March):15-18.

Wallerstein, Immanuel. 1974. *The Modern World System–I*. New York: Academic Press.

Walter, Richard J. 1968. *Student Politics in Argentina*. New York: Basic Books.

Ward, Peter. 1976. "In Search of a Home: Social and Economical Characteristics of Squatter Settlements and the Role of Self Help Housing in Mexico City." Ph.D. thesis, University of Liverpool.

Weber, Max. 1965. *The Protestant Ethic and the Spirit of Capitalism*. New York: Chicago Scribner's Sons.

Webster, Steven S. 1977. "Kinship and Affinity in a Native Quechua Community." In *Andean Kinship and Marriage*, ed. Enrique Mayer and Ralph Bolton, pp. 28-42. Special Publication no. 7. Washington, D.C.: American Anthropological Association.

Weinart, Richard S. 1977. "The State and Foreign Capital." In *Authoritarianism in Mexico*, ed. José Luis Reyna and Richard Weinart, pp. 109-118. Philadelphia: Institute for the Study of Human Issues.

West, Robert C., and J. P. Cengetti. 1966. *Middle America: Its Lands and Peoples*. Englewood Cliffs, N.J.: Prentice Hall.

Whiteford, Andrew H. 1967. "Aristocracy, Oligarchy and Culture Change in Colombia." In *City and Country in the Third World*, ed. A. J. Field. Cambridge, Mass.: Schenkman.

Wilkie, James W. 1965. *The Mexican Revolution*. Berkeley: University of California Press.

Willens, Emilio. 1965. "The Structure of the Brazilian Family." In *Contemporary Latin American Culture: An Anthropological Source Book*, ed. G. M. Foster. University of California, Berkeley, WLS-B. Mimeo.

Wilson, Fiona, N.d. "The Eclipse of a Regional Oligarchy in the Central Sierra of Perú, 1960 to 1980s." Mimeo.

Wilson, Monica. 1970. *Rituals of Kinship among the Nyakyusa*. Oxford: Oxford University Press. 1st ed. 1957.

Winch, Robert F., and Louis W. Goodman. 1968. *Selected Studies in Marriage and Family*. New York: Holt, Reinhart and Winston.

Wionczek, M., Gerardo M. Bueno, and J. E. Navarrete. 1974. *La transferencia internacional de tecnología: El caso de México*. Mexico City: Fondo de Cultura Económica.

Wolf, Eric. 1965. "Aspects of Group Relations in Complex Society: Mexico." In *Contemporary Cultures and Societies of Latin America*, ed. A. D. Heath and R. Adams, pp. 85-101. New York: Random House.

———. 1967. *Pueblos y culturas de mesoamérica*. Mexico City: Era.

———. 1969. "Kinship, Friendship and Patron-Client Relations." In *The Social Anthropology of Complex Societies*, ed. Michael Banton. London: Tavistock.

Womack, John R. 1968. *Zapata and the Mexican Revolution*. Harmondsworth: Penguin.

Worsley, Peter. 1978. "Social Class in Developing Countries." Paper prepared for the Burg Wartenstein Symposium 80. Mimeo.

———. 1980. "Marxism and Culture: The Missing Concept." Occasional Paper no. 4. Dept. of Sociology, University of Manchester. August.

Wrigley, E. Anthony. 1977. "Reflections on the History of the Family." *Daedalus* (Spring):71-85.

Yanagisako, Sylvia Junko. 1977. "Women-Centered Kin Networks in Urban Bilateral Kinship." *American Ethnologist* 4, no. 2 (May):207-226.

Yedid, Marcos Caín, F. Ortíz Monasterio de Ugarte, and José Pliego Alcaraz. 1975. "El mercado de capitales: Análisis de dos activos para México." B.A. thesis, School of Economics, Instituto Tecnológico Autónomo de México, Mexico City.

Zaid, Gabriel. 1979. *El progreso improductivo*. Mexico City: Siglo XXI.

INDEX

LIBRARY OF CONGRESS CATALOGING-IN-PUBLICATION DATA

Lomnitz, Larissa Adler de.
A Mexican elite family, 1820-1980.

Bibliography: p.
Includes index.
1. Family—Mexico. 2. Kinship—Mexico. 3. Family corporations—Mexico.
4. Elite (Social sciences)—Mexico. 5. Mexico—Economic conditions.
I. Pérez Lizaur, Marisol. II. Title.
HQ561.L66 1987   306.8'5'0972   87-3037

ISBN 0-691-07737-1 (alk. paper)   ISBN 0-691-02284-4 (pbk.)